BC

WITHDRAWN

Transnational Corporations and the Latin American Automobile Industry

Selected Titles

Adventurers and Proletarians: The Story of Migrants in Latin America
Magnus Mörner, with the collaboration of Harold Sims

Authoritarianism and Corporatism in Latin America
James M. Malloy, Editor

Black Labor on a White Canal: Panama, 1904–1981
Michael L. Conniff

Discreet Partners: Argentina and the USSR Since 1917
Aldo C. Vacs

The Giant's Rival: The USSR and Latin America
Cole Blasier

The Hovering Giant: U.S. Responses to Revolutionary Change in Latin America
Cole Blasier

Juan Perón and the Reshaping of Argentina
Frederick C. Turner and José Enrique Miguens, Editors

The Life, Music, and Times of Carolos Gardel
Simon Collier

The Politics of Mexican Oil
George W. Grayson

Public Policy in Latin America: A Comparative Survey
John W. Sloan

Rebirth of the Paraguayan Republic: The First Colorado Era, 1878–1904
Harris G. Warren

Social Security in Latin America: Pressure Groups, Stratification, and Inequality
Carmelo Mesa-Lago

The State and Capital Accumulation in Latin America: Brazil, Chile, Mexico
Christian Anglade and Carlos Fortin, Editors

The United States and Latin America in the 1980s: Contending Perspectives on a Decade of Crisis
Kevin J. Middlebrook and Carlos Rico, Editors

TRANSNATIONAL CORPORATIONS AND THE LATIN AMERICAN AUTOMOBILE INDUSTRY

Rhys Jenkins

University of Pittsburgh Press

First published 1987 by The Macmillan Press Ltd

Published in the U.S.A. 1987 by the University of Pittsburgh press
Pittsburgh, Pa., 15260

Printed in Hong Kong

Library of Congress Cataloging-in-Publication Data

Jenkins, Rhys Owen, 1948–
   Transnational corporations and the Latin American
automobile industry.

   (Pitt Latin American series)
   Bibliography: p.
   Includes index.
   1. Automobile industry and trade—Latin America.
2. International business enterprises—Latin America.
I. Title.   II. Series.
HD9710.L32J46   1987   338.8'87   86–1500
ISBN 0–8229–1145–0

Contents

Contents

List of Illustrations

List of Tables

Preface

My interest in the Latin American motor industry goes back over some fifteen years. When I first started to research the industry, there were few studies of even the development of the industry at the national level, despite its importance in the development strategies of a number of countries in the region, for a decade or more. The past fifteen years has seen an immense growth of interest in the industry which has been reflected in a steady stream of publications. There has also been an expanding literature on the motor industry at the international level. However, there has still been no study which takes an overview of the industry in Latin America as a whole, the different national patterns that have emerged and the way in which the industry in the region has been conditioned by the development of the world motor industry.

When the Division de Estudios Economicos of the Instituto Latinoamericano de Estudios Transnacionales (now Centro de Economia Transnacional) first suggested that I should undertake the present study in the context of their programme on the penetration of transnational corporations in Latin America, it seemed to me an excellent opportunity to write such a synthesis. Initially it was planned that this study should be undertaken jointly by Edgardo Lifschitz and myself, and I am grateful to him for the early discussions which we had on the Latin American motor industry. My task was rendered considerably easier by the work of two groups of researchers on the Latin American motor industry. I was able to draw on the studies carried out in Argentina, Brazil, Mexico, Peru, Uruguay and Venezuela as part of ILET's programme of research on the motor industry, and to discuss some of their findings at a seminar held in Mexico City in January 1980. I was also fortunate in participating in a number of meetings of the New York SSRC Working Group on the Transnational Automobile Industry in Latin America which brought together US, Latin American and European social scientists working on the Latin American motor industry. A number of the papers presented at these meetings have recently been published in R. Kronish and K. S. Mericle, *The Political*

Economy of the Latin American Motor Vehicle Industry (1984).

I am indebted both to ILET and to the Social Science Research Council of the United Kingdom which at different times provided financial support for the project. I am also grateful to John Humphrey and Eduardo Guimaraes, on whose knowledge of the Brazilian motor industry I have been able to draw. Finally my thanks to Ruth, Megan and Sam who have ensured that the motor industry could never entirely dominate my life.

R.O.J.

1 Introduction

The motor industry has played a key role in capitalist development for most of the twentieth century. It was the leading sector in the United States in the inter-war years, it played the same role in Western Europe in the fifties and the sixties, and in Latin America it became a crucial barometer of economic progress in a number of countries in the sixties and seventies. It has been able to play such a major role because of the many links which the industry has with economic activity generally. The development of the motor industry created in the advanced capitalist countries a large number of parts and component firms producing both original equipment for the assemblers and spare parts for the replacement market. It also greatly enhanced the demand for the products of a number of other industries such as iron and steel, aluminium, rubber, plastic and glass. It has led to the growth of a vast distribution and servicing network, while the increasing use of motor vehicles has led to the growth of petrol stations and of course to the expansion of the oil industry. The ramifications of the industry are illustrated by one estimate that if all the indirect employment effects are included, there may be as many as 135 million people world-wide whose jobs depend on the motor industry (Bhaskar, 1980, p. 6).

In addition to the jobs created, the growth of vehicle production has meant radical changes in life styles in the advanced capitalist countries in the twentieth century. Distances can be covered much more rapidly at the individual's own convenience. This has led to substantial changes in urban patterns as proximity to the work-place became a far less crucial factor. Similarly the development of road transport rendered production locations much more flexible than in an earlier period when the pattern of rail links was a dominant consideration. There have also been negative consequences such as increasing air pollution from exhaust emissions. Few, if any, industries can have had a comparable impact on life in the twentieth century.

In view of its central position in capitalist development, the motor industry is particularly suitable as a focus for a study of the internationalization of capital. In 1980 there were nine vehicle manufacturers among the world's largest fifty industrial corporations (UNCTC, 1983, table II.3). All these had extensive overseas operations either through foreign subsidiaries or exports. The world's largest 22 vehicle manufacturers produced one-fifth of their world-wide output in overseas subsidiaries (not including assembly plants) in 1980 (UNCTC, 1982, table 15). The major tyre producers are even more internationalized in terms of their overseas production (West, forthcoming, table 8), while many of the largest parts producers are also heavily involved abroad.

The major transnational corporations (TNCs) control an overwhelming proportion of world-wide production (outside the socialist countries). The largest dozen vehicle manufacturers account for almost 90 per cent of the total (see Table 1.1). In tyres, twelve firms account for over 90 per cent of the world market, and the largest six of them for over 70 per cent (*The Economist*, 24/9/83, p. 67). It is also a key area of inter-capitalist rivalry between US, European and Japanese capital.

The motor industry, having played a major role in the post-war boom in the advanced capitalist countries, was particularly severely affected by the collapse of the boom in the early seventies. It is therefore

TABLE 1.1   *Leading vehicle producers, outside COMECON countries, 1983*

	Output (million)	Percent of total output
General Motors	7.77	21.5
Ford	4.93	13.6
Toyota*	3.85	10.6
Nissan†	3.06	8.4
Renault‡	2.49	6.9
Volkswagen	2.06	5.7
Peugeot-Citroen	1.74	4.8
Fiat	1.44	4.0
Chrysler	1.34	3.7
Toyo Kogyo	1.26	3.5
Honda	1.09	3.0
Mitsubishi	1.02	2.8
Mercedes-Benz	0.68	1.9
Suzuki	0.63	1.7
BL	0.58	1.6

* Toyota Group including Daihatsu and Hino.
† Nissan Group including Fuji and Nissan Diesel.
‡ Including AMC.
SOURCES   Automotive News. *1984 Market Data Book*; Automobile International, *1984 World Automotive Market*.

an interesting case of the implications of world recession and the restructuring of capital for the internationalization of capital and the future insertion of the Latin American countries in the international division of labour.

Historically the motor industry has also been of particular interest as a sector which has often pioneered new labour processes and new strategies of labour control. In the United State the conveyor belt and the five dollar day formed the basis of what came to be known as Fordism. In Europe in the sixties immigrants from Southern Europe and North Africa were employed to reinforce managerial control and divide the work-force. More recently Japan has pioneered the use of robots in the production of vehicles. The counterpart of these managerial strategies have been workers' resistance in many guises. Particularly in Britain and Italy in the sixties car workers acquired a reputation for militancy. In Latin America, especially in Argentina and Brazil, the growth of the motor industry has also led to militant working class struggles.

Not surprisingly in view of the role played by the motor industry in capitalist development in the United States and Western Europe, and the widespread economic impact described above, many *desarrollista* governments in Latin America assigned it a major part in their development strategies of import substitution in the fifties and sixties. More than any other sector, it came to exemplify the consequences and pitfalls of the developmentalist strategy. It was dominated by the major TNCs which had previously exported to the region. These produced high cost vehicles in small, inefficient plants, whose output went to satisfy the demand of a narrow upper income group. More recently, with the greater emphasis being given to the promotion of manufactured exports, as opposed to import substitution, the motor industry has again been allotted a major role by the larger Latin American countries, while it was selected as one of the four key sectoral development programmes for the Andean Pact.

As a result of these policies the industry has acquired significant weight within the industrial sector particularly of those Latin American countries which have achieved high levels of local content. In Brazil and Argentina the industry accounted for about 12 per cent and 8 per cent respectively of the value added of the manufacturing sector in the seventies. In Mexico and Venezuela the corresponding figure was around 6 per cent while in the other Latin American countries with assembly operations it was 5 per cent or less.

In Brazil direct employment in the industry, including the parts industry had reached more than 300 000 by the 1970s. If all those jobs indirectly related to the motor industry were included this figure would be more than doubled.[1] In Argentina direct employment exceeded 100 000 and the total number of jobs linked to the industry came to more than 400 000 (Sourrouille, 1980, pp. 150–1). In Mexico too more than 100 000 workers were directly employed in the industry (AMIA). Elsewhere in the region the industry was much less significant with Venezuela, the next largest, having fewer than 30 000 directly employed (Fontanals and Porta, 1979).

As can be seen in Table 1.2, the major vehicle TNCs, household names such as General Motors, Ford, Volkswagen, Fiat and Renault are all present in Latin America. For some, notably Volkswagen, Latin America accounts for a major share of their worldwide output. For others their Latin American operations are marginal. In Brazil, Argentina and Mexico the foreign subsidiaries of these TNCs are amongst the largest industrial firms in the country, giving them considerable economic and political influence.

1   METHODOLOGICAL CONSIDERATIONS

The definition of the motor industry used in the present study is a wide one. Often studies of the motor industry are concerned only with the terminal industry, that is those firms which assemble cars and commercial vehicles.[2] While this has obvious advantages in enabling one to focus on the operations of a small group of firms, the concept of the motor industry complex gives a more complete picture of the impact of the internationalization of capital (Trajtenberg, 1977; Lifschitz, 1978).

Figure 1.1 illustrates schematically the notion of the motor industry complex. It includes not only the terminal industry but also those enterprises which are principally linked to the terminals or their products. These are the parts and component industry and the tyre industry which supply the terminal industry with original equipment as well as supplying the replacement market. It also includes the distribution network of authorized dealers and the sale of parts to the replacement market, as well as repair shops and garages. It excludes other industries which supply the motor industry such as iron and steel, glass, paint, plastics and textiles, but for whom the motor industry does not account for a major share of output.

This definition of the motor industry enables us to study the dominant position which the terminals enjoy in the network of inter-

TABLE 1.2 Production by country for major TNC in the Latin American auto industry, 1983

	Argentina	Brazil	Chile	Colombia	Mexico	Peru	Venezuela
GM	—	207 544	2 206	9 344	32 934	—	42 530
Ford	56 047	166 101	—	—	43 874	—	36 911
Chrysler	—	—	—	—	42 130	—	—
Nissan	—	2 500	—	—	51 304	4 050	—
Toyota	—	—	—	—	—	4 024	12 362
VW	17 408	345 439	—	—	86 470	1 505	—
Renault*	41 603	—	2 008†	14 542	22 984	—	8 590
Fiat	19 773	146 521	—	4 263	—	—	7 869
Daimler-Benz	3 851	22 255	—	—	—	—	—
Peugeot-Citroen	19 363	—	297	—	—	—	—

* Including AMC.
† Production of joint venture between Peugeot and Renault.
SOURCE Automobile International, *1984 World Automotive Market.*

6

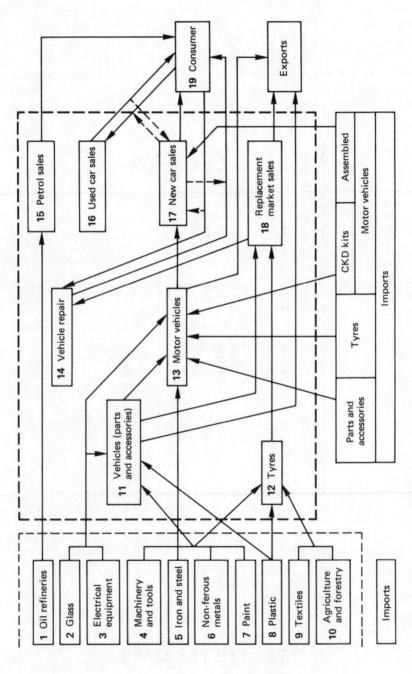

FIGURE 1.1 *Motor industry complex*
SOURCE: Lifschitz, 1978, p. 27.

industry relationships. They constitute the nucleus of the motor industry complex able, as will be seen in the course of this study, to condition the patterns of accumulation and reproduction in the other parts of the complex. This will be studied particularly in relation to the sphere of production and the relations between suppliers and terminals, although it also applies in the sphere of circulation where dealers and distributors clearly find their activities determined by the terminals.

This approach indicates that the influence of TNCs, which control the nucleus of the motor industry complex, extends much further than their direct role in production would imply. In other words the internationalization of capital is a far more extensive phenomenon than is often realized in Latin America. TNCs located in the nuclei of various industries determine what is produced by others, and can also take advantage of their dominant position to further their own accumulation and increase their profitability through depressing the returns of others.

Despite the fact that the complex needs to be analysed in its entirety, as suggested above, the existence of a nucleus implies that the firms which constitute this nucleus play a predominant role in determining the dynamic of the complex as a whole. This explains why in the chapters that follow, the terminals remain at the centre of much of the analysis.

2 THE STRUCTURE OF THE STUDY

One of the major assumptions on which the study is based is that economic change in Latin America can only be understood in the context of developments in the international economy to which the region has been linked since the Conquest. This should not be taken to imply that developments in the world economy directly determine what will occur in Latin America, but rather that external relationships form a conditioning situation that 'determines the limits and possibilities of action and behaviour of men' (Dos Santos, 1973, p. 77).

In the case of the motor industry developments in the international motor industry in the twentieth century have indeed changed the possibilities open to the Latin American countries as this study seeks to show. The relationship is not a simple and direct one, but major phases in the development of the international motor industry can be seen to coincide with changes in the development of the industry in the region. One such major change has occurred in the international motor industry since the early 1970s. This is explicitly recognized in the study which is divided into two parts. Part I deals with the period from the mid-fifties when the first attempts to integrate the local assembly industry which already existed in some Latin American countries were made, to the early seventies. Part II focuses on the changes which have taken place since the early seventies internationally and in Latin America.

Chapter 2 provides a historical overview of the development of the motor industry up to the mid-fifties, spelling out the international context in which the earliest assembly plants were set up in the region in the inter-war period, and the subsequent growth of assembly operations after the Second World War.

Chapter 3 analyses the changes that took place in the motor industry between the mid-fifties and the early seventies. At the beginning of this period the basic pattern established in the inter-war years remained largely unchanged. The industry was concentrated in a small number of advanced capitalist countries whose domestic markets were dominated by a small number of firms, protected from imports and enjoying specific spheres of influence in overseas markets. The internationalization of capital in the late fifties and 1960s led to the formation of three major producing blocs in North America, Western Europe and Japan by the early seventies, and the spread of the industry internationally both through new countries embarking on vehicle manufacturing and the extension of assembly operations.

The remaining chapters of Part I are concerned with explaining the structure of the Latin American motor industry and the patterns of capital accumulation. Chapter 4 provides the background to the decisions taken in a number of Latin American countries in the late fifties and early sixties to promote the industry, discussing both the rationale behind government policies and the specific instruments used in each case to bring about local manufacturing or increased use of local parts by assembly plants.

Chapter 5 analyses conditions of production in the motor industry comparing those in Latin America with the situation in the advanced capitalist countries. A distinction is drawn between those countries in which the motor industry is characterized by 'transnationalization by complete repetition' and those of 'incomplete repetition' (cf. Trajtenberg and Vigorito, 1981). It should be stressed that production is not simply a technical process but also a social process. In the motor industry control of labour is a central aspect of production. Various managerial strategies of labour control are discussed first with examples from the advanced capitalist countries and then in the three Latin American countries which established manufacturing operations in this period (Argentina, Brazil and Mexico). The chapter ends with a discussion of the evolution of labour productivity and wages in these three countries.

Chapter 6 turns to the problems of realization as experienced in the Latin American motor industry, focusing on the factors which limit the demand for new cars and the competitive strategies which TNC producers used to attempt to revitalize the market. The chapter ends with a discussion of the way in which production conditions and realization problems interacted to create a structure of high costs and prices for vehicles in the sixties.

Chapter 7 turns to the relations between terminals and suppliers to illustrate the way in which the TNCs located in the nucleus are able to dominate other firms in the motor industry complex. It is argued that the terminal TNCs try to reproduce the relationships with suppliers which they enjoy in the advanced capitalist countries. These relationships are used to reproduce the dominant position of the terminal and benefit them in the form of reduced costs and higher profits. This is followed by a brief discussion of the way in which preferential access to local and international capital markets also contribute to the profitability of the terminal TNCs.

Part I concludes with an analysis of the implications of the processes described in the preceding chapters for capital accumulation in the Latin American motor industry. It shows a tendency for the capacity to accumulate (as reflected in the profits generated by the terminals) to run ahead of the need for funds, so that after a short initial period, the subsidiaries become 'oriented to repatriation' (Chudnovsky, 1981). Moreover, continued dependence on imports and the failure to develop exports means that up to the early seventies the industry continued to act as a drain on the balance of payments, imposing a constraint on the accumulation capacity of the economy as a whole.

Part II focuses on the impact of the crisis and the restructuring of capital which have charactetized the international motor industry since the early seventies. Chapter 9 analyses developments at the international level. It is argued that the seventies and early eighties have seen a further internationalization of capital with the formation for the first time of a true world industry with growing interpenetration of capitals and increasing similarities of products and processes world-wide. This period has also seen an intensification of international competition with the rapid expansion of Japanese capital. As a result the major

TNCs are increasingly treating their global operations as an integrated whole. The slow growth or stagnation of demand in the advanced capitalist countries has led to growing competition for other markets and it is in this context that certain semi-industrialized countries have emerged as important exporters of motor industry products.

Chapter 10 describes the changes which have taken place in policies towards the motor industry in Latin America since the early seventies. The national import substitution strategies of the fifties and sixties have come under increasing criticism and there has been a general shift towards more open policies. In the case of the motor industry it is possible to distinguish three broad policy responses in the region. The first, while maintaining a strong element of import substitution, attempts to increase links with the international market through export promotion. This strategy has characterized Brazil and Mexico since the early seventies and Argentina until the military coup of 1976. The second response has been liberalization leading to a dismantling of the local industry, which received its fullest expression in Chile, but also characterizes Argentina after 1976. Finally the Andean Pact countries have attempted to pursue import substitution on a regional basis.

Chapter 11 discusses the changes which have taken place within Latin America as a result of the impact of the world recession, changing TNC strategies and the new state policies. It distinguishes between the same three groups of countries discussed above and draws out the implications for conditions of production, labour, suppliers, capital accumulation and the balance of payments.

By way of conclusion, Chapter 12 looks to the future of the Latin American motor industry. First the relationship of the growth of the motor industry in the region to a particular 'style of development' is established. It is argued that this style is unlikely to change in the foreseeable future and that the industry will therefore continue as an important pole of capital accumulation. Future developments in the industry internationally are discussed before finally attempting to specify the patterns which are likely to emerge within the Latin American industry.

NOTES

1. In 1970 when over 190 000 workers were employed in the terminal and parts industries there were over 90 000 in maintenance and repair and over 100 000 employed in distribution (de Oliveira *et al.*, 1979, table 77; OU, 1983, table 12).

2. Three recent studies of the international motor industry Bhaskar (1980), Maxcy (1981) and UNCTC (1982), all concentrate exclusively on the terminal industry.

2 The Origins of the Latin American Automobile Industry

The motor industry is almost a hundred years old. Its origins can be traced back to the 1880s when Daimler and Benz in Germany put their first cars on the market. The industry has come a long way in the century which followed passing through a number of distinct phases. An initial experimental period in the last years of the past century and the first years of the present, in which the German industry played a crucial role, gave way to an age of mass production initiated in the United States by Ford, with the introduction of the Model T in 1908. This revolutionized the motor industry, first in the United States and then in the rest of the world. It established that the car would not only be the plaything of the rich (at least in the advanced industrialized countries) but could become a mass consumption good. It also extended a particular form of the labour process based on the fragmentation of tasks, the de-skilling of labour and the use of the conveyor belt which has come to be known as Fordism. Finally, in the international context, the Model T was the first truly international car, produced in a number of countries and sold world-wide. The inter-war period was dominated by the US industry, but also saw the development of a protected industry in Western Europe. After the Second World War the US industry was increasingly challenged first by the Europeans and then by the Japanese. The period from the late fifties onwards was one of intensified internationalization of capital which will be discussed in a later chapter. Finally, in the seventies, the industry has entered a major crisis which has intensified international competition even further.

1   THE PERIOD TO 1945

International developments

The early years of the industry both in Europe and the United States were characterized by small scale production involving a large number of firms. Car makers were essentially assemblers buying in most of the parts and components which they used and as a result capital requirements were low and the industry was easy to enter. In these early years the number of firms embarking on vehicle production in the major countries were numbered in hundreds rather than tens. Although entry to the industry was easy, exits were also frequent and many firms went out of business within a few years.

The first decade of the twentieth century saw a shift in the major centre of the industry from Europe to the United States. The change which revolutionized the entire industry was the introduction of mass production techniques in the United States. This enabled Ford to increase production of the Model T from 12 000 in 1909 to over a million by the early 1920s. Production costs were reduced by a half within five years of the introduction of the conveyor belt, and Ford was able to reduce the price of the Model T, to one-third of its initial level over a fifteen-year period (White, 1977, table 2).

The introduction of mass production techniques led to substantial concentration and centralization of capital in the US motor industry. Ford increased its share of the market from 10 per cent in 1909 to over a half by 1921, while General Motors grew through a process of acquisitions and mergers. The number of firms in the industry began to decline in the twenties, from 88 in 1921 to 35 ten years later and only 12 by 1941 (Rae, 1959, ch. 3). By 1930 Ford, General Motors and Chrysler accounted for 90 per cent of US production.

These cost reductions were achieved through a massive increase in labour productivity in the production of automobiles. This increase in productivity was not only a result of an increasing organic composition of capital (increasing use of machinery), in the industry but also an increase in the intensity of labour involving the applications of Taylorist methods of work study, and the increased control over the pace of work which the introduction of the assembly line permitted. While initially there was an increase in the capital–labour ratio as batch production methods were replaced by mass production, in the interwar period productivity continued to increase with no significant rise in capital intensity (Maxcy and Silberston, 1959, p. 209). The development of Ford in this period exemplified the processes of de-skilling and fragmentation of industrial tasks which Taylorist principles implied. Ford was able to reduce his dependence on scarce skilled labour and thus reduce the ability of workers to resist the intensification of labour. Moreover, the introduction of the assembly line permitted not only a more technically efficient organization of production through a reduction in the time spent carrying parts, etc., but also permitted an acceleration of the pace of work since this was now removed from the control of the worker (Rothschild, 1974, pp. 33–5; Gartman, 1979).

The early introduction of mass production techniques in the United States gave US capital a huge competitive advantage over European competitors. The threat to capital in the different European countries led to State invervention both through tariffs and discriminatory taxation to protect the industry against US competition. As a result European-made cars received protection in the region of 100 per cent or more against US imports. Consequently, imports accounted for only a small share of sales on the domestic market in Europe during the inter-war period. In Britain, for instance, it was estimated that only 5 per cent of all cars registered in the country in 1938 had been imported (PEP, 1950, p. 77).

The period of mass production in the US industry also saw the beginning of the international expansion of US capital in the sector. This not only involved growing exports of vehicles from the United States but also led to the establishment of foreign subsidiaries to assemble vehicles. Ford had begun to decentralize its operations within the United States in 1909, setting up an assembly plant in Kansas City in order to reduce transport costs. International expansion soon followed with the establishment of assembly plants in Britain in 1911 and in France in 1913. In this way Ford secured important additional markets for its rapidly growing output of Model Ts. The growth of protectionism in the European motor industry in the inter-war years led to further internationalization of capital as Ford and General Motors established manufacturing operations in Europe. Ford set up a plant in Germany in 1926 and attempted to enter the Italian market in 1929, while General Motors acquired Vauxhall in the UK in 1925 and Opel in Germany four years later.[1] General Motors followed a policy of producing locally designed vehicles in both Britain and Germany, after acquisition, rather than producing American models, while Ford's major subsidiaries had significant local shareholdings although they produced the Model T. Thus the internationalization of capital in the industry was still of a relatively primitive form.

Although production levels in Europe continued to be low compared with the United States throughout the inter-war period, mass production techniques began to be introduced in the twenties and thirties, with similar results to those described for the United States. The number of firms was reduced to 22 in Britain and 21 in Germany by 1938, compared with 88 in Britain in 1922 and more than 200 in Germany in 1925. By the end of this period three firms accounted for three-quarters of the industry's output in Britain, France and Germany while the Italian industry was totally dominated by Fiat. Maxcy and Silberston have summarized the causes of this concentration and centralization of capital in the case of the British motor industry in the following terms:

> The factor that sealed the fate of the smaller concerns was the growth of mass production techniques on the part of companies such as Morris and Austin which had succeeded in producing models that were successful with the public (Maxcy and Silberston, 1959, p. 14).

and further:

> The concentration of some 75% of car production in the hands of these manufacturers and the elimination of many small producers during the 1920s had been brought about by the competitive pressure exerted by a few rapidly expanding companies benefitting from the economies of scale that accompanied the introduction of elementary mass production techniques (Maxcy and Silberston, 1959, p. 99).

Despite the introduction of mass production techniques in the European countries in the inter-war period, the much larger scale of production in the United States meant much lower levels of cost and the European industry remained relatively uncompetitive until the 1950s. In 1935 labour productivity was three times as high in the United States as in the United Kingdom, and this was reflected in prices which were about 40 per cent lower both before and immediately after the Second World War (PEP, 1950, pp. 126–8). A Ford V-8 produced in the United States was 30 per cent cheaper in France than the same model produced in Britain (PEP, 1950, p. 29).

In view of the advantages which US capital derived from the early introduction of mass production techniques and the expansion of the domestic market, it is not surprising that the US (and the Canadian subsidiaries of the US producers) dominated world trade in vehicles. By 1929 North America accounted for 80 per cent of world exports of cars and over 90 per cent in commercial vehicles. Although the position of the North American industry declined somewhat during the thirties, nevertheless it was still estimated that the United States alone accounted for 60 per cent of world exports of vehicles before the Second World War. Moreover, a significant proportion of the exports of the other leading exporting countries, Canada, Britain and Germany was accounted for by the subsidiaries of the major US companies. It has been estimated that as much as 80 per cent of the world's car production capacity was either located in the United States or owned by US companies abroad (PEP, 1950, p. 113).

Although US exports reached a wide range of countries in the pre-war period, those of other countries were heavily concentrated in those markets to which they enjoyed preferential access. In 1937, for instance, 87 per cent of UK exports of cars and 75 per cent of exports of commercial vehicles went to the British Empire. Exports to the Empire were even more significant for Canada where Ford, General Motors and Chrysler accounted for 95 per cent of production, with over 98 per cent of both car and commercial vehicle exports going to the Empire (SMMT). In the same year, half the value of French exports of vehicles were to Belgium, Spain, Algeria-Tunis and French Indo-China, while two-thirds of Italian exports were to their colonies in Ethiopia and Eritrea (PEP, 1950, Appendix VII). A similar pattern of one, or sometimes two, supplying countries dominating the market of individual countries also emerges. In 1937 the United States and Canada accounted for over 80 per cent of cars sold in South Africa, over 70 per cent in the British West Indies and around two-thirds of sales in Australia, Egypt and Sweden. The United Kingdom accounted for well over a half of car imports to British Malaya, Burma and New Zealand, over 80 per cent in Ceylon and 90 per cent in Eire, while Germany had over half of the Hungarian market and a third of imports in Denmark and Switzerland (SMMT). In Latin America the United States enjoyed complete domination of the industry. In Brazil the second largest supplier, Germany, accounted for only 10 per cent of the cars sold, in 1937, while in Argentina 85 per cent of imports came from the United States in 1938 and only 7 per cent from Germany and 3 per cent from Britain (PEP, 1950, p. 102).

As was indicated above, the position of the US motor industry in world trade in vehicles declined somewhat in the 1930s. This did not, however, imply a decline in the position of US capital which continued to expand internationally in this period. Whereas in 1929 US companies exported 536 000 vehicles compared with their overseas production of only 200 000, by the late thirties both Ford and General Motors were producing more in their foreign subsidiaries than they exported. By this time the US companies had established assembly plants in a number of countries outside Europe including Australia, New Zealand, South Africa, India, Argentina, Brazil, Chile and Mexico. European firms continued to supply these markets through exports and in a few cases entered into agreements with local body-builders. The existence of US subsidiaries in these countries tended to reinforce their competitive position *vis-à-vis* European capital.

The internationalization of the parts industry in the inter-war period was clearly related to the expansion of the US car manufacturers abroad. Expansion by US parts producers in this period was concentrated in two main areas, Canada and Europe, which were also the main areas of activity of Ford and General Motors. In Europe suppliers which set up local subsidiaries included Brigg Manufacturing Company, Edward G. Budd Manufacturing Company, Kelsey-Hayes Wheel, Electric Autolite, Electric Storage Battery, Timken Roller Bearing, Libbey-Owens Sheet Glass, while in Canada the American Auto Trimming Company, McCord Radiator and Manufacturing, Champion Spark Plug and Kelsey-Hayes set up plants. Most of this expansion took place during the twenties and there was little further new investment in the parts industry in the thirties. Moreover expansion was confined to Europe and Canada because it was only here that the US motor companies had set up manufacturing operations as opposed to assembly plants. In Latin America in contrast the expansion of the multinational companies in the parts industry did not begin until the sixties following the move towards manufacturing of vehicles in the major countries, Argentina, Brazil and Mexico.

In the tyre industry, in contrast, international expansion had followed a dynamic of its own. Large firms came to dominate the markets of the major producing countries early on in the industry's development. In the United States four firms controlled 55 per cent of the market by 1919 and in Europe, Dunlop in the UK, Michelin in France and Pirelli in Italy were establishing dominant positions at the same time. Concentration increased further in the inter-war years, and in the US four firms accounted for around 80 per cent of the market before the Second World War.

The tyre industry internationalized early with Dunlop setting up plants in a number of countries before the First World War. In the twenties there was increasing interpenetration of capital in the industry with Dunlop and Michelin building plants in the United States and

Goodrich, Goodyear, Firestone, Michelin and Pirelli investing in Britain. While the international expansion of the tyre companies in the twenties was focused on the developed countries, the thirties saw new subsidiaries being set up primarily in LDCs, especially by Dunlop, Goodyear and Firestone (West, forthcoming, table 1). Stagnant markets in the industrialized countries and the beginning of import substitution policies in some Third World countries in the face of balance of payments problems accounts for this change.

Extension of the motor industry to Latin America

It was in this period that US capital in the motor industry began to extend its activities into Latin America. Again the pioneer was Ford which set up its first assembly plants in Argentina in 1916, Brazil in 1919, Chile in 1924 and Mexico in 1925. It was followed later in the inter-war period by the other two leading firms in the United States, General Motors and Chrysler (the latter through licensing agreements). The initial moves to set up assembly plants in Latin America were undertaken primarily because of the savings which could be obtained through shipping semi-knocked down (SKD) or completely knocked down (CKD) kits as opposed to completely built up (CBU) vehicles to the region.[2] In both Argentina and Brazil the initial investment in assembly plants were made prior to any tariff advantages being granted for local assembly and were motivated primarily by lower transport costs (Wilkins and Hill, 1964, p. 91; Guimaraes, 1981, p. 3). Even in Mexico, where Ford was able to negotiate important concessions in railway freight rates, customs duties and taxes, the decision to invest may have been taken independently of these incentives (Wilkins and Hill, 1964, p. 147).

Throughout the inter-war period the plants that were set up in Latin America remained essentially assembly plants putting together imported kits. Although in theory subsidiaries were free to replace imported parts by locally produced ones where these were available locally more cheaply, the parent companies could always use their pricing practices to ensure that this rarely occurred. The interest of the parent companies were in obtaining longer production runs for the major parts and components which they produced in the United States and which were subject to substantial economies of scale. The fact that, compared with other processes in vehicle manufacturing, assembly was less subject to economies of scale and also relatively labour intensive meant that the additional costs incurred by decentralizing assembly operations were relatively low. However, the auto companies had little interest in decentralizing their other activities. Setting up a local assembly plant was therefore an attractive way of securing an important market for parts and components. Not surprisingly the subsidiaries that were set up were not geared to locating, developing or utilizing local suppliers, but rather to act as an outlet for the kits supplied by the parent company (cf. Edelberg, 1976).

The Latin American markets grew in importance in the 1920s reflecting the expansion of the road network in the major countries of the region. The signficance of these countries for capital in the motor industry can be seen from the fact that vehicle imports to Argentina and Brazil peaked in 1929 at 70 000 and 54 000, respectively (ADEFA; Guimaraes, 1981, table 1). In the case of Argentina this represented a market that was almost twice as large as Italy's and about one-third of that of France or the United Kingdom in the same year (MVMA). The difference as far as US capital was concerned was that these Latin American countries could be used to extend the production runs of parts and components in the USA, whereas the highly protected European markets could not. Another indication of the importance of their subsidiaries in the region for the US car manufacturers is that in 1923 the assets of Ford's Buenos Aires plant were valued at $8.8 million making it the company's second most important plant outside North America (Maxcy, 1981, p. 71).

Although initially assembly plants were set up in Latin America in order to reduce freight costs, by the early thirties there were also significant tariff advantages available to local assemblers. In Mexico assembly material could be imported at a tariff that was 50 per cent less than that for assembled vehicles, while in Argentina the corresponding discount was 30 per cent for CKD assembly and 15 per cent for SKD kits. Because of the low value added in assembly these nominal tariff rates represented very high rates of effective protection enjoyed by the assemblers. Despite this local assembly continued to coexist with imports of built-up vehicles. An important reason for this was that a minimum level of sales was necessary to make local assembly profitable. In the case of Argentina in the early 1930s it was estimated that a firm needed sales of about 3000 to 4000 cars a year for assembly operations to be worthwhile (Phelps, 1936). Only Ford, General Motors and Chrysler enjoyed demand in excess of this level. Thus the smaller US manufacturers and the Europeans, in so far as they participated in the market at all, did so through exports. Given the advantages which they enjoyed it is not surprising that US capital, particularly Ford and General Motors dominated the Latin American motor industry throughout the inter-war period.

While the terminal industry in Latin America developed under the control of the leading US TNCs the pattern which emerged in the parts industry was rather different. Because of the strategies followed by the terminals, the local market for original equipment in Latin America was virtually non-existent. Consequently the large US firms which supplied Ford and General Motors in the United States and which had followed them into Canada and Europe had no interest in investing in Latin America. However, the growth of vehicle usage in the region created a demand for repair shops and a market for replacement parts. This sector grew rapidly in the thirties and particularly during the Second World War. In Argentina for example, employment in the parts industry grew three times and value added two-and-a-half times between 1935 and 1946 (CONADE, 1966, table 3). These firms provided the basis for the subsequent development of a local parts industry.

The one area of the motor industry complex, apart from the terminal sector, in which significant foreign investment did take place in the inter-war period was in tyre manufacturing. As indicated above the international expansion of the tyre TNCs followed its own dynamic and was not directly linked to the investments of the terminal firms. In Latin America the growth in vehicle use created a demand for replacement tyres which led to tyre production being established in Argentina (1931), Mexico (1933), Uruguay (1936) and Brazil (1939) during the thirties, closely followed by Venezuela (1941), Peru and Cuba (1943), Chile (1944) and Colombia (1945) during the Second World War (West, forthcoming, table 12). The US tyre TNCs led this expansion of the tyre industry in the region. By 1947 there were a total of 19 tyre plants established in Latin America (West, forthcoming, table 12), most of which were either subsidiaries or licensees of the major international tyre companies. Unlike the situation in the terminal industry where, because of the economies of scale in part and component production only the final stage, assembly, was transferred by the TNCs to Latin America, in the tyre industry technological considerations led to the transfer of the whole tyre manufacturing process, although the local subsidiaries continued to depend heavily on imported raw materials.

2 POST-WAR DEVELOPMENTS

The period immediately following the Second World War was one of buoyant demand and rapid growth for the motor industry in the advanced industrial countries. In the United States it was a period of high profit rates and a number of firms considered entering the terminal industry although in fact only two did so. Independents (firms other than General Motors, Ford and Chrysler) were able to take a 23 per cent share of the market in 1948. However, these conditions soon disappeared and in the early fifties the growth of sales fell sharply and profits began to decline. By 1955 only Studebaker of the independents was still profitable, and their market share had declined to only 5 per cent. The early fifties saw the main independents merge and by the mid-fifties only Studebaker-Packard and American Motors remained in the US car industry.

In Europe the period of rapid post-war expansion lasted somewhat longer than in the United States. In Britain local demand remained buoyant well into the fifties partly as a result of the priority which post-war governments assigned to the promotion of exports, while in Europe the physical destruction of much plant and equipment in the industry delayed recovery from the war. The destruction of the industry on the Continent and the post-war dollar shortage, enabled the British motor industry to achieve a preeminent position in world trade in vehicles, exporting more than three-quarters of its total production in the early fifties. In Latin America the period immediately after the Second World War saw a surge of imports, reflecting the pent up demand for vehicles of the war years and the availability of built up reserves of foreign exchange. The experience of Argentina where imports reached a peak of 80 000 vehicles in 1947 and Brazil where they peaked at 110 000 in 1951 are illustrative of this situation (ADEFA; Guimaraes, 1981, table 2). As in the inter-war period, the bulk of these imports were supplied by the United States, with the United Kingdom playing a secondary role.

The availability of foreign exchange was short-lived and governments responded by imposing restrictions on vehicle imports. In Mexico imports of assembled vehicles and some parts which competed with locally produced parts were temporarily banned in 1947 and in the following year a licensing system was introduced for all imports of assembly material and machinery for the motor industry. In Brazil imports of more than a hundred parts were banned in 1951, and in the following year non-essential imports of built up vehicles were also terminated. Further in 1954 it was decided that imports of parts which were produced locally should no longer be permitted and high tariffs were imposed on such imports. In Argentina, the Peronist government imposed strict foreign exchange controls and gave vehicle imports a low priority in terms of allocating foreign currency.

The period immediately preceding the transition to full scale manufacturing in Argentina, Brazil and Mexico was characterized by the entry of a number of new terminal firms. Whereas up to the Second World War only the US Big Three had their vehicles assembled in Latin America in the late forties and early fifties some of the US independents and some European firms began to assemble locally. These included Willys in Mexico in 1946 and Brazil in 1954, Kaiser in Argentina in 1955, Mercedes-Benz in Argentina in 1952 and Brazil in 1953, Volkswagen in Brazil in 1953 and Mexico in 1954 and Fiat in Mexico (1951).

The competitive advantage enjoyed by US capital, particularly the Big Three, in Latin America was significantly reduced in this period. They no longer enjoyed the privileged position of the inter-war period and immediate post-war years. By the early 1950s only 60 per cent of car imports to Argentina and Brazil came from the United States (Jenkins, 1977, p. 49; Guimaraes, 1981, table 2). Even in Mexico the US Big Three found their share of the market reduced to under 60 per cent by the early 1960s (Bennett and Sharpe, 1979a, table 1).

The other significant feature of the industry's development in the immediate post-war period was the rapid growth of the local parts industry. In Argentina where the industry was already well established by the end of the war, the number of firms more than doubled between 1946 and 1954 (CONADE, 1966, table 3). In Brazil the number of firms in the parts industry increased from only 30 in 1946 to more than 500 by 1955 (Guimaraes, 1981, p. 5). In 1956 it has been estimated that the parts industry was composed of over 700 firms employing 90 000 workers (da Cruz and da Silva, 1982, p. 4). In Mexico by 1960 the parts industry was made up of over 130 firms employing more than 7500 workers (Foncerrada Moreno and Vazquez Tercero, 1969). The industry's output grew by 6 per cent per annum between 1940 and 1954 and 8 per cent per annum between 1955 and 1961 (Aguilar, 1982, table VII). This industry was largely in the hands of local capital. Its growth in the late forties and the fifties was greatly facilitated by the restrictions on imports of parts and finished vehicles described above. They provided a nucleus of firms on which it was possible to build in subsequent years in order to achieve increased levels of local content in the terminal industry. They also constituted an important pressure group for such policies which would expand their market to include original equipment as well as spares.

The only other country apart from Argentina, Brazil and Mexico to have significant assembly operations prior to 1960 was Venezuela. General Motors set up a local plant in 1948 and two years later a local firm began to assemble Chrysler vehicles under licence before being taken over by Chrysler itself in 1955. Throughout the fifties local assembly coexisted with imports which accounted for the greater part of domestic sales. Elsewhere in the region the market continued to be supplied by imports in the fifties. The same decline in the position of US capital can be observed in these countries. By 1960 the United States accounted for less than half the cars imported into Venezuela and Colombia, less than one-third in Peru and less than one-sixth in Chile (SMMT, 1961).

NOTES

1. US investment in Britain and Germany in this period raises the question of why foreign firms were permitted to enter the industry if a major objective was to protect national capital. Indeed, in the case of GM's attempted acquisition of Citroen and Ford's attempted entry into Italy the host governments discouraged the investment. In Britain and Germany it is possible that the main concern was to protect local capital against the overwhelming competitive advantage of production in the US rather than to provide complete protection from foreign capital which competed on an equal basis with domestic production.
2. There is no data on the extent of such savings in transport costs on shipments from the United States to Latin America in this period, but it is reported that in 1928 GM could export nine CKD Chevrolets to Europe at about the same shipping cost as two fully-asembled cars (Donner quoted by Maxcy, 1981, p. 71).

Part I

3 Internationalization of Capital in the Post-war Boom

1 INTRODUCTION

The post-war years and particularly the period since the mid-fifties has seen an unprecendented internationalization of capital in the motor industry. In the first decade after the Second World War, as in the inter-war years, the industry was largely nationally based with its principal production centres in the United States, Canada, Great Britain, France, West Germany and Italy. Each national industry had its own distinctive characteristics and competition between capitals from different countries was largely confined to third markets (except for the case of US investment in Europe). Since the mid-fifties the motor industry has evolved from a nationally based industry to one based on three major regional centres, North America, Western Europe and Japan, and is increasingly becoming a 'world industry'. This final development is still by no means complete but the seventies and eighties have seen major steps in this direction.

The internationalization of capital is more than simply the growth of international trade and foreign investment although these are aspects of it. It also involves the standardization of products and techniques on a world-scale as distinctive characteristics of national markets and production techniques tend to be eliminated. It is the replacement of national norms by international norms in consumption and production. It also has a reflection in the internal organization of the transnational corporation where many firms have abandoned the structure which initially predominated of having a separate international division, as international operations grow and are seen as integral to the firm's overall operations. It is in this sense that one can speak of the creation of a world industry involving competition between capitals

27

on a world-scale and the incorporation of new areas of production in the international division of labour.

The present chapter concentrates on the period up to the early seventies which saw the emergence of three regional blocs within the industry in the developed countries and the extension of manufacturing operations to a number of peripheral countries and the establishment of assembly industries in many more countries. Developments since the early seventies which have led to the emergence of a single integrated world motor industry will be discussed in Chapter 9. This has also been a period in which the role of the industry in peripheral countries has begun to change with a much closer incorporation into the production process of the transnational corporation. Each of these phases in the development of the industry has seen an intensification of the competitive struggle.

The major change in the period up to the early seventies was the extension of the valorization of capital on a regional basis. Whilst this is usually commented upon in the context of European integration with the development of the EEC, it also occurred in North America which was constituted as a single production area with the US–Canada Automotive Agreement of 1965. The Japanese case is somewhat different since the formation of a regional industry coincides with the formation of a national industry both in time and in space. Japan which had scarcely begun to develop a motor industry in the late fifties had by the early seventies emerged as a major regional centre for the industry. The intensification of competition to which the internationalization of capital gave rise in this period was also reflected outside the major producing centres in the development of the industry in a number of Third World and semi-industrialized countries. This chapter will therefore deal with development first in each of the three major producing centres and finally in other areas.

2   NORTH AMERICA

The US motor industry having experienced a boom in the immediate post-war years began to face more difficult conditions in the early fifties. The independent producers were soon eliminated in the new competitive conditions leaving General Motors, Ford and Chrysler in control of 95 per cent of the US car market by 1955. However, the conditions which had permitted a sustained growth of the industry in the period before the Depression were not to be repeated in the fifties.

The full employment conditions of the post-war period made it more difficult to intensify labour through speed-ups etc. At the same time there was no rapid change in production technology which would have increased productivity substantially. The fact that the market for cars was increasingly becoming a replacement market also depressed the rate of growth. Profit rates fell in the terminal sector from 22.6 per cent between 1946 and 1950 to only 15.8 per cent in 1951–4 as market conditions tightened.[1]

Within the United States the companies attempted to maintain profitability by increasing the size of cars (since larger cars were more profitable to produce), and adding on the maximum number of accessories. Also faced with a slowly growing stock of cars in use they attempted to increase the rate of replacement by reduced durability and frequent model changes (White, 1971, ch. 12). These strategies were accompanied by a greater emphasis on expansion overseas where growth and profits prospects were better. In the late fifties and early sixties the Big Three car manufacturers all showed a sharp increase in the importance of their overseas operations relative to US production. Between 1953 and 1963 production overseas increased from 7 per cent to 17 per cent of world-wide production for GM, 15 per cent to 28 per cent for Ford and from virtually nothing to 17 per cent for Chrysler. The bulk of this foreign expansion was in Europe. GM's Overseas Policy Group had realized as early as 1944 that overseas markets would become at least as important as that of North America and expanded the range of cars produced by its subsidiaries in West Germany and the UK. Ford which already had important subsidiaries in West Germany and the UK expanded these although it closed its French subsidiary in the fifties. Chrysler which until 1958 had been primarily a North American company exporting to other areas, had by 1963 acquired a minority holding in Barreiros in Spain and a majority holding in Simca in France. The company's dependence on the US market had made it vulnerable. 'The sales volume fluctuations on the domestic market were particularly damaging to a company of Chrysler's size, and the growth and volume potential of Europe began to appear attractive.' (Young and Hood, 1977, p. 46.) Essentially it was felt that if Chrysler was to avoid the fate of the independents it would have to follow the path of Ford and GM in becoming internationalized.

While the Big Three spearheaded the international expansion of US capital in the motor industry in this period it was a much more extensive movement. In the late fifties and early sixties plant and equipment expenditures abroad by US subsidiaries in the transport equipment industry (mainly the motor industry including components) grew rapidly, more than doubling between 1959 and 1960 and doubling again by 1965 (*Survey of Current Business*, various issues). The same expansion of overseas activities is evident from the number of new subsidiaries set up by US multinationals, which increased sharply in the late fifties to reach a peak in the early sixties. A similar, although less pronounced, pattern also emerged in the tyre industry (see table 3.1).

A second important feature of the US car industry in the late fifties was the sharp increase in import penetration. In the immediate post-war period the United States continued to enjoy a substantial technological advantage over the European producers. In 1950 labour productivity in the US motor industry was between three and six times as high as in Europe (Silberston, 1965, table 5.8). As a result imports of cars to the United States accounted for less than 1 per cent of total sales in 1955 and imports of trucks were non-existent. The fifties saw substantial changes in the European motor industry. Production grew rapidly particularly of cars in each of the major countries. At the same time production techniques developed through the introduction of automatic transfer lines and the addition of control devices to standard engineering machines, a process which had become general in Europe by 1960 (Jenkins, 1972, pp. 264–8). Consequently labour productivity increased significantly in Europe reducing the gap compared with the United States to about 2:1 by 1959 (Silberston, 1965, table 5.8).

The first manifestation of the intensified international competition to which the recovery of the European motor industry was to give rise was

TABLE 3.1   *Number of subsidiaries of US MNCs set up by industry of subsidiary*

	Motor vehicles and equipment			Tyres		
	Total	Europe	LDCs	Total	Europe	LDCs
1946–50	13	6	5	12	4	7
1951–3	9	3	2	5	3	2
1954–5	8	2	4	4	2	2
1956–7	9	1	4	1	0	1
1958–9	39	11	21	11	6	4
1960–61	28	12	12	7	4	2
1962–3	47	17	21	7	1	4
1964–5	46	14	15	4	0	3
1966–7	35	21	8	5	2	2

SOURCE   Vaupel and Curhan (1969).

the rapid growth of exports, especially from France and West Germany in the late fifties. Volkswagen took the lead with a strategy of aggressive international expansion from the mid-fifties. The main target for this expansion was the United States where the share of imported cars (almost entirely European) increased rapidly to over 10 per cent in 1959. This expansion was made possible not only by the recovery of the European industry and the narrowing of the productivity differential with the United States, but also by developments in the US industry itself. In particular, the Big Three having effectively eliminated the threat posed by the Independents in the immediate post-war period focused their attention on the more profitable large car sector. As a result this left a gap at the bottom end of the market which the major European manufacturers were able to exploit. Although the introduction of the compacts in 1959 led to a sharp fall in the share of imports on the US market, it was never again entirely dominated by local manufacturers in the way in which it had been until the mid-fifties and in 1968 the share of imports again passed the 10 per cent mark.

An important step in the internationalization of capital in the motor industry in this period was the creation of an integrated North American industry. Although US capital had dominated the Canadian motor industry since the inter-war period, producing over 80 per cent of all cars, CVs and parts by the late 1920s (Wilkins, 1974, p. 75), it was still possible to speak of a separate Canadian industry until the mid-sixties. The US–Canada Automotive Products Agreement of 1965 effectively integrated the industry in the two countries. Prior to the agreement imports into Canada from the United States were subject to a tariff of 17.5 per cent, while Canadian imports into the United States paid a duty of 6.5 per cent. As a result the US companies produced most of the vehicles sold in Canada within that country, despite the fact that this inevitably meant smaller production runs because of the limited size of the Canadian market. The agreement eliminated tariffs between the two countries with the specific aim of permitting greater specialization in order to take advantage of economies of scale. The agreement covers both finished vehicles and parts to be used as original equipment.

The result was a rapid growth of trade in both vehicles and parts between the two countries as the manufacturers rationalized their activities allocating the production of certain models to their Canadian subsidiaries. In the ten years following the signing of the agreement US exports of vehicles to Canada grew more than tenfold while Canadian exports to the US increased more than twenty times. A less spectacular but significant growth of trade in parts also occurred in this period (Toder *et al.*, 1978, tables 2.10 and 2.11). The fact that the agreement was designed primarily to serve the needs of US capital in the terminal sector is clear from the limitations which were introduced. The duty free imports of parts applies only to shipments for original equipment, and the agreement is limited to products containing less than 50 per cent of material from outside North America. This effectively prevents European or Japanese firms from supplying the whole North American market from an assembly plant located in either Canada or the United States without paying import duties. Moreover, the agreement is limited to companies established in the base year, in effect General Motors, Ford, Chrysler and American Motors, and the Canadian government can prevent other companies from importing duty-free. Since the agreement only permits the motor manufacturers to import duty-free, and does not allow completely free trade in vehicles, it has permitted the US manufacturers to continue to charge higher prices in Canada. This has occurred, it has been suggested, because the Canadian market is more protected from Japanese and European competition (White, 1977). Nevertheless, despite such price discrimination, from the point of view of production, the North American market is now completely integrated.

3   WESTERN EUROPE

Up until the late fifties the basic pattern established in the inter-war period remained unchanged in the European motor industry. The industry in the major producing countries was highly protected with tariffs on cars of over 30 per cent in France, Britain, Italy and West Germany. As a result import penetration of the domestic markets of the major producers was extremely low. In the early fifties car imports accounted for less than 5 per cent of new registrations in each of the major European countries and as late as 1960, imports were still under 10 per cent in each market. In the case of commercial vehicles import penetration was even less with imports exceeding 5 per cent of sales only in Italy by 1960 (see table 3.2). A similar situation existed in the tyre sector and in the parts industry with the bulk of sales coming from local production. Each major national market was dominated by local capital with a participation by US capital in West Germany and the UK.

Three factors were crucial in changing this situation in the sixties.

First there was a reduction in tariffs particularly through the creation of the EEC. Tariffs on intra-EEC trade in cars were totally eliminated by 1968, while those on imports to other countries were also substantially reduced.[2] This led to a considerable increase in import penetration in the vehicle markets of the major European producing countries in the sixties and early seventies largely as a result of the growth of intra-European trade (see Table 3.2).

A second factor was the increased penetration of the West European industry by US capital as part of the process of overseas expansion described above. One of the main areas towards which this expansion was directed in this period was Western Europe. Established firms grew aggressively while a number of US firms set up subsidiaries in European countries for the first time. The US subsidiaries increased their share of the EEC market from 16 per cent at its formation in 1958 to 26 per cent six years later (Karssen, 1968), while in Britain, Ford and Vauxhall (GM) increased their share of the car market from 35 per cent in 1955 to 42 per cent by 1964 (Silberston, 1965, table 5.3). Between 1960 and 1968, Ford and General Motors invested about $1500 million each in expanding their European operations. In 1960 alone 60 per cent of the plant and equipment expenditure of US firms in the transport equipment industry abroad was in Europe. More than one-third of the foreign subsidiaries set up by US TNCs in the transport and equipment industry were in Europe in the period 1958–62 and half the tyre

TABLE 3.2   *Imports as a percentage of new vehicle registration*

	USA	UK	W. Germany	France	Italy	Japan
			Cars			
1955	0.7	2.2	4.0	2.4	1.9	21.1
1960	7.6	7.0	9.1	4.1	4.8	°2.4*
1965	6.1	4.9	17.9	13.9	11.6	2.2
1970	14.7	14.3	22.5	19.8	27.7	0.7
1973	15.2	27.4	25.9	20.8	27.9	1.1
			Commercial vehicles			
1955	0.1	0.6	2.5	0.6	2.2	3.2
1960	0.4	1.3	2.8	2.9	5.2	°0.3*
1965	0.9	1.0	4.6	7.6	15.9	°—†
1970	4.1	4.3	13.3	13.5	14.9	°—†
1973	8.2	12.5	19.5	17.6	30.7	°—†

* 1961.
† Less than 0.05.
SOURCE   Trade association data.

subsidiaries (see Table 3.1). This period saw the take-over of Simca and Rootes by Chrysler, the entry of Goodyear and Firestone into France and Italy, Goodyear and Uniroyal into West Germany and Uniroyal into France, while in the components industry Perkins was taken over by Massey-Ferguson and Cummins entered the UK industry. It was of course this wave of US investment in Europe which sparked off the discussion of the American Challenge in the late sixties.

The third factor to have a major effect on the development of the motor industry in Europe in this period was the changing demand conditions within the industry. This was most marked in the case of the car industry where the rapid growth in demand after the Second World War came to an end by the mid-fifties, and the market ceased to be a sellers' market. The rate of growth declined further in the late sixties as the potential for increasing car ownership diminished and replacement demand increased in importance. As Friedman (1977, ch. 13) argues for the case of Britain, this stage in the product cycle led to an intensification of competition in the industry. This intensification of competition was accompanied by a marked downward trend in profitability in the industry. In Britain, for instance, profit rates were highest in the early post-war years, falling in the late fifties and then declining even further in the sixties (Silberston, 1965, p. 276; Rhys, 1972, table 10.5).

The breakdown of national monopolies and oligopolies, increased penetration by US capital and the slow-down in market growth all contributed to increasing competition in the European motor industry in the sixties and early seventies. This was marked by a change in the competitive strategy of European capital in the industry. Whereas the problems of the fifties had been production, in the sixties problems of realization became increasingly important. As one commentator on the industry in this period wrote, 'The new configurations in Europe have led manufacturers to put a new emphasis on marketing. The accent on engineering remains, but the shift towards styling with annual model changes has begun' (Wierzynski, 1968, p. 121). This change was most marked on the Continent where in the fifties the major firms had produced a very small range of models. Perhaps the most spectacular case was Renault which in 1961 produced only the Dauphine on a large scale and within ten years developed a range of ten models. Similar policies were followed in the sixties by other companies, notably Volkswagen, Peugeot and Fiat.

The changed strategy of the major car manufacturers in the sixties had in fact two complementary aspects. The first was to increase the number of models produced by each firm and the second was to change models more frequently, compared with the situation in the fifties when it was common for models to stay in production for well over ten years before being discontinued. Both these strategies implied a loss of economies of scale for the European manufacturers. A large range of models meant that annual production of each model would be less while more frequent model changes reduced production runs over the entire life of a model. This gave a substantial competitive advantage to larger firms which could offer more models and change them more frequently, and put pressure on the smaller manufacturer.[3]

The strategic response of European firms intensified the trend to concentration and centralization within Europe. The sixties saw a spate of mergers in the industry. The result was the creation of a small group of large European vehicle manufacturers which were important transnational corporations in their own right.

Although centralization of capital in the European motor industry in the fifties and sixties continued to occur primarily on a national basis with no significant international mergers or take-overs within Europe, in other respects there is evidence of a clear trend towards the creation of a European motor industry as opposed to the separate national motor industries of the post-war period. This trend manifested itself in a number of ways. First, as has already been noted, there was an increasing interpenetration of domestic markets of the main producing countries by firms based elsewhere in Europe reducing the dominant position of local firms in national markets. As a result the leading firms came increasingly to regard Western Europe rather than France or West Germany as their domestic market.

Secondly, the US companies began to regard their European operations as an integrated whole and not to see each one as an isolated subsidiary. This trend was a response to the new market conditions and greater competitiveness of the motor industry in the sixties. In each European country US firms ranked behind the major national firms in terms of their volume of car production in the sixties. In 1965 for instance, Opel produced less than half the number of cars manufactured by VW in West Germany and Ford had less than a quarter of that number. In Britain Ford was well behind BMC, Vauxhall produced one-third of the number of cars produced by BMC, and Rootes which was in the process of being acquired by Chrysler, just over a quarter. In France too, Simca, by then controlled by Chrysler, was the smallest of the four manufacturers producing less than half the number of cars made by Renault. Thus paradoxically increased competition, which had been partly provoked by the activities of the US companies, in fact left them in a relatively weak position.

An important reason for this weakness was the fact that the subsidiaries of the US companies in the different European countries operated largely in isolation from one another. An article written as late as 1965 could comment that:

> There is little integration of production or interdependence between the major manufacturing plants of the American vehicle companies throughout the world. It is not the practice for a plant in one country to specialize in the production of other components for supply to the other manufacturing units (*Motor Business*, 1965).

With all the present talk of 'world cars' it is easy to forget that international integration of the operations of the major motor manufacturers is less than two decades old.

The integration of their European operations was a logical step to combat their competitive disadvantage on the part of the US transnationals. Taking their British and West German plants together the output of both Ford and General Motors (Opel and Vauxhall) were greater than that of all the other European car manufacturers with the exception of VW and Fiat, while Chrysler (Simca and Rootes) came behind BMC and Renault but ahead of the other French and German producers.

The pioneer in this trend towards international integration was undoubtedly Ford which set up Ford of Europe as a first step in the integration of its European operations in 1967. Within a few years the company had developed a common range of cars in its European operations as opposed to two quite separate model ranges in Britain and West Germany. GM and Chrysler were somewhat behind Ford in moving towards integrated European operations. Chrysler declared its intention of centralizing styling, product planning and engineering in order to create a unified European model range but was slow to move towards integration of production partly because of the financial difficulties of the parent company. The first step in this direction was the Chrysler 180 designed in Britain and produced in France which was introduced in 1970. In the same year GM followed Ford in setting up a European headquarters. Nevertheless, with the exception of Ford no car manufacturer had developed this kind of international integration very far by 1973.

That the move towards integrating their European operations was a reflection of the relative weakness of the US firms in the competitive European market emerges clearly in the case of Ford. The company took its first steps towards integrating its British and West German subsidiaries as a direct response to the weakness of the latter in the German market (CIS, n.d., p. 23).

A third aspect of the constitution of a European motor industry in the late fifties and 1960s has been the growth of production and commercial links, short of full-scale merger between firms from different countries. These included a joint company to build engines formed by Renault, Peugeot and Volvo, a sales and technical agreement between MAN and Saviem and joint companies between Citroen and Audi-NSU to develop the Wankel engine. These agreements were a means by which economies of scale in research and development and in the production of certain parts and components could be realized without a full-scale merger of all the companies' activities. These covered both car and commercial vehicle sectors of the industry and were another way in which national self-sufficiency in the industry was broken down. However, it was not until the 1970s that this was taken a step further through a series of international mergers in the industry.

The tendency for cars to become increasingly European (as opposed to French, German etc.) in design is most evident with the small hatchback cars introduced in the seventies by VW, Fiat, Renault and Ford. The trend in this direction was already underway in the sixties. The individualistic designs of the Beetle and the Mini were becoming few and far between while the US model of cautious cost-conscious design was increasingly being adopted by the major European manufacturers (Ensor, 1971, ch. 2). Moreover, increasing market interpenetration meant that in designing new cars, firms could not afford to neglect the need to sell throughout Europe. While in the early seventies one industry commentator argued that 'there is no logical reason to suppose that all cars will begin to look alike or look "European"' (Jenkins, 1972, p. 184), the experience of the past decade suggests the contrary.

While the increasing standardization of the industry's product within Europe is more immediately visible, the standardization of production techniques has been equally significant. In the sixties the use of standard limited purpose machines as a basis for automatic transfer lines which had been pioneered by Renault followed by the UK manufacturers became generalized within the European industry (Jenkins, 1972, p. 265). This is not to say that plants in different countries employ identical production techniques. Even within one country there will be significant differences between firms as each seeks to reduce costs ahead of competitors. However, the sources of differences between firms in Europe now are different positions in the competitive struggle rather than different national solutions to production problems.

4 JAPAN

The third major bloc within the motor industry which developed in the late fifties and sixties was Japan. Unlike North America and Europe this development did not involve the integration of previously separate national markets, but rather came about through the development of a dynamic new industry which had barely existed in the early fifties. In 1952 and 1953 a number of Japanese firms signed technical contracts with foreign manufacturers – Nissan with Austin, Hino with Renault, Isuzu with Rootes and Mitsubishi with Willys Overland. Many of the firms which were subsequently to become major producers in Japan thus started life in the fifties assembling CKD kits under licence from European and North American manufacturers. There was, however, no foreign investment in the industry and it has been suggested that foreign firms, especially the US companies were not interested in investing in Japan, partly because of the experience of having been forced out of the Japanese market by the Automobile Manufacturing Law of 1936 and partly because they saw greater opportunities for growth in Europe at that time. A further factor which may have limited the interest of foreign capital in Japan was the heavy emphasis on three-wheel commercial vehicles in Japan during the fifties (Duncan, 1973).

The sixties was a period of rapid growth in car ownership in Japan and this was reflected in the expansion of local production. New registrations of cars grew more than fifteen-fold between 1960 and 1970 and production increased even faster. The growth of commercial vehicle sales and output was less spectacular but nevertheless substantial. Despite the rapid growth of the domestic market foreign capital was not allowed to enter the terminal industry until the liberalization of the early seventies. This was a deliberate policy on the part of the Japanese state of preventing the industry from being faced with direct competition from foreign capital until it was in an extremely strong competitive position. Thus in the post-war period it had been established that foreign capital participation in the motor industry should be limited to 7 per cent of the share capital for an individual entity and 20 per cent in total. Thus even when the rapid growth of the Japanese motor industry made it an obviously attractive market for foreign capital, controlling interests were not permitted.

Under the auspices of the Ministry of International Trade and Industry (MITI) a process of centralization of capital was promoted in the Japanese motor industry from the mid-sixties. Prince was taken over by Nissan in 1966 and Fuji Heavy Industries joined the group two years later, while Toyota acquired Hino in 1966 and Daihatsu in 1967. An attempt was made to form a third group to include Mitsubishi, Isuzu and Fuji but this did not come off, while it was thought at one stage that Suzuki would join the Toyota Group. Despite the failure of these two attempts, the result of these government sponsored moves was a significant increase in concentration in both car and CV production.

The international expansion of the Japanese industry began in the late sixties with the growth of exports, at first with a heavy emphasis on CVs but later increasingly of cars. The increased emphasis on exports came at a time when the growth rate of the domestic market was beginning to slow down, and the export drive was spearheaded by Toyota and Nissan, the two firms which dominated the internal market. The growth of exports came at a time of rapid productivity growth in the Japanese motor industry. Between 1965 and 1973, output per man in the Japanese industry increased at an average annual rate of more than 10 per cent, and the level of productivity rose from less than that in the Western European countries to a level not far below that of the United States (CPRS, 1975, chart 24). The expansion of exports in this period was largely of CBU vehicles and there was little expansion of overseas production by Japanese capital. CKD units for assembly abroad accounted for less than 20 per cent of Japanese vehicle exports in the early seventies.

Despite the limitations on foreign capital entering the terminal sector of the industry in Japan in the sixties there was some foreign investment in the tyre and parts industries. Goodrich, Firestone, Uniroyal and General all had minority interests in Japanese tyre and rubber manufacturers. In the mid- and late 1960s a number of foreign companies became involved in joint ventures in the Japanese parts industry. These included Eaton, Borg Warner, GKN and TRW. However, substantial foreign penetration of the Japanese motor industry did not occur until the seventies.

The sixties saw the establishment of Japan as a major vehicle manufacturing centre. However, it remained a relatively isolated bloc and could not be regarded as part of an internationally integrated industry. Imports were virtually non-existent from the early sixties while the industry only began to become an important exporter towards the end of the period. Moreover, there was little penetration of the Japanese industry by foreign capital in this period, while Japanese capital had not really begun to invest abroad on a significant scale. Finally, in a number of respects, the nature of the Japanese market differed significantly from both the West European and the North American market in this period. One manifestation of this was the continued importance of three-wheelers in Japan until the mid-sixties. Another aspect was the importance of very small cars (less than 360 cc) which accounted for more than 20 per cent of car production in the late sixties, in sharp contrast to the emphasis on large cars in North America and the predominance of medium sized cars in Western Europe.

5   EXPANSION OF THE INDUSTRY INTO NEW AREAS

The recovery of the European motor industry after the Second World War and the narrowing of the productivity gap between Europe and the United States in the fifties led not only to increased competition in Europe and North America as was seen above, but also to an intensification in the struggle for markets outside the main producing blocks. This led to a breakdown of the old pattern of market divisions based on colonial preferences, geographic proximity and cultural links. In Latin America, as was seen in the last chapter, US capital came to be increasingly challenged by European firms.

Two important trends in the international motor industry since the late fifties have been the growth of certain new centres of vehicle manufacturing, outside the traditional producing countries, and the expansion of assembly operations on a world-wide scale. The intensification of competition for markets outside of North America and the European producing countries made it possible for certain states with potentially important domestic markets to attract foreign capital to set up a local motor manufacturing industry. The most important examples of this process have been Argentina, Brazil and Mexico in Latin America, Spain in Southern Europe, India in Asia and Australia and South Africa among the former British Dominions.

Vehicle production in these seven countries increased from less than 300 000 (produced mainly in Australia) in 1955 to over 2 million in 1970 and over 3 million by 1973. The countries' share of world vehicle production rose sharply from 2.1 per cent in 1955 to 7.5 per cent fifteen years later. The growth of vehicle manufacturing in these countries was a result of deliberate government promotional policies and international competition between US and European TNCs to control new markets. All seven countries had Ford and General Motors assembly plants set up in the twenties and thirties but the transition from assembly to manufacturing production really took place in the period from about 1955 to 1965.[4] This transition to manufacturing was undoubtedly related to the increased competition which the recovery of the European motor industry created for the major US manufacturers.

In the early fifties Ford and General Motors decided not to engage in manufacturing in either Spain or India preferring to close down their assembly plants there. However, by the late fifties it had become apparent that failure to undertake local manufacture in important potential markets would lead to the government carrying out its plans with the aid of other transnationals. In 1961 Henry Ford II declared:

Whether we like it or not Africa, Asia, Latin America are going all-out into the industrial age . . . If we want to share in those markets, rich and vast as they will some day surely be . . . we are going to have to go in with our capital and tools and know-how and help them get the things they want (Wilkins and Hill, 1964, p. 414).

A very similar point of view was expressed by General Motors' Vice-President, T. A. Murphy, in evidence to the Senate Subcommittee on International Trade:

There is no question that if General Motors or other US automotive firms were to turn their backs on market participation through overseas facilities, multinational firms based in other countries would be alert and quick to act to fill the need (US Senate, 1973).

Thus, whether the US companies chose to participate or not (as in the case of Spain and India), by the mid-sixties all these countries had developed manufacturing with a local content of over 50 per cent. In all cases there was a strong presence of European manufacturers who before the Second World War had not internationalized their production at all. VW had subsidiaries in Brazil, Mexico, South Africa and

Australia and Mercedes-Benz in Argentina, Brazil, South Africa and India. The French companies (Renault, Peugeot and Citroen) and Fiat were most active in Argentina, South Africa and Spain while the British forerunners of British Leyland concentrated on South Africa, India and Australia. Everywhere except in India the Europeans were in competition with the US transnationals – Chrysler in Spain, and all the Big Three elsewhere as well as American Motors and International Harvester in some countries.

The development of the motor industry in the late fifties and sixties followed very similar lines in all seven countries. The industry was granted high levels of tariff protection and restrictions were imposed on imports of built-up vehicles. Competition to control the local market usually resulted in a large number of firms entering the industry with a consequent fragmentation of the market and lower levels of concentration than were found in the larger markets where the industry was well established. As a result of this market fragmentation and the small size of the total market production runs for individual companies were low and costs correspondingly higher than in the developed countries. Production was almost exclusively intended for the domestic market and the integration of the local subsidiaries into the international operations of the parent companies was purely as a market for imported parts and components. Finally, by the late sixties the industry in all countries had come to be virtually entirely under the control of foreign capital despite the existence of a significant presence of national capital in the early days.[5]

The development of vehicle manufacturing in these countries meant also the growth of a parts and components industry which had previously been limited largely to the production of replacement parts and some items of original equipment which had been deleted from the CKD packs supplied to local assembly plants. The parts industry which was thus created came under a substantial degree of foreign control either directly through ownership of local subsidiaries by transnationals or indirectly through licensing agreements with foreign suppliers of technology. Major transnational parts manufacturers such as Eaton, Bendix, Borg Warner, Lucas, Bosch and others set up subsidiaries as these countries developed their automotive industries. The Latin American countries are discussed in more detail later. In both Spain and Australia there was an extensive foreign presence in the parts industry (Cuadernos del Dialogo, 1971, pp. 28–9; Stubs, 1972, ch. 8). Only India again appears as an exception with a much lower level of foreign involvement in the industry.

Apart from the seven countries discussed above, the other major area in which vehicle production developed in the late fifties and sixties were the socialist countries of Eastern Europe and the Soviet Union. With the exception of Yugoslavia, which in many respects bears a closer resemblance to the group of countries just discussed than to the rest of Eastern Europe in terms of automotive development, there has been no direct foreign investment in the industry. Nevertheless there has been a substantial trade in technology between the major transnationals in the industry and the Soviet Union and the Eastern European countries.[6]

These technical cooperation agreements have laid the basis for the development of the Soviet Union and Eastern Europe as a fourth major vehicle producing area which may in future increasingly become an integrated part of the international motor industry. These developments will be discussed in Chapter 9.

While development of vehicle manufacture in this period was confined to a small number of semi-industrialized countries and the Soviet Union and Eastern Europe, the second trend noted above, the growth of assembly operations, was much more extensive. As with the development of manufacturing the growth of assembly operations involved state intervention in the form of import restrictions and local content requirements to force some integration of locally produced parts. By the seventies most Southern European and Third World countries had some requirement of this kind (see Table 3.3). The number of countries in which the motor manufacturers have assembly plants either directly owned or operating under licence increased from 42 in 1960 to 86 in 1976 and the total number of such operations went up from 170 to more than 600 over the same period. By the mid-seventies it was estimated that assembly and production of vehicles in these plants accounted for more than 20 per cent of world production.

The growth of assembly operations is also a manifestation of the intensified competition between firms to control new markets. As with those countries which have developed manufacturing operations, it has led to a large number of firms setting up plants. Because the initial investment requirements are fairly low these are often owned by local licensees. The transnationals secure a market for parts or CKD kits exported from the home country and obtain preferential access to the protected domestic market. Thus in the initial stages of developing a local assembly industry the parent company can retain production of those parts and components most subject to economies of scale in the home country while only decentralizing those processes (such as assembly) and parts (such as tyres and radiators) which are not subject

TABLE 3.3   *Trade restrictions and imports into selected developing countries, 1978**

Country	*Trade restrictions‡*			*Cars in use ('000)*	*Car imports† ('000)*
	Local content	*Import resitrictions*	*Export requirements*		
Greece	●	●		650	90
Portugal	●	●		888	34
Spain	●	●		6 530	15
Turkey	●	●	●	602	4
Yugoslavia	●	●		2 142	69
Argentina	●	●	●	2 500	2
Brazil	●	●	●	6 750	1
Chile	●	●	●	295	17
Colombia	●	●	●	470	21
Mexico	●	●	●	2 829	95
Peru	●	●		320	3
Venezuela	●	●	●	1 100	86
India	●	●		850	1
Indonesia	●	●		540	16
Iran	●	●	n.a.	600	163
Israel		●		333	29
S. Korea	●	●	●	185	30
Kuwait				280	40
Malaysia	●	●	n.a.	525	75
Pakistan	●	●	●	200	5
Philippines	●	●	●	374	32
S. Arabia				350	140
Taiwan	●	●		n.a.	56
Thailand	●	●		375	25
Algeria		●		650	9
Egypt	●	●		310	21
Libya	n.a.	n.a.	n.a.	387	55
Morocco	●	●		375	21
Nigeria	●	●		400	62

* All countries with over 180 000 cars in use in 1978 outside North-West Europe, North America and Japan are included.
† Includes some CKD kits.
‡ Import restrictions apply to non-tariff measures which deal solely with imports.
n.a. = information not available.
SOURCE   Jones (1981), table 9.

to great cost penalties when produced at low levels of output. The high rates of effective protection which tariffs on imports of CBU vehicles usually give to local assembly activities and the captive market makes local assembly on these terms attractive especially when compared with the alternative of losing the market to competitors.

With time, however, there has been a shift from local assembly to manufacturing in Third World countries. As already indicated a number of countries made the transition to manufacturing in the period 1955 to 1965. This has reduced the share of assembled vehicles in the total produced in less developed countries from 92 per cent in 1960 to less than half by the mid-seventies.

6 CONCLUSION: INTERNATIONALIZATION OF CAPITAL AND THE DEVELOPMENT OF THE AUTOMOBILE INDUSTRY

This chapter has indicated that internationalization of capital in the motor industry in the period up to the early seventies involved the constitution of three major producing blocs and increasing competition between capitals for control of new areas of vehicle production outside these blocs. In conclusion, we shall consider how these tendencies manifested themselves in international trade flows within the industry, in the strategies of overseas production and export of the major companies in increased integration between firms and finally in the level of national and international concentration in the industry.

The period saw a rapid growth in world trade in vehicles. Exports of the major producers have increased at a significantly higher rate than production since the early fifties. Between 1955 and 1970 exports as a share of world production of vehicles increased from 11.6 per cent to 26.2 per cent. This was reflected in the growing importance of overseas markets as opposed to the domestic market for all the major producing countries.

In terms of the development of three identifiable blocs in the motor industry the qualitative change in the direction of trade which accompanied this rapid growth was even more significant. In 1955 trade consisted almost entirely of exports from North America and Western Europe to the rest of the world. Trade both between the major producing blocs and within each bloc was relatively insignificant. By 1970, however, the situation had changed radically. Although exports from the major Western European countries to the rest of the world continued to be the largest single flow, trade between Canada and the US dwarfed other exports from North America. Trade between the major European producing countries also contributed a significant portion of world trade in contrast to the situation fifteen years earlier. Finally the beginning of interpenetration between the different regional blocs can be seen in the growth of exports from both Europe and Japan to North America (see Figures 3.1 and 3.2).

A second aspect of the internationalization of capital in this period has been the increased share of output by the major companies which is produced by foreign subsidiaries. In the fifties, overseas production by the major European vehicle companies was extremely limited with foreign markets being served almost exclusively through export. By the early seventies the major European TNCs in the terminal sector were in many cases selling as much or more from overseas subsidiaries as through exports (see Table 3.4). The trend towards increasing reliance on overseas production is evident from the example of the West German motor industry. Overseas production as a share of total production by the German motor industry increased over the period 1960 to 1973 from 2 per cent to 17.3 per cent for cars and 8.1 per cent to 25.1 per cent for commercial vehicles. Over the same period the ratio of exports to foreign production fell from 23.4:1 to 2.8:1 for cars and 5.6:1 to 1.8:1 for commercial vehicles.

As Table 3.4 also indicates US companies rely entirely on overseas subsidiaries in pentrating foreign markets and as was mentioned above these operations grew rapidly especially in the late fifties and early sixties. The Japanese firms in contrast relied entirely on exports to penetrate foreign markets and were still more dependent on their domestic market then the European manufacturers. This reliance on exports reflected the recent character of the internationalization of the Japanese industry which only began exporting on a significant scale in the late sixties.

The sixties also saw a substantial internationalization of the operations of the major firms in the component industry. Not surprisingly in view of the international expansion of the terminals and the development of manufacturing in a number of countries which previously only had assembly operations major US companies such as Borg Warner, Clark Equipment, Eaton and TRW which until the fifties had been almost entirely based in the US expanded overseas. At the same time, the major European companies such as Associated Engineering, Chloride, Lucas and Bosch also expanded their overseas operations substantially. Within Europe this was given a further impetus by the increas-

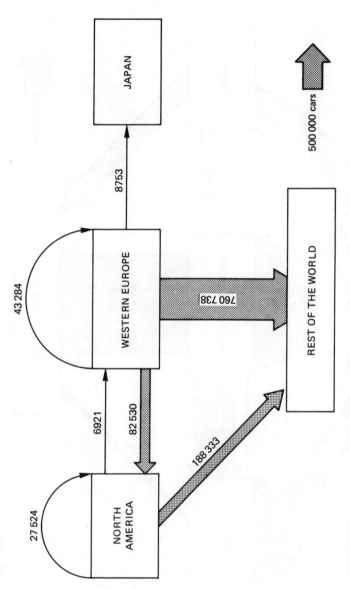

FIGURE 3.1 *Major international trade flows in cars, 1955*

48

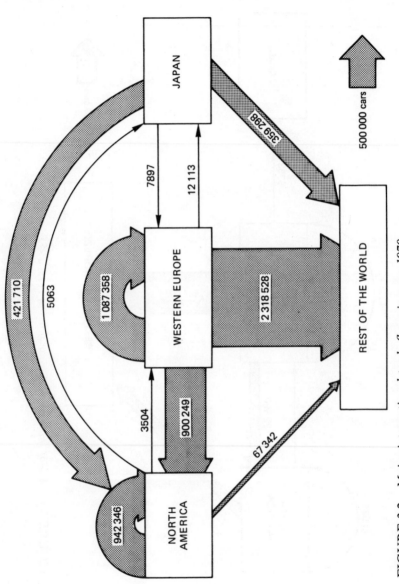

FIGURE 3.2 *Major international trade flows in cars, 1970*

JAPAN

WESTERN EUROPE

NORTH AMERICA

REST OF THE WORLD

359 298

7897

12 113

421 710

5063

1 087 358

2 318 528

3504

900 249

942 346

67 342

500 000 cars

TABLE 3.4   *Distribution of vehicle sales between domestic market, exports and foreign subsidiaries, 1973*

	Domestic sales	Exports	Sales of foreign subsidiaries
GM	75	—	25
Ford	64	—	36
Chrysler	57	—	43
VW	27	47	26
Daimler-Benz	48	45	7
Renault	43	26	31
Peugeot	55	20	25
Citroen	49	26	25
Fiat	44	27	29
BLMC	52	27	21
Toyota	65	35	—
Nissan	64	36	—
Toyo Kogyo	54	46	—
Honda	79	21	—
Isuzu	73	27	—

SOURCES   Company Reports and Bhaskar (1980), table 4.7.

ingly European basis of the terminal industry as firms sought to diversify their supplies.

Increased international integration of the industry in this period occurred mainly within the three major blocs and particularly within Western Europe. There are two aspects to this integration. One is the integration of operations in different European countries of the kind pioneered by Ford. The second is the increasing number of links between European firms which in this period involved the creation of joint companies, or marketing and production agreements rather than mergers or take-overs. Figure 3.3 illustrates the major links which existed around 1970. This underlines three points. First, with the exception of the long-established US investment in Europe (plus the more recent entry of Chrysler) links are within the major blocs rather than between them. Secondly, links within Europe do not usually involve ownership of subsidiaries in other major producing countries. Finally, Japan is virtually totally isolated from both North America and Western Europe. As will be seen in Chapter 9 the situation changed radically in the 1970s.

As was indicated above the intensification of competition in the motor industry in the sixties led to concentration and centralization of

50

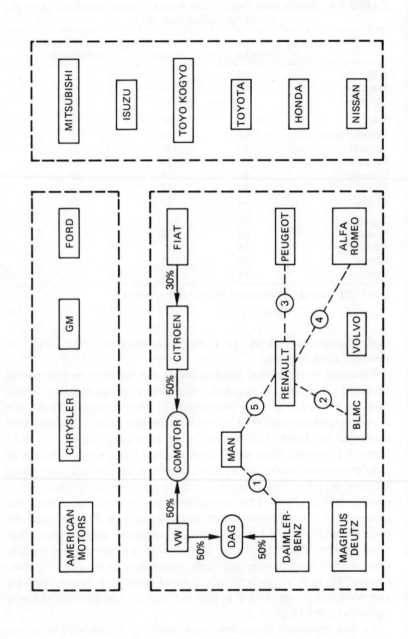

▢ Terminal firm

⬭ Other firm

→ Ownership with percentage shareholding indicated

---- Other link

1 Daimler-Benz and MAN have a technical cooperation agreement.

2 Pressed Steel Fisher division of BLMC makes parts for Renault.

3 Peugeot-Renault joint test circuit and planned jointly owned factories to produce engines and gearboxes.

4 Cooperation in marketing between Renault and Alfa Romeo.

5 Production and marketing agreement between Renault's Saviem truck subsidiary and MAN.

FIGURE 3.3 *Links between major motor manufacturers, c. 1970*

capital in the terminal industry of the major producing countries. At the same time, however, the increasing interpenetration of national markets as a result of the expansion of trade in fact reduced market concentration as indicated by the share of the largest firms in total sales. This raises the question of the effect of concentration and centralization at the national level on the extent to which a small group of firms have dominated the industry at a world level.

If one takes aggregate figures for the share of total world vehicle production accounted for by the leading companies then the motor vehicle industry has been highly concentrated since before the Second World War. In the inter-war period and the early post-war years this reflected the dominance of US production within the global total and the domination of GM and Ford within the United States. In 1954, before the internationalization of the European motor industry described above, more than two-thirds of all the vehicles produced in the world were manufactured in the US and Ford and GM accounted for more than 80 per cent of US production. Together with their foreign subsidiaries these two firms accounted for almost 65 per cent of world production of cars and commercial vehicles (IMF, 1964, table VII). By 1963 the share of the United States had declined to less than 45 per cent of the total and despite the internationalization of their operations described above, that of GM and Ford had also declined to 49 per cent (see Table 3.5). The next decade saw a further erosion of the market share of these firms, largely as a result of increases in the shares of Chrysler, Toyota, Nissan and to a lesser extent Renault and Peugeot. This is consistent with the picture presented above of intensified international competition in the industry during the sixties and early seventies. Moreover, if one focuses on not just the largest two firms but on the largest eight or fifteen firms, it can be seen that there has been a consequent increase in concentration in the industry during this period. The share of the largest eight firms in total vehicle production increased from 73.1 per cent in 1963 to 76.5 per cent in 1973, while fifteen leading companies increased their share from 83.0 per cent to 90 per cent over the same period. The development of concentration in the industry is therefore more complex than is suggested by data which has been used to show a decline in concentration in the industry since the late fifties or early sixties.[7] In fact while concentration has declined at the highest level, the share of world output controlled by a relatively reduced group of firms has increased significantly.

TABLE 3.5 *Leading vehicle producers, outside COMECON countries, 1963 and 1973*

		1963		1973			
Rank	Firm	Output ('000)	Percentage of total output	Output ('000)	Percentage of total output	Firm	Rank
1	GM	5 974	30.0	8 684	23.5	GM	1
2	Ford	3 692	18.5	5 871	15.9	Ford	2
3	Chrysler	1 322	6.6	3 450	9.3	Chrysler	3
4	VW	1 210	6.1	2 335	6.3	VW	5
5	Fiat	950	4.8	2 260	6.1	Fiat	7
6	BMC	750	3.8	1 161	3.1	BMC	9
7	Renault	668	3.4	1 452	3.9	Renault	8
8	AM	511	2.6	562	1.5	AM	14
9	Citroen	476	2.4	773	2.1	Citroen	11
10	Daimler Benz	345	1.7	548	1.5	Daimler-Benz	15
11	Toyota	318	1.6	2 692	7.3	Toyota	4
12	Peugeot	289	1.5	795	2.1	Peugeot	10
13	Nissan	268	1.3	2 271	6.1	Nissan	6
14	Rootes	200	1.0	739	1.9	Toyo-Kogyo	12
15	Volvo	117	0.6	563	1.5	Mitsubishi	13
Total output (excluding COMECON)		19 905	100.0	36 984	100.0		

SOURCE   IMF (1964), table A and Company Reports.

NOTES

1. Average of net profit (after tax) as percentage of net worth (White, 1971, table 15.2).
2. The UK, which remained outside the EEC at this time reduced its tariff on car imports from 30 per cent in 1960 to 11 per cent in 1973.
3. Cf. Menge (1962) on the importance of model changes in eliminating the Independents in the United States.
4. Australia was a partial exception to this with manufacturing production by GM, beginning in the late forties and other US manufacturers increasing local content when as a result of the dollar shortage the local subsidiaries which had dominated the market before the Second World War found themselves unable to compete with British imports. Ford and Chrysler did not achieve full local manufacturing until the late fifties, however, and BMC began manufacturing in 1956 and VW in 1960.

5. India was a partial exception to this with only two firms with a foreign shareholding but its industry was also the least dynamic.
6. For more details on relations between the auto TNCs and the Soviet Union and Eastern Europe, see Maxcy (1981) pp. 165–73 and UNCTC, 1982, pp. 112–17.
7. See UN (1978), table III-52 which shows a decline in the Herfindhal index of concentration for the automobile industry between 1957 and 1973 and UN (1978), table III-53 which shows a decline in the share of the three leading firms as a percentage of the world's twenty largest firms between 1962 and 1972.

4 Implantation of Motor Manufacturing in Latin America

1 INTRODUCTION

It was in the context of the intensified international competition in the motor industry from the mid-fifties described in the previous chapter that a number of Latin American states took steps to promote the development of local manufacturing activities, while others began to regulate and promote assembly activities in order to make increasing use of locally produced inputs. This chapter examines the way in which these policies interacted with the international system conditioning the emergence of a particular structure in the Latin American motor industry.

2 RATIONALE FOR DEVELOPING THE INDUSTRY

The factors which led to several Latin American states adopting measures to promote the development of the motor industry from the mid-fifties are inextricably linked to the insertion of their economies into the international system. The foreign exchange reserves built up during the Second World War were quickly rundown in the late 1940s, and although the commodity boom associated with the Korean War provided a brief respite from external pressures, the deteriorating terms of trade which faced most Latin American countries in the mid-fifties led governments to focus their attention on ways in which the balance of payments could be improved.

The motor vehicle industry was a prime candidate for an extension of import substitution in the larger Latin American countries. In both Brazil and Mexico the industry accounted for a substantial share of all

55

imports–14 per cent in Brazil in 1951 and 13 per cent in Mexico in 1950. (AMIA, 1976, p. 164; de Oliveira and Popoutchi, 1979, p. 20). In Argentina where government policy severely restricted imports in the post-war period, the effect was a substantial increase in the average age of the stock of cars to over eighteen years by 1955 (Sourrouille, 1980, table 4).

In addition to its obvious significance as a drain on foreign exchange there were a number of further reasons for choosing the motor vehicle industry as a prime target for industrial promotion. In Argentina, Brazil and Mexico import substitution in non-durable consumer goods was largely completed by the early fifties. To renew the dynamic of capital accumulation it was necessary to embark on new key sectors. Consumer durables was therefore identified as an area of expansion and within this cars were clearly the most important in terms of their sales value. Given also that the attraction of foreign capital to promote industrialization was much in vogue amongst the developmentalist governments in Latin America from the mid-fifties, the motor vehicle industry which was identified with some of the world's largest TNCs and characterized by increasing competition, again seemed an obvious sector to develop.

Assembly plants already existed in many Latin American countries but they had failed to have a significant dynamizing effect on capital accumulation and existed primarily as a means by which imported CKD kits could be put on the domestic market.[1] The local content of the vehicles which they assembled was low. In Brazil locally produced parts accounted for only 18 per cent of the total weight of the assembled vehicles in 1953 (Almeida, 1972 quoted in Guimaraes, 1981, p. 6), while in Mexico imports accounted for 80 per cent of all purchases by the assembly plants in 1960 (Lifschitz, 1979, p. 24).

Despite the lack of a direct impetus to the development of suppliers, a significant parts industry had emerged in Argentina, Brazil and Mexico serving primarily the replacement market. Thus at the time that it was decided to promote the development of vehicle manufacture in these countries there were already 500 parts producers in Brazil, 400 in Argentina and 200 in Mexico (Lifschitz, 1982, p. 11). This sector, controlled primarily by local capital, constituted an important pressure group in favour of government legislation requiring the assembly plants to increase their local purchases.

Government officials emphasized a number of ways in which the development of the industry would dynamize the accumulation process. The wide range of inputs used in vehicle assembly meant that linkages could be created across a broad range of industries such as steel, glass, rubber and plastics as well as the components industry. Having been at the centre of capitalist development for decades it was also commonly regarded as a technologically sophisticated industry the development of which would upgrade the technological level of domestic industry. It was also hoped that because of its size and linkage effects it could make a major contribution to the generation of new jobs. (See Bennett and Sharpe, 1979a on Mexico; Sourrouille, 1980 ch. 1 on Argentina.)

Inter-country rivalry within Latin America also played a part in generalizing the process of promoting the motor vehicle industry. Given the political rivalry between Argentina and Brazil for influence in the region, it was inevitable that if one developed an automotive industry, the other would soon follow suit. Similarly, the development of the automotive industry in these countries both indicated the possibilities open to Mexico and put pressure on the Mexican government to develop its own industry. As Raul Salinas Lozano, the Minister for Industry and Commerce at the time was later to point out.

If we had not begun to integrate the industry at that time, we would have been required to 'negotiate' the import of those products which we did not produce including vehicles (Vázquez Tercero, 1975, pp. 7–8).

In the smaller Latin American countries both the pressures for and possibilities of developing a local manufacturing industry were less acute. In Chile, Colombia, Peru, Uruguay and Venezuela the market was supplied primarily by imports until the sixties. The restricted size of the domestic market, however, meant that they did not constitute such a heavy drain on foreign exchange as in Brazil or Mexico. It also meant that full manufacturing would not be feasible because of the very short production runs which this would entail. Moreover, the supplier industry (with the exception of tyres where a number of TNCs had established subsidiaries in the thirties and forties) was virtually non-existent, reducing the interest of local capital in the development of high levels of local content. Nevertheless in the sixties all these countries adopted policies to promote local assembly, with increasing incorporation of locally produced parts and components.

3   GOVERNMENT POLICIES TO PROMOTE THE MOTOR VEHICLE INDUSTRY

In broad terms the policies followed by the different Latin American states in developing a local motor vehicle industry were very similar. They involved protectionist measures using either prohibitively high tariffs or an outright ban on imports which were not included in the programmes of local production, a requirement that local content should be increased over a period of several years, and preferential tariffs (or total exemption from import duties) for parts and components as well as capital goods which constituted part of an approved production programme. In addition, in a number of countries, they were associated with direct subsidies and further tax exemptions for the participating companies. Finally the promotion of the industry took place within the general framework of the liberal foreign investment legislation which was introduced in most Latin American countries in the late fifties and early sixties.[2]

The first government to begin a comprehensive programme for the development of a local motor industry was Brazil's which in 1956 set up the Grupo Ejecutivo de la Industria Automovilistica (GEIA) responsible for promoting the industry. GEIA set local content targets for the industry which were to rise from between 35 per cent and 50 per cent of vehicle weight in 1956 to 90–95 per cent by 1961. At the same time, firms participating in the programme were offered certain fiscal incentives such as exemption from duties and taxes on imports of parts and machinery, and special credit facilities from the National Development Bank. The Argentinian government, which had in the early fifties under Peron begun to promote a local motor industry, embarked on a comprehensive policy for the industry in 1959. As in the case of Brazil, local content requirements were set which would increase from between 55 per cent and 70 per cent of the c.i.f. value of vehicles in 1960 to 80–90 per cent by 1964. The last of the three major Latin American countries to promote a nationally integrated motor industry was Mexico, which began to rationalize its assembly industry in the early sixties, cutting the number of models assembled locally by half, and then in 1962 requiring 60 per cent of the direct costs of vehicles (including the engine) to be accounted for in Mexico within two years. Again firms which set up under the programme were exempted from import duties on parts and machinery, and granted an 80 per cent reduction in the federal assembly tax.

Although Argentina, Brazil and Mexico were the only Latin American countries to develop motor manufacturing as opposed to assembly operations in this period, a number of other Latin American countries began systematically to promote the development of assembly operations with increasing levels of local content in the early sixties. In Chile a number of assembly plants were set up in the northern port of Arica in the late fifties and early sixties, and in 1962 the government created the Comisión para el Fomento de la Industria Automotriz to take charge of the development of the industry. Local content requirements were set which would rise from 30 per cent of the f.o.b. value of the vehicle in 1963 to 58 per cent by 1968, for cars and in 1966 similar norms were laid down for commercial vehicles. In Venezuela local assembly began in 1948, but throughout the fifties the greater part of local demand was supplied by imports. In 1962 imports were prohibited almost completely and local content requirements increasing from 13.5 per cent of vehicle weight in 1963 to 40 per cent by 1970 were set. In Peru in 1963 tariff protection for local assembly of vehicles was increased sharply and firms setting up CKD assembly operations were offered a number of fiscal incentives. Local content requirements were set at 10 per cent of the c.i.f. value of imports in 1965 rising to 30 per cent by 1970. The only other country which developed significant local assembly operations in this period was Colombia where two firms set up in the early 1960s under special contracts with the government. No specific local content requirements were set and by the late sixties integration was only around 25 per cent. Finally in 1964, Uruguay which had previously relied entirely on imported vehicles, imposed high duties on imports of built-up vehicles, leading to the development of a local assembly industry. This operated with a minimal level of local content until the early seventies when increasing levels were required by further legislation.

The cases of Brazil and Mexico provide a vivid illustration of the extent to which government subsidies and tax exemptions contributed to the promotion of industrial development in the sector. One estimate indicated that in Brazil 89 cents were granted in exchange and fiscal subsidies for each dollar invested in the industry in the period 1956–61 (Almeida, 1972, p. 41). A calculation for Mexico indicates that the subsidy received by the industry between 1966 and 1972 came to between 50 per cent and 60 per cent of the value of investment in that period. The author concludes that the rapid growth of the Mexican auto industry was paid out of government generosity (Gudger, 1975, p. 228ff).

4 THE TERMINAL INDUSTRY

The immediate result of government legislation to promote the development of a local motor industry in the various Latin American countries was a flood of new firms setting up. Generally speaking all the firms which met the requirements of the promotional legislation had their investment plans approved and no attempt was made to limit the number of firms entering the industry. In Argentina 23 firms submitted proposals of which 21 actually produced some vehicles. In Brazil 17 proposals were accepted by GEIA of which 11 began production, while in Mexico 10 firms received government approval of which two subsequently withdrew. The situation in countries which promoted assembly operations with a certain level of local content was if anything worse. Twenty companies set up in Chile, 16 in Venezuela and 13 in Peru during the early- and mid-sixties. Thus the characteristic fragmentation of the Latin American motor industries between a large number of manufacturers was established at the outset, through a combination of intense oligopolistic rivalry between the leading transnationals in the industry and a failure on the part of the Latin American states to intervene to control entry into the industry.

The failure of Latin American governments to limit entry into the terminal industry in the late fifties and sixties is crucial to the subsequent development of the industry and deserves further consideration. The official rationale which was commonly offered is best expressed in the words of an Argentinian government official closely involved in motor industry policy:

The means adopted in order to achieve these objectives was through the operation of an open competitive regime, whereby there would be room for all those interested parties who complied with certain common requirements. The most capable and efficient firms should survive the struggle for a small but eager market, without prior exclusions or discretion on the part of government officials which would permit erroneous interpretations. Clear instructions were received from the President on this point. Only meeting, or failing to meet, the basic requirements and agreed plans should give rise to differential treatment (Vila, 1962, quoted in Sourrouille, 1980, p. 51).

A similar view that competition would eliminate the least efficient firms and, at the same time, bring about price reductions was also expressed in Mexico (Bueno, 1971, p. 95).

It is clear, with hindsight, that in an industry such as the Latin American motor vehicle industry which is dominated by foreign-owned oligopolies, competition will not bring about a more rational industrial structure through the elimination of firms. However, it is not only with hindsight that this has become clear. In the case of Mexico there was a definite proposal to limit the number of firms and models which would be produced locally. Government officials were well aware that foreign subsidiaries can produce at a loss in the hope of achieving a larger market in the future while offsetting these losses against the tax liabilities of the parent company (NAFINSA, 1960, p. 56).

In fact the Mexican decision to reject the advice of its own technicians was a consequence of the many pressures which the TNCs were able to bring to bear on the government. These came not only from the assemblers themselves but also from their suppliers and dealers in Mexico and from the home states. US Embassy officials told the Mexican Director and Sub-director of Industries that the exclusion of any of the US assemblers could be interpreted as 'not very friendly acts' and the US Ambassador warned the Secretary of Industry and Commerce that in such an event a strong reaction could be expected from the State Department. Similar pressures were brought to bear by the Japanese government on behalf of Nissan using continued access to the Japanese market for Mexican cotton, as a lever with which to obtain the acceptance of the firm's production plan (Bennett and Sharpe, 1979a).

Although detailed information of such pressures is only available in the case of Mexico[3] the objective situation which made such pressures possible were not unique to that country. They derived essentially from two aspects of Mexico's insertion into the world economy and the development strategy which the government pursued. First the reliance on foreign capital to promote import substituting industrialization made it essential to maintain a favourable 'climate for investment', so that measures which could be interpreted as indicative of hostility to foreign capital were ruled out. Secondly, despite import substitution, the Mexican economy remained crucially dependent on access to foreign markets for its primary products in order to obtain the capital and intermediate goods necessary to continue the process of accumulation.

In addition to its fragmentation between a large number of terminal firms, a second characteristic feature of the industry in those Latin American countries which have increased levels of local content is the almost total domination of the terminal sector by foreign capital. In the assembly phase a number of locally owned firms produced under licence from foreign capital, and even after the initial move towards increased local integration there continued to be a significant involvement by local capital. In the course of the sixties, the major auto TNCs increased their penetration of the market, taking over licensees, acquiring independent national firms and driving out national competitors. In Argentina in the early sixties two-thirds of output was produced by firms with more than 50 per cent local capital. In Brazil one-fifth of output was by local firms and the largest producer was Willys, a company with a 42 per cent Brazilian shareholding and not part of a large transnational. In Mexico more than one-third of the industry was in national hands and in Chile almost 90 per cent. Of the other countries, Colombia had two locally owned assembly plants in the early sixties and when Peru and Venezuela began to promote the industry in the mid-sixties, there was a significant representation of local firms producing under licence.

By the early seventies, the situation had changed dramatically as Table 4.1 indicates. In the three largest Latin American countries only the state owned firms, IME in Argentina and DINA and VAMSA in Mexico remained in local hands and none of these enjoyed leading positions in the market. In the countries where assembly operations continued albeit with increasing local content, a similar situation existed, although minority foreign-owned firms were slightly more important. The trend, however, was clearly one of displacement of local capital from the terminal sector.

TABLE 4.1   *Foreign ownership in the terminal motor industry, 1972.*
Share of production by per cent

	Majority foreign owned firms	Minority foreign owned firms	Locally owned firms
Argentina	97.3	—	2.7
Brazil	100 °	—	—
Chile	96.3	—	3.7
Colombia	44.9	55.1	—
Mexico	84.6	6.5	8.9
Peru	77.2	22.8	—
Venezuela	67.4	3.2	29.4

SOURCE   Trade association data.

5 THE PARTS INDUSTRY

In addition to creating a particular structure in the terminal sector the interaction between internationalizing tendencies in the world motor vehicle industry and national measures to promote the industry within Latin America had major consequences for the parts and components industry. As was mentioned earlier there already existed, in the larger Latin American countries, a significant number of parts manufacturers, largely locally owned and producing primarily for the replacement market. There also existed a number of tyre manufacturers, either foreign-owned or, in a few cases, producing under licence, which not only supplied the replacement market but also were amongst the first firms to have their products incorporated into locally assembled vehicles. For the tyre manufacturers the move into manufacturing did not bring about major changes, for the parts industry, however, change was dramatic.

In the first place the decision to achieve high levels of local content within a few years meant that a rapid expansion of parts production would have to take place. In both Brazil and Mexico legislation restricted the extent to which the terminals were allowed to produce parts 'in house', thus reserving a substantial market for the auxiliary industry. In Argentina on the other hand no such limitations were enforced. In all three countries production and employment in the parts industry increased rapidly.[4] This growth was accompanied by major structural changes in the parts industry.

Prior to the establishment of domestic manufacturing the parts industry concentrated on technologically relatively unsophisticated products and those for which there was a substantial replacement market. It was now necessary, however, to produce more complex parts and components for incorporation as original equipment. This was often achieved by the terminals persuading their home country suppliers to follow them into overseas markets. Thus the late fifties and early sixties saw a wave of investment by foreign parts producers in Argentina, Brazil and Mexico. As a result the predominantly nationally owned parts industry came increasingly under foreign control and a dualistic structure emerged with a relatively small number of large companies producing original equipment, either under foreign ownership or under licence while a considerable number of smaller, locally owned companies continued to produce for the replacement market, and supply some simple parts as original equipment. By the early seventies foreign capital accounted for roughly half the output of the parts industry in all three countries (de Oliveira *et al.*, 1979; Jenkins, 1979; Sourrouille, 1980).

In the smaller Latin American countries increasing local content also provided a stimulus to the development of parts production. In some cases this has involved investment by the major component TNCs to produce more complex parts, but in general the share of TNCs in parts production is much less significant in these countries than in Argentina, Brazil and Mexico, reflecting the predominance of simpler parts amongst those incorporated as original equipment and produced for the replacement market. Most of the TNCs which have entered the parts industry in these countries tended to do so as progressive increases in local content requirements made it necessary to incorporate more complex parts. Examples include the entry of Rockwell Standard in Chile in 1968, and Robert Bosch in Peru in the early seventies.

NOTES

1. A study of the procurement practices of US firms in the Mexican motor vehicle industry in the fifties and early sixties concluded that they failed to act as a catalyst for the development of local suppliers (Edelberg, 1976).
2. See Jenkins, 1984, pp. 182–5 for a discussion of this legislation.
3. There is some evidence to suggest that in Argentina the US companies pressured for changes in the initial government legislation before beginning car production there (Jenkins, 1984a).
4. Employment in the parts industry increased at an average annual rate of 6.6 per cent in Brazil (1956–64), 24.7 per cent in Argentina (1959–65) and 17.9 per cent in Mexico (1965–70). Own calculation from da Cruz and da Silva (1982); ADEFA, 1969 and Aguilar (1982), table XII.

5 Conditions of Production

1 THE PRODUCTION PROCESS IN THE MOTOR INDUSTRY

In this section the production process in an integrated car plant in the advanced capitalist countries will be described. This will provide the necessary background for subsequent discussion of vehicle production in Latin America and the extent to which different phases of the production process have been transferred there.

The conventional view of car production identifies it with the moving conveyor belt and routine, monotonous work, the pace of which is dictated by the machine. This characterization is, however, an oversimplification and corresponds only to particular parts of the production process, particularly final assembly. In aggregate not more than a quarter of the total blue-collar work-force in the industry work 'on the line'. Even in an assembly plant less than three-quarters of the workers are line workers (Widdick, 1976, p. 8).

A typical integrated car factory engages in a number of stages prior to final assembly, each with its characteristic production process. The main types of processes involved in addition to assembly are stamping of sheet metal to form body parts, casting of engine blocks etc., forging of high strength parts and machining of engine and transmission parts. The sequence of operations and the different departments and plants in which they are carried out are illustrated in Figure 5.1.

Body stamping takes place in a press shop in which sheet steel is pressed under heavy pressure into the required shape. The steel passes along a line of presses or through a multi-stage press to give it its final form. The basic capital equipment involved are the presses which are very expensive but have a long life (twenty to thirty years) and the dies which give the panel its particular shape. The length of life of dies which have to be changed with alterations in body-styling depend on the volume of output produced. The durability of dies is a subject of considerable controversy among commentators on the industry with estimates varying from 400 000 to 7 million.[1] As will be seen below the

66

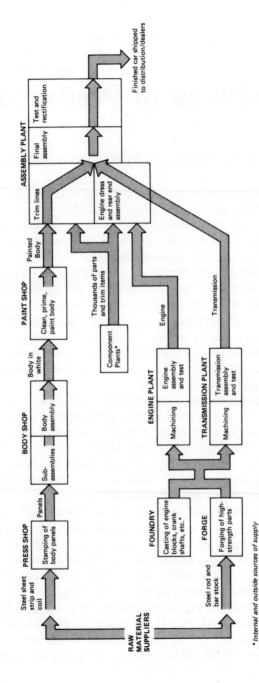

FIGURE 5.1 *Automobile production – sequence of operations*
SOURCE: CPRS, 1975, chart 2.

*Internal and outside sources of supply

length of life of dies is an important element determining economies of scale in the industry. Stamping operations in the developed countries are now largely automated with mechanized feeding and exit of panels and often completely automatic lines. It is estimated that only 10 per cent of the labour required to produce a car is in this department.

Castings for cylinder blocks, crankshafts and many transmission parts may be produced by the terminals in their own foundries or bought in from outside suppliers depending on the level of vertical integration of the company. The practice varies from country to country and company to company. Most large companies have their own foundries but they also buy a wide variety of castings since no foundry produces the whole range of castings required in vehicle manufacture. Parts requiring exceptional strength are heated in furnaces and drop forged to approximately the right dimensions. Castings and forgings are then machined to the fine tolerances required in the machine shops of engine and transmission plants. Although machining has generally been highly automated by the larger firms which make extensive use of automatic transfer machines, sub-assembly continues to require a considerable amount of labour. In total, production of engines, transmissions and axles account for about 25 per cent of the total labour force and for a significant part of total investment (CPRS, 1975, p. 15).

Steel panels and stampings are welded together into sub-assemblies and finally into a rigid body in the body shop. Up to the 1970s this was a relatively labour-intensive operation with sub-assemblies being welded on tracks known as buck lines (if the body is stationary during assembly) or gate lines (if the body is moving). About 30 per cent of the total work-force is employed in the body shop (CPRS, 1975, p. 14). The 'body in white' is then cleaned, primed and painted in the paint shop. Cleaning, priming and at least the initial enamel coat are applied automatically. Labour requirements are relatively low, less than 10 per cent of total labour, but painting is a skilled job because of the need to obtain a high quality finish (CPRS, 1975, p. 15).

Following painting the body passes along the trim line where a large number of parts and bought-in components are installed. The body then moves to final assembly where the engine, transmission and power train are installed. This is an area which requires careful coordination since bodies arriving on one line have to be matched with the correct engines, etc. arriving on the other. It is therefore an area of potential bottlenecks and a source of interruptions to production. The vehicle then passes on to final trim where items such as the tyres and battery are installed. This is the most labour-intensive area in car production since most operations are carried out manually. Direct labour accounts for as much as half of total costs in an assembly plant (ECLA, 1973, table 21), and about one-fifth of the total work-force is employed in the assembly plant (CPRS, 1975, p. 16).

Although it is common to regard modern, dynamic industries such as motor manufacturing as a preserve of skilled labour, this is not in fact the case. In the United States only 21 per cent of GM workers are skilled workers while in France the corresponding proportion at Renault was 23 per cent (Widdick, 1976, p. 8; Krutzky, 1977, p. 151). The remainder are classified either as semi-skilled or unskilled. Although the majority of auto workers fall into the semi-skilled category, this is not an indication that they require a lengthy period of apprenticeship or training. Back in 1925 Henry Ford estimated that 79 per cent of his workers could become proficient in the tasks required of them within eight days, and as many as 43 per cent within a single day (Beynon, 1973, p. 116). Indeed a major objective of Ford's development of standardized parts and assembly line production in the early decades of the twentieth century was to eliminate the control of skilled workers over the labour process by reducing the need for craftsmen (Gartman, 1979). Things have not changed much since then and the time required to train most car workers continues to be minimal.

The nature of the labour process in the motor industry explains not only why the greater part of the work-force in the industry requires minimal levels of skill, but also the advantages of mass production of vehicles in terms of reduced unit costs. The large capital investment required particularly in the presses and dies for the press shop, and in automated equipment for the machine shop, means that uninterrupted production of a large number of vehicles is required in order to spread the cost of fixed capital.

Table 5.1 indicates a number of estimates of the minimum efficient scale of production of cars under US and UK conditions in the late sixties and early seventies. Assembly is generally regarded as the process least subject to economies of scale and it appears that with an output of 200 000 cars there is no great cost penalty. Estimates of economies of scale in body stamping vary considerably and as was indicated above this depends on the assumptions made concerning the useful life of dies and of the effects on costs of writing off dies over a shorter time period. It appears that costs do not fall a great deal beyond an output of around 400 000 to 500 000, although there are some

TABLE 5.1 Estimates of minimum efficient scale in car production

Author	Year	Country	Casting	Machining	Stamping	Assembly	Overall 1 Model	Overall Complete range
Patten	1971	UK	1000	250	500	300	500	1000
White	1967	US	small	260	400	200	400	800
Rhys	1971	UK	200	1000	2000	400	–	2000
University of Bristol	mid-1970s	UK	1000–2000	400–1000	500+	200–400	200+	1000+
CPRS	1975	UK	100	500	n.a.	250	500	–
Ebner	1974	US	n.a.	250–400	200–400	200–400	350–400	1100–1500

SOURCES Bhaskar (1980), table 4–2; CPRS (1975) table 4; Toder et al. (1978) tables 5–2 and 5–6.

savings at higher scales. Dies can be rotated in order to obtain full utilization of presses and used up over a longer period of time (White, 1977, p. 183). For machining estimates for the production of one engine model are in the range from 250 000 to 400 000 with higher figures where more than one engine is produced. The large design, development and tooling costs of new engines means that manufacturers keep engines in production for a number of years. There is no general agreement on economies of scale in casting but this is not a serious problem because of the availability of outside foundries from which castings can be bought if the firm's production is not otherwise sufficiently large.

The drive to mass production derives not just from the exigencies of the production process, however, but also from the competitive strategies of the major producers. The minimum efficient scale for producing one car model in the 1970s was in the region of 400 000 to 500 000. However, the marketing strategies of the major manufacturers stress the need to supply a whole range of models. Reliance on a single model would be extremely risky since one market failure could spell disaster for a company. Moreover, in the normal course of events existing customers would be lost as they traded-up to a more expensive model. A range of two or three basic models therefore requires production runs of at least half a million cars a year.

Commercial vehicle production has historically tended to be less highly mechanized than car production despite the fact that the same basic processes are usually involved.[2] Consequently it is not subject to economies of scale to the same degree as car production but there have been far fewer studies of the exact level of the m.e.s. While light commercial vehicles and vans are often related to car models produced by the same firm and can therefore take advantage of the same engines and components, this is not the case for medium and heavy lorries. The importance of economies of scale in CV production depends on the level of vertical integration in the industry. It is possible for a small CV producer to survive at little cost disadvantage where there is a well developed component industry from which it can buy engines, gearboxes and axles. At levels of production of less than 5000 vehicles a year labour-intensive production methods are probably most efficient. It was estimated in the late sixties that economies of scale existed for medium-sized trucks (3–8 tons) up to a range of 20 000 to 40 000 vehicles and for heavy trucks and buses up to around 5000 (Baranson, 1969, p. 24).

In comparison with cars, the m.e.s. in truck production tends to be lower relative to average annual production indicating that more plants of an optimum scale can be supported by a given market in the truck sector, than for cars. This is particularly true in less developed countries where there tends to be a proportionately greater emphasis on truck production. More significantly costs do not appear to rise as sharply below the m.e.s. as they do for car production, making it easier for smaller firms to survive. Moreover, until fairly recently there has not been the same emphasis on frequent model changes in the truck sector as in cars so that this has not been such an important factor in accentuating the advantages of larger scale.

2 PRODUCTION PROCESSES IN THE LATIN AMERICAN MOTOR INDUSTRY

In discussing vehicle production in Latin America in this period it is possible to identify two extreme patterns. One involves the reproduction of the type of integrated vehicle factory described in the previous section and includes all the major operations – stamping, casting, forging, machining and assembly.[3] This is the pattern which typified the major producers in Brazil and Argentina from the 1960s.[4] The other extreme arises where the terminal firm is simply an assembly plant which imports most of the parts and components which it uses and buys in a few parts from local suppliers.[5] This situation was typical of Chile, Colombia, Peru, Uruguay and Venezuela in the sixties or early seventies.[6] An intermediate situation, which was found in Mexico, is one where the terminal firm is not simply an assembler but also sets up an engine plant but does not engage in major stampings.

The different types of terminal operations found in Latin America are obviously related to the local content requirements imposed by different states which were discussed in the last chapter. Levels of local content of up to about 35 per cent can be achieved without the terminal firm being more than an assembly plant, since assembly itself accounts for about 10 per cent of the cost of the vehicle and parts which can be bought in such as wheels, tyres, batteries, radiators, upholstery etc. can account for a further 25 per cent (Jenkins, 1977, pp. 90–91). Integration beyond this level involves the development of a machine shop to produce engines and transmissions which brings the level of local integration up to 60 per cent. Finally the establishment of a press shop and body shop can bring the level of local content to over 90 per cent.

The differences between integrated production and truncated production in the motor industry are reflected in differences in the commerical flows which characterize the motor industry in different Latin American countries (see table 5.2). In Argentina and Brazil imported parts accounted for only some 4 per cent of the value of sales by the terminal firms in 1970, while locally bought parts, components and raw materials account for more than half the total. In Peru and Venezuela on the other hand, imported parts account for around half the value of output while locally produced parts account for less than a third. There is also a higher level of vertical integration within the Argentinian and Brazilian industry, where the value added by the terminals is 40 per cent or more of the value of sales, than in Peru and Venezuela where the ratio is less than 30 per cent.[7] Mexico, as expected occupies an intermediate position, in terms both of its reliance on imported inputs and the extent of local purchases. Its low value added is a reflection of the Mexican government's policy of preventing vertical integration by the terminal firms apart from the production of engines.

TABLE 5.2   *Value added, local purchases and imports as percentage of value of output in selected countries, 1970*

	Value added by terminals	Local purchases	Imports
Argentina	45.0	51.0	4.0
Brazil	40.6	55.4	4.0
Mexico	27.7	44.3	28.0
Peru	28.6	24.1	47.3
Venezuela*	17.0	33.0	50.0

*1977.
SOURCES   Lifschitz, 1982, table 2; Fontanals and Porta, 1979, table 16.

These differences are significant not only for what they reveal about the structure of the motor industry in different Latin American countries, but also for their implications for the way in which the major auto TNCs view the operations of their subsidiaries in different Latin American countries. In countries such as Peru, subsidiaries are primarily a means of realizing surplus value produced in the advanced capitalist countries through the export of kits or parts or major components. They contribute, in aggregate, to the achievement of large scale production of crucial parts and components by the TNC in its home country or other major production base. In Brazil and Argentina, however, such exports are extremely limited confined to a few specialized parts or materials. The strategy of the TNCs is therefore focused on the production and appropriation of surplus value within the countries concerned.

In the smaller Latin American countries therefore the main considerations for the motor manufacturers concern their relations with the state, on which their continued access to imported parts, as well as the reservation of the domestic market for locally produced vehicles through protectionist policies, depend.[8] Given suitable government policies they are able to derive a double advantage. First, they are able to sell their CKD packs to local subsidiaries or licensees at highly favourable prices. This is ensured by the system of 'deletion allowances' whereby the omission of a particular part from a CKD kit leads to a reduction in the price of the pack of less than the value of the omitted part. Taken to its logical conclusion this implies that a firm could import an empty CKD pack and pay, say, 50 per cent of what it would pay for the complete pack. This strategy has two beneficial effects for the TNC. First, it makes it more difficult for local suppliers of parts to undercut the deletion allowances given by the terminal and is therefore a disincentive to local production. Secondly, even when parts are deleted, the pricing policy pursued ensures that the parent company continues to obtain considerable revenues from sales to their assembly plants. For example in Colombia in 1977, the value of CKD packs imported was almost 90 per cent of what would have been paid for importing completely built up (CBU) vehicles despite the considerable degree of local parts production by that date (Ronderos Tobon, 1981, table 3.8).

The second advantage is the ability to charge high prices for the assembled vehicles in markets which are highly protected from import competition. As will be seen below this means that high costs can be passed on to consumers. In this situation of truncated production therefore, relations with labour are of secondary importance compared with relations with the state.

It is not the case, however, that the plants which were set up by the motor manufacturers in Latin America in the late fifties and sixties were exact replicas of those which they owned in Europe or North America, even in those countries which embarked on integrated production. This difference is highlighted in the following description of a General Motors plant opened in Mexico in the mid-sixties, given by an official of the UAW.

I had made a careful tour of the plant. It was worse than archaic.

> Worse, because it was deliberately archaic, with the obsolescence carefully built in ... Overall, it would appear to have less than 10 per cent of our productivity back home ... The salient fact is that the presses in Buenos Aires, like the machines in Toluca, were not antiquated, brokendown wrecks. The machinery there was also newly built – but not to produce ... I asked him (an engineer in the United States on his return home) about the Foot-Burt machinery I had seen in the Latin American plants. 'Oh', he answered, 'that is our special low production machinery' (Leo Fenster quoted in Frank, 1972, p. 109).

Given the small size of the local market and its fragmentation between a large number of companies, the firms had little choice but to scale down plants well below the levels which were considered necessary to take advantage of economies of scale. In the sixties the major TNCs in Argentina, Brazil and Mexico had plants which in no case were designed to produce as many as 100 000 vehicles and in a number of instances had a capacity of 20 000 or less. Given that the estimated minimum efficient scale for producing a single model, under developed country conditions was over 200 000 units, and that these Latin American plants produced a variety of different models, the extent of down-scaling is clear.

As the above quotation implies, adaptation to lower volume production is not simply a matter of reproducing a small scale replica of the standard plant, but also leads to changes in the nature of the labour process involved. Most obviously production tends to be less automated in Latin America. A comparison of the use of general purpose, non-automatic machinery in the motor industry in Brazil and the United States showed that whereas almost half the machines used in Brazil were non-automatic, in the United States the proportion was less than one-fifth (Morley and Smith, 1977, table 3). Similarly, in Argentina the plants were equipped with universal, single station hand control equipment which could be used to machine different parts (Nofal, 1983, p. 161).

Manual loading, unloading and handling of materials were far more common in the Latin American plants than in the United States. Similarly welding which was often automated in the US was carried out using hand-held equipment in Argentina and Brazil. The main advantage of the non-automated method was the greater flexibility in view of the more frequent need to change models (Morley and Smith, 1977). It has also been observed that painting is carried out using hand-held spray guns in Brazil in contrast to the prevailing practice in the advanced capitalist countries (Morley and Smith, 1977, p. 256). The area in which production techniques were most similar to those found in the advanced capitalist countries was assembly reflecting the limited extent of automation in assembly plants generally in the sixties. Even here, however, there were some differences in that assembly lines in Latin America tended to produce a much wider variety of models, to have slower line speeds and to involve longer work-cycles for each worker (Nofal, 1983, pp. 163–4).

In the countries in which the activities of the terminal were confined almost entirely to the assembly of CKD kits with the incorporation of a few locally produced parts, scales of production were even lower, often only a few thousand units a year. In these cases assembly was extremely labour intensive with the capital required being confined to the buildings in which assembly was carried out and some tools. In these cases production could usually be increased by hiring more workers, so that the concept of capacity was rather flexible.

The use of less mechanized production techniques often (but by no means always as the description of the GM plant in Mexico bears out) involved the use of second-hand equipment. The most extreme examples were Willys Overland in Brazil and Kaiser in Argentina. Both these firms which had attempted unsuccessfully to compete with the Big Three (GM, Ford, Chrysler) in the United States, transferred complete plants to Latin America. Other firms also made partial use of second-hand machinery. Ford, for example, imported second-hand machinery from Canada to set up its Argentinian subsidiary. In 1967 almost a quarter of the equipment in use in the Argentinian motor industry was over ten years old, and since the bulk of the investment in the industry took place after 1959, this must indicate a significant use of used machinery (Jenkins, 1984a, p. 52). Extensive reliance on second-hand equipment when the industry was set up in the 1950s has also been reported in Brazil (Baer, 1976, p. 127). In Mexico two of the terminal firms were reported to have used second-hand machinery (Bueno *et al.*, 1971, p. 118).

In summary therefore it can be said that motor industry production in Latin America in this period differed in a number of ways from production in the advanced capitalist countries. In those countries which undertook integrated production, a formal similarity in terms of the processes undertaken, hid important differences in the nature of the labour process. Latin American plants tended to be less mechanized because of the need for greater flexibility in the face of smaller markets and shorter production runs for each model. The partial exception to this generalization was final assembly where the development of mechanized techniques in the advanced capitalist countries was still limited, and there was therefore a greater similarity between them and Latin America. In the case of countries engaged in truncated production, the differences were much more apparent. The production activities of the terminal firms were much more limited, in the extreme case confined to assembly, and the plants continued to rely heavily on imported kits. In these cases assembly activities tended to be even less mechanized, in the extreme case being an almost artisan-like activity.

3   STRUCTURE OF THE LABOUR FORCE

It was seen above that the motor industry in the advanced capitalist countries does not rely heavily on skilled labour. The question that now arises is whether in view of the differences in the labour processes of the industry in Latin America described in the last section and the differences in local conditions, the same holds for the Latin American motor industry. One line of argument holds that dynamic industries, of which the motor industry is a prime example, have a privileged labour force which, because of the high skill requirements in the industry, is protected from the competition of those workers which make up the industrial reserve army, and is therefore able to secure higher wages and better working conditions than workers in the so-called traditional industries (Cimillo *et al.*, 1973, pp. 144–7; Quijano, 1974; Lifschitz, 1982, pp. 43–6).

The evidence on the level of wages in the motor industry gives certain plausibility to this thesis. In Argentina, Brazil and Mexico, the average wage in the motor industry as a whole was between two-fifths and two-thirds greater than the manufacturing average. If only the terminal firms are taken into account then wages are more than 75 per cent higher in Argentina and more than double the manufacturing average in Brazil and Mexico (see table 5.3). In the parts (and body-building) industries the level of wages is much closer to the manufacturing average, while in the tyre industry it is comparable with or even higher than in the terminal industry.

If such high levels of wages in the terminal industry are a reflection of the industry's heavy reliance on skilled labour, this implies that the differences observed in the labour process between the Latin American plants and those in the home countries of the major auto TNCs must

TABLE 5.3   Index of average wages in the motor industry, 1970
(Manufacturing = 100)

	Argentina	Brazil	Mexico
Motor industry	142.3	161.1	166.4
Terminal industry	176.9	212.0	206.0
Parts industry	98.4	138.8	120.2
Tyre industry	199.8	179.0	287.5

SOURCE   Lifschitz, 1982, tables 4, 5 and 6; 1978, table VIII.

have led to a greater use of skilled labour in Latin America. Since the major differences between the Latin American plants and those in the advanced capitalist countries is the lower degree of mechanization, accompanied by the use of outdated, second-hand machinery from the developed countries, the question is whether technological developments in the West, and particularly the replacement of manually operated machines by automatic ones, has led to substantial deskilling in the motor industry.

It is difficult to maintain that there has been a general trend towards deskilling in the motor industry. In the case of engine plants the introduction of automatic transfer lines tended to eliminate much of the direct labour of operatives engaged in short duration, repetitive tasks, while there was a growth in more skilled work associated with the operation and maintenance of the whole system (Abernathy, 1978, pp. 102–7). Similarly in the paint shop, automation has tended to eliminate unskilled work while skilled labour continues to be used in tasks such as putting on the final coat.

On the other hand, in assembly the variety of models, less detailed division of labour and longer work cycles which this involves places greater demands on workers in Latin America than on the typical assembly line in the advanced capitalist countries (Nofal, 1983, p. 166). Although this may mean that learning time is somewhat longer in Latin America (Nofal, 1983, p. 187), it is by no means clear that this is such as to render assembly a skilled occupation in the region compared with other countries.

The evidence therefore seems to suggest that the less mechanized production processes used in Latin America would not require a significantly higher proportion of skilled workers than are found in the advanced capitalist countries. Indeed, managers in Brazil are reported to be wary of using transfer lines in their machine shops, precisely because of the need for skilled workers such as electricians and machine makers with such systems, and their high cost relative to machine operators (Morley and Smith, 1977, p. 254).

Of course the most convincing evidence on this point would be a comparison of the extent to which skilled labour is employed in Latin American vehicle factories. Unfortunately, the detailed evidence which would be required is unavailable. However, estimates for one Brazilian plant indicated that just over a quarter of manual workers were considered skilled (Humphrey, 1982, table 3–2). This is not much higher than the figures quoted earlier for the United States and France and further undermines the thesis that the majority of car workers in Latin America are highly skilled.

Furthermore, although skilled workers in the Brazilian motor vehicle industry are highly paid compared with unskilled workers in the industry, their wages are not particularly high compared with those of skilled workers in other industries. Unskilled workers, however, are considerably better paid in the auto industry than in traditional industries such as textiles (Humphrey, 1982, pp. 68–70). Thus far from the high average level of wages in the motor industry being a correlate of reliance on a high proportion of skilled labour, it is precisely the high level of wages paid to unskilled workers that needs to be explained.[9]

Although there is no direct evidence on the skill distribution of the labour force in the Argentinian and Mexican motor industries it is unlikely, given the similarity of production processes, that it will differ significantly from that found in Brazil. Moreover, given that wage differentials between skilled and unskilled workers were narrower in Argentina and Mexico than in Brazil, the use of skilled labour is equally unlikely to explain high average wages in these countries.[10] In order to explain the relatively high wages found in the motor vehicle industry, therefore, we must turn to the strategies applied by management to control labour.

4 LABOUR CONTROL STRATEGIES

A disciplined labour force is of crucial importance in a car factory. Although direct labour costs are a relatively small proportion of the total costs of producing a car,[11] uninterrupted production is important for operations to be profitable. There are two main reasons for this. Given the large-scale commitment of fixed capital in the form of presses, machines and other equipment, it is extremely costly to have them lying idle for lengthy periods of time. Secondly the highly interdependent nature of production in a car factory means that a disruption caused by a small number of workers in one specific area of the factory can lead quite quickly to production being stopped throughout the company. Paradoxically, the assembly line through which capital gained increased control over the labour process by dictating the pace of work, also made production increasingly vulnerable to disruption by small groups of workers (Gartman, 1979, pp. 204–5).

Labour control has therefore been a crucial consideration of management strategy throughout the industry's history. Forms of labour control have differed through time and between countries in response to specific local conditions and technological change, as well as in response to workers' resistance. A number of different models can be identified. In doing so it will be useful to bear in mind the distinction made by Friedman (1977) between management strategies of 'Direct Control' and 'Responsible Autonomy'. The Direct Control strategy 'tries to limit the scope for labour power to vary by coercive threats, close supervision and minimising individual worker responsibility'. Responsible Autonomy

attempts to harness the adaptability of labour power by giving workers leeway and encouraging them to adapt to changing situations in a manner beneficial to the firm. To do this top managers give workers status, authority and responsibility. Top managers try to win their loyalty, and co-opt their organizations to the firm's ideals (that is, the competitive struggle) ideologically (Friedman, 1977, p. 78).

These strategies are not necessarily mutually exclusive but can be applied differentially to different groups of workers.

A classic example of the direct control strategy is that employed by Ford in the United States in the inter-war period. In the early years of the company's existence the labour process was under the control of the skilled workers who were able to determine the intensity and productiveness of their work. Increasing division of labour in the Ford shops and continuous harassment by foremen marked the first steps in imposing direct control even before the First World War. The introduction of the mechanical assembly line in 1914 enabled management to dictate the pace of work and increased control over workers by further eliminating skilled labour. This made it possible for Ford to draw in workers from the industrial reserve army of immigrant workers who were flooding into the country. The increasing intensity and dehumanization of work led to new forms of workers' resistance, reflected in high rates of absenteeism and labour turnover (Gartman, 1979). This was countered by the introduction of the $5 day. By offering higher wages than other industries Ford was able to pick and choose the most suitable workers and subject them to the discipline of intensive work, knowing that they faced the permanent threat of replacement from the available pool of unskilled labour. This strategy of direct control combined high wages, job insecurity and resistance to unionization.

A variant on this strategy was applied by Fiat in Italy in the 1950s and 1960s. It differs from the example of Ford just discussed in that it involved the defeat of a strong communist-dominated trade union in the firm in the mid-fifties, rather than involving resistance to incipient attempts at unionization as in the United States. Fiat used a number of mechanisms to control and coerce its workers in this period (Partridge, 1980). Workers were offered an anti-strike bonus for quiescent behaviour; militants were sacked and blacklisted making it extremely difficult for them to obtain work in other industrial firms in Turin; a hierarchical system in which foremen had considerable discretion in recommending promotions and bonuses was used to force up production; divisions were encouraged between the newly arrived immigrants from Southern Italy and the native Piedmontese workers. This combination of sanctions against the militants, rewards for good behaviour, (which included the relatively high wages received by Fiat workers, as well as fringe benefits such as housing, health and recreation facilities) and 'divide and rule' strategies, enabled Fiat to increase the intensity of work and introduce new technology to the benefit of the firm's profitability. A crucial factor in Fiat's successful implementation of this strategy was the defeat of the communist union which had controlled the *Commissione Interna* (CI) (shop-floor workers' committee) until 1955. 'After this defeat the CI lost virtually all independent character, functioning almost as a body of lower management' (Partridge, 1980, p. 426).

The Responsible Autonomy strategy also comes in different guises. One example is the 'gang system' which operated in certain parts of the UK motor industry in the post-Second World War period. This involved a substantial element of real autonomy for workers in the industry. The gangs had an elected leader who would negotiate with top managers to produce a given output. Often the gang would distribute work and discipline members collectively. Generous bonuses were given for output above the contracted amount. This system reduced the need of supervisors and foremen and gave management greater flexibility in incoporating new materials and tasks where necessary. The adoption of this system was a reflection of the strong position of workers in the industry but also offered a solution to the technical problems which management faced at this time (Friedman, 1977, pp. 313–15). In the 1960s, faced with tightening market conditions and increasing competition, management pushed to restore a greater element of direct control in the UK motor industry which was carried out through the introduction of the Measured Daywork system.

In contrast the Quality Control Circles, which are a characteristic feature of the Japanese system of management control (and which have become increasingly popular in recent years amongst managers in other countries including Argentina and Brazil where they have been introduced by Ford and VW in the 1980s) (Nofal, 1983, p. 137; VW do Brasil, Annual Report, 1983), were introduced after the defeat of the democratic unions in the Japanese motor industry in the early fifties, and their replacement by Company unions. Their introduction came about as a result of management concern over sabotage, absenteeism and high turnover with the disillusion of workers following the defeat of their unions (TIE, 1983, pp. 13–14). Quality Control Circles had a double advantage from the point of view of management, both providing useful suggestions for increasing productivity and giving a sense of participation to the workers. Rather than the intense supervision on which the direct control strategy is based, the Japanese approach gives greater responsibility to workers to diagnose problems, repair equipment and spot defects, thus reducing the need for supervisors and repairmen (Altshuler *et al.*, 1984, p. 137). The life-long employment offered by these companies, together with the numerous allowances and bonuses provided by the company are also used to increase workers' identification with the firm. Nevertheless this goes along with union control (and even persecution of independent-minded workers) over the labour force (Hermele, 1982, pp. 8–10).

The above discussion illustrates that managerial strategies of labour control and workers' struggles are conditioned by both the stage of development of the motor vehicle industry (technological developments, market conditions) and the overall political economy into which the industry is inserted. The same is true in the case of the Latin American motor industry and particularly those of Argentina, Brazil and Mexico which will be the focus of our attention. In terms of the development of the motor industry itself, it is possible to identify three key phases. The first covers the period when manufacturing is first

established and the industry experiences rapid growth in very favourable market conditions. The second phase is a period of restructuring
and retrenchment when the initial 'easy' market conditions come to an
end and competition intensifies. Finally there is a third period, coincid-
ing with the international crisis in the industry and the new forms of
integration which emerged in the 1970s.[12]

The main thesis advanced here is that each of the phases in the
development of the industry in Latin America will be characterized by
different strategies of labour control and that the focus of workers'
struggles will also tend to change with the evolution of the industry. Of
course, as will be seen below, there will be variations from country to
country in response to the different overall situation found in each one.
In the growth phase, particularly where a backlog of demand has built
up, the main concern of management is to supply the market at all
costs. At an extreme a car can be sold at any price no matter what its
quality. This has a number of implications as far as labour control
strategies are concerned. As was seen in the UK example above, such
favourable market conditions predispose management towards a strategy of Responsible Autonomy. In the case of the Latin American
countries this is likely to have been reinforced because production was
being built up from scratch with new processes being introduced as
local content increased and flexibility of workers to meet new conditions and undertake new tasks was at a premium. In addition the
novel nature of the industry and its labour force probably contributed
to a low level of militancy in this phase. It is to be expected that
workers' demands would be mainly focused on wage issues.

There is some evidence to support these generalizations. In Brazil in
the early years (prior to the 1964 military coup) there was little
industrial unrest in the industry. Auto firms adopted a policy of small,
frequent increases in wages to diffuse wage demands. Opportunities
existed for effective promotion as the result of the growth of the
industry although it was recognized that the situation could change as
the industry reached maturity (Rodrigues, 1970). In Argentina the
period up to the mid-sixties has been characterized as one of tranquil
labour relations (Evans *et al.*, 1984, pp. 134–5). In Mexico too
industrial unrest in the terminal industry was virtually non-existent in
this phase, with only one strike at Chrysler (Automex) between 1965
and 1972 (Middlebrook, 1978, table 2; Aguilar, 1982, table XXXIX).

The extremely favourable market conditions in the industry were
fairly shortlived (lasting longer in Mexico because the state controlled
production through quotas). (See below Chapter 6.) The result was that

when the economy went into a down-turn car workers were no longer largely immune from its effects. In Argentina the total number of hours worked in the industry fell for the first time in 1963, although the labour force was still greater at the end of 1963 than it had been a year earlier. In 1967 the number of workers employed fell below the level at the end of 1966 (ADEFA). Chrysler, Fiat, GM and IKA all reduced their work-force by several hundred during 1967 (own investigations). In Brazil there was a reduction of almost 10 per cent in the work-force between 1962 and 1963, and another fall in 1967 (ANFAVEA). In Mexico there was a slight fall in 1969 followed by a more substantial decrease in 1975 (AMIA).

The less favourable market conditions in this phase led to an intensification of competition in the industry and major restructuring including the elimination of a number of firms. This was reflected in a tightening of managerial control as increases in productivity, rather than production at any cost became a primary consideration. Thus there was a movement from Responsible Autonomy to greater Direct Control accompanied by measures to increase labour productivity such as line speed ups and rationalization.

These developments led to a greater level of potential conflict in capital–labour relations in the industry. They also led to a change in the nature of workers' struggle towards a greater emphasis on issues related to job security and conditions of work. Describing the auto workers in Argentina in this period Evans *et al.* (1984, p. 136) write:

> The effect of these changes was to erode the basic conditions underlying the docility of the labour force in the pre-1965–1966 period, and the typical grievances associated with the automotive labor process came more to the fore, exacerbated now by company speedup and rationalization in response to sharpened competition.

The number of hours lost as a result of strikes and other causes (not accidents or illness) increased substantially in the Argentinian motor industry from 272 000 hours in 1964 to 1 009 000 hours in 1969 (ADEFA, 1970, p. 6). The main kinds of grievance articulated by auto workers which led to strikes or serious labour conflicts were related to lay-offs and speed-ups or production reorganizations (Evans *et al.*, 1979).

Although in Brazil there was a similar trend towards increased lay-offs and pressure to speed up production, this was not reflected in increased workers' militancy and strike actions. The reason for this is simple. The transition from the early boom years of the industry to the period of consolidation and restructuring in Brazil was followed soon after by the 1964 military coup. This brought with it severe repression of trade union activity and changes in the legal position of workers which constrained the expression of working class grievances until the first stoppages of 1973. Nevertheless both lay-offs and speed-ups were major problems for auto workers in this period. The auto companies, freed from the restrictions on firing labour which had been imposed by the Lei da Estabilidade[13] pursued a deliberate policy of labour rotation. It was not uncommon for one-fifth or more of a firm's labour force to leave in the course of a year (Humphrey, 1982, table 3.8). This practice of labour rotation was frequently denounced by workers' organizations in Brazil.

Changes in the intensity of work are difficult to measure directly. There is, however, substantial evidence of a subjective or anecdotal nature to indicate that the intensity of work was increased in the industry. Interviews with workers carried out in the mid-seventies indicated that a significant proportion of the work-force thought that their workloads had increased since entering the plants where they worked. This was particularly marked among assemblers where 50 per cent of those interviewed reported increased workloads (Humphrey, 1982, p. 84). The pressure to increase productivity in the industry contributed to dangerous working conditions, and in Brazilian industry generally a sharp increase in industrial accidents accompanied the 'miracle' of the late sixties and early seventies (Wurtele, 1979, p. 77).

The later development of the motor industry in Mexico and the more gradual growth of production in the early years, meant that the end of favourable market conditions in the industry almost coincided with the crisis which affected the motor industry world-wide in the 1970s. In the seventies increased militancy was associated again often with issues of lay-offs and speed-ups. The first such conflict broke out in Automex (Chrysler) late in 1969 over the dismissal of workers and in order to improve working conditions. Industrial conflicts became increasingly common in the industry from 1972 onwards (Aguilar, 1982, table 39). These conflicts frequently included demands for the reinstatement of sacked workers, or relating to working conditions (Aguilar, 1982, table 37). The use of temporary workers (*eventuales*) by the auto TNCs became an issue of conflict, for example at Nissan in 1972 and GM in the following year (Juarez, 1979, pp. 232, 237). Workers have achieved some success in this area particularly at Dina and Nissan, where the number of permanent workers were increased to 90 per cent by the late seventies (Roxborough, 1984, p. 171). Speed-ups became increasingly common in the industry. It was reported that GM was gradually increasing the pace of work at its Mexico City plant from 1972 (Wurtele, 1977, p. 46), while in 1977 the Ford union threatened to go out on strike in response to speed-ups in the company (Roxborough, 1984, p. 172) and increasing concern over these issues is found in other unions in the industry. An indirect indicator of the intensification of work in the Mexican industry, is the increased incidence of accidents noted at the plants of Ford (Tlanepantla), Nissan and Volkswagen in the early and mid-seventies (Aguilar, 1982, tables 42, 43 and 44).

The specific strategy of labour control adopted by management in each of the major Latin American countries depended on the local conditions which they found there. The Brazilian strategy has been compared with that followed by Ford in the United States in the inter-war period.[14] There are a number of similarities. First the trade union movement in Brazil was relatively weak after the military coup of 1964. Not only did government legislation and direct repression weaken the organized power of the working class, but the levels of unionization in the auto industry were extremely low, indeed the lowest in Latin America (see table 5.4). A low level of unionization was accompanied by relatively high wages and high labour turnover, again paralleling the situation in the Ford plants in the US in the twenties and thirties. 'Labour rotation' was central to the strategy of management in the Brazilian motor vehicle industry. It enabled managers both to control labour costs in the industry and to increase productivity. Wage costs could be kept under control by firing workers who, because of their duration of employment, had moved up to the top of the wage scale for their particular grade and hiring new workers who would start at the bottom. At the same time the resulting job insecurity, which was

TABLE 5.4 *Unionization in the Latin American auto industry, 1975*

	Number employed	*Unionized workers*	*Percent organized*
Argentina	52 004	33 000	63.5
Brazil	101 905	32 634	32.0
Colombia	4 532	2 598	57.3
Mexico	37 292	25 620	68.7
Peru	3 936	2 149	54.6
Venezuela	9 400	6 002	63.9
Total	209 069	102 003	48.8

SOURCE Wurtele, 1977, table 7.

reinforced by the ready availability of replacements because of the high wages which the industry paid, ensured that management could enforce discipline in the plants and hence dictate the intensity of work. This basic system of labour control was buttressed by the use of informers to weed out potential militants, while the high level of rotation itself made it difficult to build up trade union organization.

Although there was an initial attempt made in Argentina to keep the unions weak in the early years of the industry's development by affiliating them to SMATA, the car mechanics union, and creating company unions, in order to keep them out of the hands of the powerful UOM, conditions in Argentina never permitted the successful implementation of the type of labcur control strategy applied in Brazil. The level of unionization in the industry was twice as high as in Brazil (see Table 5.4). Moreover, company unions such as SITRAC and SITRAM emerged as highly politicized and militant unions in the late sixties, while SMATA also was far from being the quiescent force which had been planned. Not only were auto workers in Argentina highly unionized but there was also a high level of rank and file involvement in union affairs. This was true not only of the company unions but also of SMATA which, for a number of reasons, was much less centralized and subject to control from the leadership than other Peronist industrial unions (Evans *et al.*, 1984, pp. 138–9).

The strength of workers' organizations was one reason why the type of strategy used in Brazil could not be applied in Argentina. The setting of production standards and job evaluation which were the exclusive prerogative of management in Brazil were determined by committees which included union representatives in Argentina (UAW, 1970).[15] This no doubt facilitated worker resistance to attempts to speed-up production in the Argentinian industry. The general conditions in the labour market in Argentina were also not so conducive to the implementation of a Fordist strategy. Unemployment and underemployment has historically been much less marked than elsewhere in Latin America. Thus the threat of dismissal is much less potent than elsewhere. Moreover the gap between auto industry wages and those in manufacturing as a whole was less marked in Argentina than in Brazil or Mexico, making the industry less attractive to workers.

Faced with a strongly organized trade union movement, the auto companies in Argentina were unable to impose the kind of direct control strategy used in Brazil. However, the permanent crisis of the Argentinian motor industry since the mid-sixties means that a Responsible Autonomy strategy is also difficult to implement since frequent recessions lead to workers being laid off and this makes it difficult to build up the kind of loyalty to the firms which such a strategy requires.[16] What the history of the Argentinian auto industry shows is the extreme difficulty of finding an adequate strategy of labour control. Although the level of unionization in Mexico is the highest found in the auto industry in any Latin American country, the implications of such a high degree of organization is rather different from that found in Argentina. Within the Mexican auto industry there are considerable differences between the unions in different plants. While some unions are relatively democratic and militant, others have been characterized as oligarchic (Roxborough, 1984a). Particularly in the latter group, shop-floor organization is very weak. In these plants the situation resembles that found in Fiat in Italy from the mid-fifties with close cooperation between the union bureaucracy and management. Indeed at Chrysler the General Secretary of the union during the 1970s was a former production manager (Roxborough, 1984a). The considerable influence enjoyed by Mexican unions over hiring, promotion and the allocation of fringe benefits, particularly cheap housing, as well as the closed shop provision which implies that a worker expelled from the union must also be fired by the firm, means that the trade union bureaucracy can play a major part in the labour control strategy. This is particularly the case in oligarchic unions. Indeed, in cases of unfair dismissal it is not unusual for the dismissed worker to cite the union as a co-defendant with the company in claims for unfair dismissal. In a sample of cases before the labour courts it was found that it was far more common for the union to be cited as a co-defendant (29 per cent of cases) than for it to give clear support to a dismissed worker (11 per cent of cases) (Roxborough, 1984a, p. 154). Particularly in the oligarchic unions, where strike action is rare, the union bureaucracy uses the traditional methods of co-optation and coercion to control shop-floor militants. Chrysler (Automex) is an extreme case in which coercion and intimidation of workers was used, and a corrupt union leadership was involved in selling jobs at the plant (Juarez, 1979, pp. 228–30). The control which the CTM exercises in Toluca where both Chrysler and GM have plants means that any worker who runs foul of the CTM at one of these plants is unlikely to get another job (Roxborough, 1984, p. 182).

Unlike the situation in Brazil, employment in the Mexican motor industry is characterized by low levels of labour turnover. Despite the fact that the work-force of Mexican car factories is divided between permanent workers (*obreros de planta*) and temporary workers (*obreros eventuales*) who are contracted for the production of a certain number of vehicles or a fixed period of time (up to eleven months), the general tendency is for firms to re-hire temporary workers when their contracts come to an end (Roxborough, 1984, p. 119). Thus temporary workers may have worked for the same company for several years and do not necessarily indicate a high turnover rate. In the mid-seventies the proportion of workers in a number of auto plants who had temporary contracts ranged from 15 per cent to 50 per cent of the total labour force (Roxborough, 1984, table 3–8). Why did the auto companies rely so heavily on temporary workers only to re-employ them year after year? This system offered the companies three major advantages. It gave them greater flexibility if they needed to lay off workers. It also reduced labour costs by eliminating the need to pay certain fringe benefits and to increase wages in accordance with the number of years worked. Finally it operated as a kind of 'probation system' ensuring good behaviour by the workers and enabling the firms to weed out potential militants before giving them permanent status. Restricting the use of temporary workers was a major target of union demands in the 1970s, and some of the more militant unions were able to impose restrictions on management's right to employ *eventuales*. Most of the firms in Mexico have attempted to impose direct control strategies. This has been relatively successful in those plants where the undemocratic nature of the unions has guaranteed their cooperation with management. It has also been successful at VW where, despite an independent union, internal dissension has weakened labour. Indeed, in many respects the VW plant at Puebla is the most clear example of direct control since it is a relatively modern plant with a deskilled labour force (with 40 per cent temporary workers and a significant number of women workers) and no union control over the labour process (Quiroz, 1980; Roxborough, 1984a, pp. 122–3). In other plants with militant, democratic unions, workers have to some extent been able to resist the attempts at direct control and maintain some control over the labour process.

It is interesting to note here the situation in the two state-owned companies, DINA and VAM, where management has adopted a paternalistic approach emphasizing worker participation (through factory committees in the case of DINA and an emphasis on human relations in VAM) which is much more akin to a Responsible Autonomy strategy (Quiroz, 1980). In these two firms trade unions have enjoyed some control over the labour process since the sixties (Roxborough, 1984a, p. 123). This does not seem to have come about as a result of workers' demands and the VAM union has no record of militancy. That these two firms should not have resorted to direct control to the same degree as the others can readily be explained. The fact that they are state-owned reduces the immediate competitive pressure on them compared with private capital, while at the same time making it possible to present the interest of the firm as the national interest.

In conclusion then, the changing conditions in the industry in all three countries as competition intensified led management to emphasize direct control. In Brazil, because of the weak position of the labour movement after the 1964 military coup, they were successful in doing so, adopting a Fordist strategy of high wages, labour rotation and opposition to trade unions. In Argentina on the other hand, the strength of workers' resistance and the specific economic conditions meant that throughout this period management had little success in this respect. In Mexico a more diversified picture emerges with some firms successfully implementing direct control where collaborative or internally divided unions existed, while others met stiffer workers' resistance.

5 PRODUCTIVITY AND WAGES

Latin American trends

One of the most striking confirmations of the success of the labour control strategies applied in Mexico and Brazil and the problems which management experienced in exercising control over labour in Argentina is the relative evolution of productivity and wages in the three countries. A successful strategy could be expected to result in substantial increases in productivity, while maintaining the growth of real wages at reasonable rates (from the point of view of management), certainly below the rate of increase in productivity. Taking the period from the mid-sixties when integrated production had been achieved in all three countries (to avoid problems arising from variations in the level of local content), it can be seen that productivity increased rapidly in both Brazil and Mexico (table 5.5). In Brazil the crude index of number of vehicles produced per person employed almost doubled between 1966 and 1974, while in Mexico it increased by almost 60 per cent over the same period. In Argentina on the other hand, productivity only increased by some 10 per cent. Brazil and Mexico also had the lowest rate of increases in wages in this period, with real wages

TABLE 5.5   *Index of labour productivity and real wages (1966 = 100)*

	Argentina		Brazil		Mexico	
	Productivity	Real wages	Productivity	Real wages	Productivity	Real wages
1966	100.0	100.0	100.0	100.0	100.0	100.0
1967	111.9	110.6	105.0	99.0	98.3	96.3
1968	113.0	105.7	116.0	101.5	111.9	108.3
1969	119.4	104.1	127.5	103.1	123.7	114.4
1970	116.3	100.8	148.6	111.9	135.6	113.2
1971	130.0	103.3	168.1	106.0	135.6	126.3
1972	127.3	91.9	188.8	116.8	139.0	131.1
1973	127.7	100.8	197.7	112.9	132.2	122.6
1974	109.9	106.5	198.9	100.3	157.6	100.3

SOURCES   Argentina: own elaboration from ADEFA data; Brazil: de Oliveira *et al.*, 1979, tables 17 and 18; Mexico: own elaboration from AMIA data; ILO, *Yearbook of Labour Statistics, 1975.*

(deflated by the index of the cost of living) barely higher in 1974 than in 1966. In Argentina, however, although the rate of growth of real wages was also relatively low it was not much below the small increase in productivity.

What this data shows is that in Brazil and Mexico workers in the motor industry did not benefit from the increase in productivity in this period. The most obvious limitation of these figures is that they aggregate all workers in the terminal industry and therefore give no indication of the dispersal of wages between different groups of blue-collar workers and white-collar workers, nor any differences in the evolution of the wages of different groups. They are, at best, therefore, a crude measure of the trend in the rate of exploitation in the industry. Nor do the crude data indicate the causes of the rapid increases in productivity in Brazil and Mexico. The previous discussion emphasized the role of speed-ups, rationalization and the counteracting tendencies of workers' resistance in determining productivity levels in car production. These are of course by no means the only factors which can influence labour productivity. In particular the modernity of plant, which is related to the rate of capital accumulation, and the scale of output, are of crucial significance in the case of the auto industry.[17]

However, it is worth noting two points in this context. First for much of the period under consideration new investment was relatively limited. The reason for this is simple. The massive investments made in the early years to establish integrated manufacturing facilities in these countries left the industry with substantial excess capacity. In Brazil the industry's capacity was over 300 000 vehicles by the early sixties, whereas production did not reach this figure until the end of the decade (Mericle, 1978, table 4). In Argentina the industry had a capacity of 220 000 by the beginning of 1963 (CONADE, 1966, p. 46), a level of production that was not exceeded until the early seventies. The situation was the same in Mexico with capacity to produce over 200 000 vehicles by 1965, but output below this level throughout the sixties (de la Isla, 1968). The situation was even more marked in the case of engines, the major area in which the terminals in Mexico undertook new investments. By 1967 the industry had a capacity of 600 000 engines a year (Jenkins, 1977, p. 210). These levels of output would only be reached in the mid-seventies with significant exports of engines from Mexico.

As a result the auto TNCs in these countries were able to expand production in the mid- to late-sixties without undertaking major new investments. In Brazil, apart from a slight upturn in 1967 associated with the introduction of new models by Chrysler and GM, investment remained low until 1970 (Guimaraes, 1981). In Argentina investment in the industry peaked in 1962 and then remained low for the rest of the decade, whilst in Mexico new investment declined substantially after 1964–5, until 1972 (Jenkins, 1977, tables 5.2 and 5.3; AMIA, 1976, p. 170). Nevertheless in both Brazil and Mexico substantial increases in labour productivity occurred in the late sixties, suggesting that more modern machinery alone could not have been the major cause.

The second point relates to the scale of production in the industry. It is true that between 1966 and 1974 production increased fourfold in Brazil and threefold in Mexico and that for individual firms the increases were even greater. Given the importance of economies of scale in the motor industry, it is certainly to be expected that such a growth in production would contribute to reducing costs. However, such reductions in costs are achieved by spreading fixed costs, including pre-production costs of design and development over a large number of units. Since the bulk of labour is a variable cost (83 per cent according to Toder *et al.*, 1978, table 5.4), the reductions in labour cost and conversely the increase in labour productivity, simply as a result of a change in the scale of production, is likely to be limited. Even a tenfold increase in output (from 10 000 to 100 000 vehicles a year) would only lead to an increase of less than 50 per cent in labour productivity in an assembly plant (CEPAL, 1973, table 22). In engine assembly it has been estimated that even a forty-fold increase in output (2500 to

100 000 vehicles) would only increase productivity by between a quarter and a third (Pratten, 1971, p. 139). (Estimates of labour productivity here are calculated on the basis of data on changes in labour costs with variations in output.)

The limited investment in new technology/machinery in the Latin American motor industry in the latter part of the sixties, and the fact that changes in the scale of production are unlikely to have led to a very large increase in labour productivity in the industry serve to underline the importance of the control of labour in explaining increasing productivity in the Brazilian and Mexican motor industries. In other words, an important part of the observed increase in productivity in the industry must have been the result of the intensification of work which managerial strategies were designed to bring about.

While the evolution of real wages (deflated by the cost of living) is relevant from the point of view of workers, in that it indicates the extent to which they are compensated for the increased intensity of work and greater productivity, from the point of view of capital what is relevant is the evolution of wages in relation to the price of the goods which they produce. If increased productivity leads to proportionately lower prices as in the competitive model, then the gains from such increases are diffused throughout the economy. If, on the other hand, oligopolistic conditions prevail then firms may be able to retain part or all of the gains from productivity increases since prices are not subject to downward pressure (cf. Sylos Labini, 1962).

Since motor vehicle prices in all three countries increased at a slower rate than the overall cost of living, the result of deflating wages by the index of vehicle prices is that the increase in wage costs (defined in terms of the firms' output) is more rapid than the increase in real wages. Table 5.6 shows that Brazil has been most successful in keeping the rate of increase of wage costs below the increase in productivity. In Mexico, although there have been fluctuations on a year to year basis it appears that over the whole period wage costs have moved more or less in line with productivity. Finally Argentina shows the most adverse trend with a steady increase in the ratio of wage costs to productivity from 1968 onwards. This was clearly a major factor in the profitability crisis experienced by the Argentinian motor industry in the early seventies (see Chapter 8).

TABLE 5.6   *Index of real wage costs and wage–productivity ratio*

	Argentina		Brazil		Mexico	
	(1) Real wage cost	(2) Wage–productivity ratio	(1) Real wage cost	(2) Wage–productivity ratio	(1) Real wage cost	(2) Wage–productivity ratio
1966	100.0	1.000	100.0	1.000	100.0	1.000
1967	115.4	1.031	97.0	0.924	99.1	1.008
1968	107.7	0.953	98.8	0.852	114.2	1.021
1969	130.8	1.095	105.7	0.829	124.0	1.002
1970	146.2	1.257	117.8	0.793	129.1	0.952
1971	169.2	1.302	122.4	0.728	140.2	1.034
1972	157.7	1.239	141.3	0.748	144.8	1.042
1973	184.6	1.446	155.5	0.786	146.9	1.111
1974	176.9	1.610	137.2	0.690	148.4	0.941

NOTES   Column (1) calculated by dividing average wages by the index of vehicle prices.
Column (2) calculated by dividing column (1) by the productivity index from Table 5.5.
SOURCES   Argentina: own elaboration from ADEFA data; Brazil: de Oliveira *et al.*,
1979, table 19; Mexico: own elaboration from AMIA data and Lifschitz, 1979, table 39.

International comparisons

Despite the success of the vehicle manufacturers in increasing the
intensity of work and the productivity of labour in the industry in this
period in Brazil and Mexico, levels of productivity remained well below
those found in Western Europe, not to mention the United States and
Japan. International comparison of labour productivity in the industry
is a complicated issue. There are two major problems. First, the output
of the industry is heterogeneous including different sizes of cars, trucks
and buses. Given that the distribution of output between these different
categories varies from country to country (e.g. the predominance of
large cars in the USA and small cars in France and Italy), a comparison
of the crude number of vehicles produced per person employed may be
misleading because it implicitly gives all vehicles the same weight. An
alternative procedure is to give explicit weights to each category of car
and commercial vehicle. While this is an improvement on the unad-
justed measure there is still the problem of determining the weights to
be used. One such set of weights, based on the estimated labour content
of different vehicles in the UK has been used in comparisons of labour
productivity in Western Europe, Japan and the USA (Pratten and
Silberston, 1967).[18] This is the weighting that has been applied here to

the Latin American countries to make them directly comparable with the calculations for the other countries.

The second problem of such international comparisons is the considerable variation between countries in the level of vertical integration in the terminal industry. A high level of bought out content inflates the apparent labour productivity of the terminals concerned. In the case of the auto industry in the advanced capitalist countries this problem has been overcome by calculating productivity on the basis of the total number employed in both the terminal and parts and components industry. Thus a country where a relatively high proportion of the terminals' parts are bought out, would show relatively more workers in the parts industry and less in the terminal industry, but the calculation of productivity would not be affected. In the Latin American case there is an added complication that a proportion of the parts used by the terminals are not produced locally but are imported. This is not a major problem in Argentina and Brazil where the high level of local content requirements make the situation similar to that found in the developed countries.[19] In the case of Mexico, however, failure to take into account the extent of imported parts and components would lead to considerable over-estimation of labour productivity in the industry, since over 40 per cent of the terminal industry's purchases come from abroad. In Table 5.7, the figure for labour productivity for Mexico has been

TABLE 5.7   *Labour productivity in selected countries, 1965, 1973, 1974*

	1965	1973/4
Argentina	2.9	2.3
Brazil	1.4	3.1
Mexico	1.9	2.5
UK	5.8	5.1
USA	13.9	14.9
Germany	7.1	7.3
France	6.1	6.8
Italy	7.4	6.8
Japan	4.4	12.2

NOTE   Weights used were cars < 1000 cc 95; 1000–2000 cc 100, > 2000 cc 120; CVs < 4 tons 90; 4–10 tons 150; > 10 tons 250. In the case of Mexico CVs were classified as < 3 tons, 3–9 tons and > 9 tons. In Brazil CVs were classified into utility and light; medium and heavy, but the exact divisions in terms of weight were not available.
SOURCES   UK, USA, Germany, France, Italy, Japan: CPRS, 1975, p. 80. Argentina, Brazil and Mexico: own calculation from output data of ADEFA, ANFAVEA and AMIA, employment data from Sourrouille, 1980; de Oliveira *et al.*, 1979 and ANFAVEA; Aguilar, 1982, Vázquez Tercero, 1975, p. 21 and AMIA.

deflated by about one-third (based on the ratio of imports to the value of sales in the terminal industry in the years concerned).

Table 5.7 compares labour productivity in the major Latin American countries with that of the main vehicle producing countries for 1965 and 1973. The choice of years was dictated by a number of considerations. First data was available for the advanced capitalist countries for 1965 and 1973, the latter being a peak year for production in the developed countries. Secondly by 1965 integrated manufacturing had been established in all three Latin American countries, and it is very near to the year which was chosen for beginning to calculate the crude indices of productivity discussed earlier (1966). Finally 1974 rather than 1973 was chosen to compare the Latin American productivity levels, since output was higher in that year than in 1973 in all three countries. Thus it seemed appropriate to compare the two years which precede the beginning of the crisis making its impact felt in the countries concerned.

A number of features of Table 5.7 deserve mention. First it bears out our earlier crude analysis of the development of labour productivity in the Latin American countries. Productivity increased most rapidly in Brazil, followed by Mexico. In the case of Argentina productivity fell between 1965 and 1974 paralleling the fall in the crude productivity index for the terminals over the same period (although the latter increased between 1966 and 1974). The table also indicates that productivity levels in Latin America were about one-third of continental European levels and about one-fifth of Japanese and US levels in the early seventies. Although the gap between Brazilian and Mexican productivity and US and European levels has been narrowed since the mid-sixties, it remained large, while the spectacular increase in productivity in Japan over the same period puts the Brazilian and Mexican performance in perspective.

The lower labour productivity in Latin America is not surprising in view of what was said earlier in this chapter about the use of less mechanized techniques and second-hand equipment in the region. Thus the increasing intensity of labour was used to partially compensate for the deficiencies of the industry in terms of its capital equipment. It is also one aspect of the relatively high prices of vehicles produced in Latin America compared with their countries of origin. A number of other factors also impinge upon the high price of Latin American vehicles. In order to analyse cost and price formation in the industry it is necessary to integrate the analysis of the sphere of production carried out in this chapter with the sphere of circulation. It is to this that we turn in the next chapter.

NOTES

1. White (1971); CPRS (1975), p. 14. White is quoted elsewhere as saying that 'it is impossible to get a straight story on dies' (Toder *et al.*, 1978, p. 143).
2. Although it should be noted that the production of CV bodies may be separate from the production of the chassis.
3. This corresponds to Trajtenberg and Vigorito's notion of 'transnationalization by complete repetition' in which production in two areas is similar and there are no necessary trade links established (1981, pp. 34–5).
4. In Argentina of the three largest firms in the late sixties, IKA Renault carried out all five operations, Fiat all but casting and Ford all but forging. The other smaller producers all had stamping, machining and assembly facilities (DNEI, 1970, p. 13).
5. This corresponds to the notion of 'incomplete repetition' where only the final or simplest stages of production are transferred with the consequent maintenance of strong commercial links between the two areas (Trajtenberg and Vigorito, 1981, p. 35).
6. See Fernandez-Baca Llamosas *et al.*, 1979, table 39 for a list of locally produced parts incorporated by the terminal firms in Peru in 1970.
7. The level of vertical integration in Argentina and Brazil is still relatively low compared with the United States and Western Europe where bought-out components and raw materials account for less than half the value of vehicles (Rhys, 1972, ch. 3). The UK motor industry has a lower level of vertical integration – not dissimilar to that calculated for Argentina and Brazil (Jones, 1981, table 19).
8. See the case study of Chile by Johnson (1967) which argues that the profitability of assemblers was determined primarily by the ability to obtain import licences for parts rather than efficiency of operation.
9. There is some evidence to suggest that the same pattern also characterizes the Argentinian motor industry. Among a sample of workers dismissed from the motor industry who found work subsequently in manufacturing, skilled workers tended to have wages at least as high as those received in the motor industry, while unskilled workers received significantly lower wages in their new employment (Nun, 1979, table 7).
10. In the mid-seventies the differential in wages between the highest paid toolmakers and unskilled workers was more than 4:1 in Brazil. The ratio of highest to lowest paid hourly workers varied between 2:1 and 3:1 in Mexico and was below 2:1 in Argentina (data on individual plants from IMF, 1976). See also Humphrey (1982) p. 110 for a comparison of wage structures in Brazil and Argentina in the early sixties.
11. For a car produced in the UK in the early 1970s labour costs were estimated at around 14 per cent of total costs (Jones, 1981, table 19).
12. This third stage will be discussed in more detail in Part II.
13. The law by which workers dismissed 'without due cause' were entitled to a

lump-sum payment equal to one month's wages for each year employed. This was replaced in 1966 by the Fundo da Garantia do Tempo de Servico (FGTS) which, although giving dismissed workers approximately the same lump-sum, was now funded by a levy on the employers paid monthly. This removed the disincentive to laying off workers which the previous system had created since under FGTS the levy had to be paid irrespective of dismissals.

14. What follows is based on Humphrey, 1982.

15. These rights were lost following the 1976 coup. The companies also began to apply a deliberate strategy of labour rotation similar to that used in Brazil (Nofal, 1983, pp. 153, 155).

16. Four Argentinian auto factories dismissed each year an average of 15 to 20 per cent of their labour force between 1960 and 1968 (Nun, 1979, p. 21).

17. This is not to suggest that these factors are themselves independent of the struggles of capital and labour. The introduction of new technology or the expansion of plant are often accompanied by changes in working practices, and increased intensity of work.

18. An alternative set of weights has been used by Jones and Prais which gives a greater weight to large cars and to CVs than the Pratten and Silberston weights and also uses a more detailed break-down of CV categories (see Jones and Prais, 1978).

19. In the early seventies imports were 3 per cent of parts purchases in the USA and 7 per cent in Britain.

6 Market Conditions and Price Formation

A major feature of the conditions for realizing surplus value in a number of Latin American countries as far as the motor industry is concerned, has been a change from an initial situation in which the key problems were those of getting vehicles produced while selling what was produced was easy, to one in which problems of realization became much more significant. This is particularly marked in the case of the evolution of the car market where the creation of a 'backlog demand' in periods in which the industry was subject to severe import restrictions was followed by a period of local production and derestriction. This is of course closely related to the nature of the commodity as a use value, namely the fact that it is a consumer durable good. The specific use value of CVs on the other hand, primarily as a means of production in the transport industry, leads to a rather different situation in this market. In what follows the main emphasis will be on cars.

1 DEMAND CONDITIONS AND PROBLEMS OF REALIZATION

A significant feature of the demand for cars is that as a durable consumer good, it is not entirely consumed in the year in which it is bought. In other words, at any given moment in time there is a stock of cars in existence on the roads that is different from the new purchases of cars made in the preceding twelve month period. This is recognized in conventional models used to analyse and predict the demand for cars which are based on the stock-adjustment principle. New car purchases can be broken into two elements. The increase in the stock of cars (i.e. the net addition to the existing number of vehicles in circulation) depends on the difference between the actual stock and a desired, optimum stock of cars. To this must be added a further element which goes to replace vehicles taken out of circulation and which therefore depends on the rate of depreciation of the stock.

The social demand for cars as expressed in the desired car stock is likely to depend on a number of variables. These include the level of per capita income, the price of cars, the extent of the development of the road network, the availability and cost of other forms of transport and the distribution of income. Over time with growing income levels and an expanding road system the desired stock of cars will increase, other things being equal. Indeed, for capitalist countries there is a remarkably close correlation between the level of per capita income and the number of cars in circulation per inhabitant. However, the actual stock of cars may diverge from the desired stock of cars for a period of time. In particular, in the Latin American context it has been the case that because of restrictions on imports to counter balance of payments problems, there has been a divergence between the actual and desired stock of cars in particular periods in certain countries. This has major implications for the analysis of the conditions for realization in the initial years of the development of a local car industry in the Latin American countries. If such a development leads to a relaxation of the import constraint then extremely favourable market conditions result because for a period of several years there is a backlog of demand as a result of the pre-existing divergence between the actual and desired stocks.

In a number of Latin American countries, the situation in the late fifties and early sixties, at the outset of vehicle production, was such that a backlog of demand existed. If the international relationship between car density (cars per inhabitant) and per capita income is taken as an approximation for the desired level of the car stock, then an impression of the situation in different Latin American countries can be obtained by looking at their position *vis-à-vis* this regression line.[1] Of the main Latin American countries, Argentina, Colombia and Chile were the ones which showed the most marked shortfall in the stock of cars given their income levels in the late fifties. Mexico showed a less pronounced deficiency, while Brazil, Peru and Venezuela were all fairly close to, or even slightly above the expected level (ECLA, 1970).[2] In the case of both Peru and Venezuela, a favourable foreign exchange situation in the post-war period can account for the fact that the actual stock of cars seems to have kept pace with the desired stock as incomes increased. In Argentina, Chile and Colombia, however, import constraints were much greater in this period. Argentina probably represents the most extreme case with rising incomes between the 1930s and the mid-1950s being accompanied by a decline in the vehicle stock (in terms of new car equivalents) (Sourrouille, 1980, graph 1).

A further factor contributing to the backlog of demand in a number of Latin American countries was the age structure of the vehicle stock. Thus not only was there a numerical decificiency, but a large part of the stock that did exist in those countries which had been subject to import constraints was itself very old. In Argentina in 1954 almost two-thirds of all cars on the road were more than 15 years old. In Chile in 1959 almost 60 per cent of cars were more than ten years old (Jenkins, 1977, pp. 131, 137). In Colombia, as late as the mid-sixties, over 60 per cent of the vehicle stock was more than ten years old (ADEFA, *Informe Estadistico, No. 327*). Even in Brazil, where there was no apparent quantitative deficiency in the car stock, the age structure was also highly unfavourable.

While this backlog of demand existed, firms which could obtain access to the local market had no difficulty in selling cars. There are a number of illustrations of this fact from the early history of the Latin American motor industry. Vehicles like the VW Kombi and Willys Rural in Brazil and the IKA Estanciera in Argentina, which in terms of design would be classified as CVs, were widely used as passenger cars because of the unsatisfied demand that existed. New cars commanded very high prices. In Argentina in 1960 and 1961, 100 000 cars were sold at an average price of almost US $5000, despite the fact that more than one-third of them were under 850 cc and would have cost less than $1000 in their countries' of origin (Sourrouille, 1980, p. 81).

A further indication of these market conditions was the limited depreciation rate reflected in the prices of used vehicles. Second-hand car prices in Argentina and Brazil in the late fifties and early sixties were much higher in relation to those of new cars than in the advanced capitalist countries (cf. Jenkins, 1977, pp. 131-2; Guimaraes, 1981, pp. 24-5). It was not uncommon for waiting lists to build up for new cars in these early years. Firms were also able to operate at or near full capacity, and failure to do so was usually a result of supply problems and not a reflection of difficulties of realization.

It is difficult to pinpoint an exact date when the backlog of demand in the various countries in which it had been found was eliminated. In any case it is probably more accurate to speak of a gradual change from a situation of easy market conditions to much tighter conditions over a period of several years, than to identify a single cut off date. What is indisputable is that after a few years such a change did occur and that it led to an intensification of the competitive struggle in the countries concerned and a much greater emphasis on realization problems.

One approximate indicator of the ending of a period in which the existence of a backlog of demand is significant, is the date when the actual vehicle stock ceases to be below the desired stock. On the basis of international comparisons it can be said that this occurred in Argentina in 1962.[3] In Chile and Colombia, the other countries in which the backlog of demand was most pronounced, continued dependence on imported components prevented the industry from growing rapidly to eliminate the backlog which persisted through the 1960s. In Mexico strong demand conditions persisted for most of the sixties as a result of the government's policy of production quotas and price controls. By the early seventies, however, the situation seemed to have changed (Jenkins, 1977, pp. 138–40). In Brazil, despite the fact that on the basis of a straightforward international comparison the vehicle stock was higher than the expected level, other estimates suggest that a backlog existed until 1962.[4]

Once the initial backlog of demand is eliminated, demand comes to depend more closely on changes in per capita income and in the price of cars in relation to other commodities. The question that then arises is how sensitive is car demand to changes in incomes and prices? In the advanced capitalist countries the income elasticity of demand for cars has been estimated at around 3.0 (although the results of individual studies have ranged from 1.0 to 4.0 in the USA and 2.0 to 4.0 in the UK) (White, 1971; Rhys, 1972). The price elasticity of demand is in the range 0.5 to 1.5 with a mid-point of 1.0. Does car demand show a similar degree of responsiveness in the Latin American countries?

The evidence from a number of studies seems to suggest that the price elasticity of demand in a number of Latin American countries is lower than the figures quoted above. In Argentina, for instance, the price elasticity estimated by different methods and for different periods was in the range 0.3 to 0.5 (Jenkins, 1977, p. 133; Sourouille, 1980, p. 88). Roughly similar figures have been found in the case of Brazil (ranging from 0.1 to 0.5 depending on the exact specification of the model used) (Baumgarten, 1972, pp. 285–6). In Mexico the price elasticity was found not to be significantly different from zero (Jenkins, 1977, p. 140).[5] In Peru higher elasticities were found ranging from 1.4 to 4.7 but these were calculated on the basis of the demand for different categories of vehicles and would therefore be biased upwards compared with the elasticity for cars in aggregate (Fernandez-Baca *et al.*, 1979).

The pattern as far as income elasticity is concerned is not so clear.

The various estimates available for Argentina, Brazil and Mexico are all in the range from 1.9 to 3.8 (Behrman, 1972; Jenkins, 1977, pp. 132–40; Sourrouille, 1980, p. 88; Guimaraes, 1981). However, the exact values are sensitive to the model used and the time period chosen. The most directly comparable results, using a similar model, indicated that the income elasticity of demand was also lower in Latin America than in the United States (Behrman, 1972; Jenkins, 1977). Certainly, as in the case of price elasticity, the evidence contradicts rather than supports the view that has been put forward to the effect that both elasticities are likely to be higher in Third World countries than in the advanced capitalist countries (Nowicki, 1968).

The low price elasticity of demand for cars in most Latin American countries clearly has important implications, particularly in the context of the oligopolistic structures of the terminal industry in these countries. Since lower prices do not lead to a large expansion of the market for cars, any price cut, if it is to lead to an increase in sales revenues must also involve a substantial increase in the firm concerned's market share. However, in an industry dominated by transnational oligopolies each firm has the capacity to follow the price cuts of its competitors (even to the point at which local losses have to be cross-subsidized by the parent company). There is therefore a strong incentive to avoid price competition and concentrate on other competitive strategies (cf. the kinked oligopoly demand curve). This is reinforced by the existence of a highly protected market in most Latin American countries which give ample margins for increasing prices.

2   INCOME DISTRIBUTION AND THE DEMAND FOR CARS

While in the advanced capitalist countries the diffusion of car ownership to lower income groups means that income distribution is not a major factor in explaining the demand for cars, in Latin America it continues to be the luxury good *par excellence*. To a far greater extent than most other consumer durables, ownership of cars is restricted to a small, well off section of the population. One broad indication of this situation is the number of inhabitants per car in the region. Despite the rapid growth of the vehicle stock in the sixties, there were still only slightly more than one car for every 40 inhabitants in Latin America by 1970. The situation in the major producing countries is illustrated in Table 6.1. The most favourable situation was found in Argentina where there was one car for every 15 inhabitants, and the least favourable in

TABLE 6.1   *Number of inhabitants per car in Latin America, 1970*

Argentina	15.3
Brazil	42.7
Chile	55.5
Colombia	118.4
Mexico	41.1
Peru	60.2
Uruguay	23.9
Venezuela	16.0

SOURCE   ADEFA, 1972, p. 27.

Colombia where there was fewer than one per hundred. These figures compare with between two and five inhabitants per car in North America and Western Europe. In terms of the proportion of families owning cars it can be estimated that at most one family in four owned a car in Argentina in 1970 (assuming 3.8 persons per family and no multiple car ownership), while in Brazil at the same time only one family out of every eleven owned a car (Guimaraes, 1981).

In fact there is considerable multiple ownership of cars amongst the richest groups in Latin America so that simply dividing the number of cars registered by the number of families would tend to overestimate the extent to which ownership is diffused. In Brazil in the early seventies, for instance, the average number of cars per car-owning household was 1.12, and for the top 3 per cent of households the average was 1.69 (Guimaraes, 1981, p. 46).

Given the limited extent of car ownership and the highly unequal distribution of income in Latin America, it is only to be expected that ownership will be heavily concentrated among the upper income groups. Evidence from Brazil in the early seventies and Mexico in 1963 shows that this is the case. In Brazil the top two deciles of the income distribution accounted for 80 per cent of the cars owned, while in Mexico fewer than 10 per cent accounted for 60 per cent of car ownership (Wells, 1977, table 1; Jenkins, 1977, table 6.2).

Since the highest income groups tend to own larger cars than lower income groups and to buy new rather than second-hand cars, the concentration of expenditure on cars is bound to be even greater than the concentration of ownership. Data from surveys of consumer expenditure in various Latin American countries in the sixties and early seventies bear this out. In Argentina the top 18 per cent of households accounted for more than 70 per cent of all spending on cars (Jenkins, 1977, table 1). In Mexico the top 14 per cent of households in the metropolitan areas (Mexico City, Guadalajara and Monterrey) and the top 8 per cent in other urban areas accounted for more than 85 per cent of expenditure on cars in those areas (Lustig, 1979, tables 3 and 9). For the other countries information is not available separately on cars. Nevertheless expenditure on transport equipment generally is highly concentrated, with 11 per cent of families accounting for more than 80 per cent of expenditure in Brazil and 5 per cent of families making up three-quarters of the total in Chile (Morley and Smith, 1973, tables 4.1 and 4.3; Jenkins, 1977, table 6.3). Finally in Peru the top two deciles account for over 60 per cent of expenditure on vehicles and similar products (Fernandez-Baca *et al.*, 1979, table 3a).

At the other end of the income distribution car ownership is virtually non-existent. In Brazil in the early seventies the poorest half of the population owned only some 5 per cent of all cars while in Mexico in the early sixties the bottom three-quarters accounted for 14 per cent of the total (Wells, 1977, table 1; Jenkins, 1977, table 6.2). A similar pattern emerged from consumer expenditure surveys. In Argentina the poorest half of all families accounted for about 5 per cent of all expenditure on cars. While in Mexico there was virtually no expenditure on cars amongst this group (Jenkins, 1977, table 6.1; Lustig, 1979, tables 2 and 9). The data on expenditure on transport equipment in Chile (the poorest two-thirds of families accounting for 1.6 per cent of expenditure) and vehicles and similar products in Peru (the poorest 40 per cent accounting for just over 5 per cent of expenditure) presents the same picture (Jenkins, 1977, table 6.3; Fernandez-Baca *et al.*, 1979, table 3a).

In Latin America sales of new cars are particularly dependent on a very restricted upper income segment of the population. One way of looking at this is to compare new car prices with the average income of different income groups. In Argentina, for instance, it was only the top 10 per cent of families which had an annual income greater than the average price of a new car in the early 1960s (Sourrouille, 1980). A similar situation existed in Mexico in the late sixties and Brazil in the early seventies.[6] In Peru new car prices in the early seventies were far in excess of the average income of the ninth decile (the average income of the top 10 per cent was not available) (Fernandez-Baca *et al.*, tables 3a and 74).

It is impossible to establish an exact relationship between car prices and the level of income which needs to be achieved in order to buy a new car, because of the other variables involved, of which the availability and terms of credit are particularly important. Any realistic ratio between new car prices and annual income is certain to be less than one in order that an income group should constitute a potential market for new cars. In Latin America, therefore, the market for new cars, with the per capita income levels and income distribution structure that prevailed in the sixties and early seventies, must have been confined to a section of the richest 10 per cent of the population.

After the initial replenishment of the stock of cars in the early years of the industry's development in those countries in which a significant backlog of demand existed, subsequent sales of new cars therefore came to depend on selling new cars to a small élite who in most cases already owned cars. Thus although the stock of cars continued to grow and the greater part of production went to increase the stock rather than to replace scrapped units, nevertheless as far as new cars were concerned, the demand of the buyers was in fact a replacement demand. This, as will be seen below, created certain problems of realization for capital in the industry. In so far as ownership diffusion did occur, and it clearly did as the rising number of cars per inhabitant indicates, this reflected the extension of ownership of used cars to income groups below the very rich. However, as the data quoted earlier on the distribution of ownership and expenditure indicates, this was still restricted to middle income groups. This was facilitated by the sharp increase in the depreciation rates on used cars once the backlog demand was met.

Not only does the relationship between income distribution and the demand for cars mean that the market for new cars is restricted to a small fraction of the population. It also implies that greater income inequality leads to a greater demand for cars and that conversely a progressive redistribution of income tends to restrict the market for cars. This is clearly the case in all the countries for which we have information where it is the highest income groups which spend the highest proportion of their incomes on cars so that such expenditure is more concentrated than income itself. Thus an upward redistribution of income leads to an expansion of the car market. The extent of this effect has been illustrated by studies of Brazil and Mexico.

In Brazil a more regressive distribution of income in which the top 10 per cent of families increased their share of income at the expense of the bottom 40 per cent increased the rate of growth of demand for transport equipment by almost one-third, compared with the situation in which all groups maintained their income share, and was more than double the rate of growth that would have been achieved by a redistribution away from all other groups towards the bottom 40 per cent (Morley and Smith, 1973, table 4.5). These comparisons under-estimate the effects of different changes in income distribution on the demand for cars, expenditure on which is more highly concentrated than on transport equipment generally. The range of redistribution covered is also limited since even in the most progressive case, middle and upper income groups continued to grow at almost half the rate of growth of average income.

In Mexico it has been found that if the whole increase in income was concentrated in the top income groups in the urban areas the growth in the demand for cars would be over a hundred times higher than if income growth were concentrated at the bottom end of the income distribution (Lustig, 1979, table 8). This is a vivid illustration of the already mentioned fact that lower income groups are virtually excluded from the market for cars.

3 EXTERNAL MARKETS

In addition to the limitations of the domestic market, a further problem for realization in the industry in this period was its inability to export. Of the major producers only Mexico exported on a significant scale in this period, while in Argentina and Brazil exports were totally marginal in relation to production for the domestic market (see Table 6.2). This can, of course, be attributed in part to the low productivity and high cost of the industry in Latin America rendering it uncompetitive in international markets. However, given the extent to which the Latin American auto industry was by this time under the control of the major terminal TNCs, and the degree to which these TNCs control internatio-nal vehicle markets and trade, it is important to locate this lack of exports in relation to the role assigned to the Latin American countries

TABLE 6.2   *Exports as a proportion of sales*

	Argentina	*Brazil*	*Mexico*
1966	0.4	0.5	1.7
1967	1.0	1.1	2.1
1968	1.2	0.1	2.0
1969	1.1	0.3	3.5
1970	1.3	0.6	5.3

SOURCES   ADEFA; MacDonnell and Lascano, 1974, table 6; de Oliveira *et al.*, 1979, table 15; AMIA.

in the international division of labour of the TNCs. This was primarily as a sphere for investment in order to gain access to domestic markets from which they would otherwise be excluded and as a market in which to realize surplus value through exports of parts and components produced in their major domestic production bases. They were not interested in Latin American production competing with the output of their domestic plants at this stage.

In order to ensure that there would be no unwanted competition from Latin American exports, it was common for the auto TNCs to include explicit restrictions on the markets in which subsidiaries or licensees could sell, in the technology contracts which they made. In Argentina a study of 146 contracts found that 81.5 per cent of them either limited the territory for which the licence was granted or explicitly restricted exports (Raddavero, 1972). The types of restrictions used included: forbidding any exports; requiring prior authorization for exports; permitting only exports of parts in finished vehicles; and restricting exports to certain countries. Similarly in Chile a study of 17 automotive industry contracts found a high incidence of restrictive clauses. Of the total, nine (53 per cent) prohibited exports and a further five (24 per cent) permitted exports only to the countries of the Andean Pact or the Latin American Free Trade Area (Baharona *et al.*, 1976, tables 21–24). In Peru 47 per cent of the 19 contracts studied in the auto industry imposed restrictions on exports (Fernandez-Baca *et al.*, 1979), while in Mexico, out of 16 contracts between terminal automotive manufacturers and foreign firms only five were entirely free from export restrictions (Jenkins, 1977, p. 212). Given the strategies of the auto TNCs in this period therefore, the limitations of the domestic market in terms of realization could not be overcome through an aggressive strategy of expansion into international markets.

4 COMPETITIVE STRATEGIES

In the last chapter managerial strategies in the sphere of production were discussed, focusing particularly on labour control strategies. It was argued earlier in this chapter that after an initial period in which realization was not a major problem in a number of countries because of the backlog of demand, subsequently it assumed growing significance as an area towards which mangerial strategy had to be directed. In this section we shall consider the various strategies used in the industry in order to create favourable conditions for realization.

Before doing so it is useful to consider a number of conditioning factors which influenced the circumstances under which surplus value was realized in the Latin American countries. As already mentioned the demand for cars was highly inelastic in response to price changes. It was also seen that the market for new cars became increasingly a replacement market in the sixties. This implied first that reductions in prices were unlikely to lead to a significant expansion in the market,[7] and secondly that ways had to be found to persuade existing car owners to replace their vehicles in order to maintain the demand for new cars. With 60 per cent of the top income decile in Brazil (the only income group with a sufficiently high average income to constitute a market for new cars) already owning a car by 1972 (Wells, 1977, table 2) the importance of persuading consumers to change cars is quite apparent.

In addition to these aspects of car demand which influenced the types of strategies adopted by capital in Latin America, there were also significant barriers to entry in the industry, particularly in those countries where major investment had been made in manufacturing facilities. First the considerable excess capacity which existed in the industry throughout the 1960s in these countries acted as a major disincentive to entry by new firms and an effective threat to keep them out by increased production if necessary (cf. Guimaraes, 1981, pp. 39–40). If this did not prove a sufficient deterrent any new entrant would also have to overcome considerable institutional resistance to the creation of an additional firm because of the growing awareness in the governments of the countries concerned that the industry was already excessively fragmented and that what was needed was a rationalization of the existing firms rather than any further entries. This awareness, together with the high levels of protection from imported vehicles which the industry had been granted, meant that its strategies could be implemented without having to be too concerned about the threat of new competition.

The dominant position which foreign capital, in the form of the major auto TNCs achieved in the industry in Latin America in the sixties was a further factor conditioning the type of strategy which emerged. Since the 1920s in the United States and the 1950s in Western Europe, competitive strategies in the car industry have been dominated by model competition (that is styling changes and the production of a 'full line' of models), large scale advertising and consumer credit. Price leadership rather than price competition has been the norm, as in the case of General Motors in the United States (White, 1971, 1977; Rhys, 1972).

During the sixties the motor industry in Latin America came to be increasingly characterized by the forms of oligopolistic competition which are found in the advanced capitalist countries. This tendency was particularly marked in the two countries with the highest level of local integration, Brazil and Argentina. It was associated with three other important developments in the industry, namely the end of the initial boom in car production based on the pent-up demand built up during the period of restricted supply prior to the commencement of local manufacture, the entry of the US Big Three into car production, and the elimination of locally owned producers.

In the late fifties and early sixties the number of models produced in both Brazil and Argentina was relatively small, fewer than two per firm, and in so far as there was an excessive proliferation of models this was the result of a large number of firms in production (Lenicov, 1973; Guimaraes, 1981). By the mid-sixties, however, in both Argentina and Brazil, competition between capitals came to rely increasingly on the traditional oligopolistic methods of increasing demand. The most clear evidence of this is the proliferation in the number of models produced and the rate at which new models were introduced within a short space of time (Table 6.3). More than twice as many new models were introduced in the period 1966–70 as in 1961–5 in both countries. This is all the more spectacular when it is remembered that in Argentina there was a sharp reduction in the number of firms producing cars in the

TABLE 6.3   *Model proliferation and model changes in Argentina and Brazil,*
1961–71

| | Argentina | | Brazil | |
	New models introduced	*Total models produced*	*New models introduced*	*Total models produced*
1961	2	20	1	9
1962	9	26	5	14
1963	5	27	4	16
1964	4	26	6	21
1965	5	27	6	23
1966	15	40	11	25
1967	10	42	10	25
1968	6	36	2	14
1969	16	53	20	31
1970	14	53	11	32
1971	6	49	16	42

SOURCES   ADEFA; Guimaraes, 1981, table 14.

early sixties. As demand for new cars came increasingly to rely on persuading existing owners to replace their vehicles, the twin strategies of providing a range of models and of introducing new models at frequent intervals gained in importance.

Model changes are a means of accelerating the 'moral depreciation' of the existing stock of cars, persuading the rich to replace last years' model with this in order to dynamize the market for new cars. This strategy is accompanied by an attempt to offer a full line of cars, that is a range of at least three or four models, because of the risks of dependence on a single model and the need to retain customers who trade up (or down) to a different size category when they buy a new car.

Another factor which helped to increase the number of models produced and the frequency of model changes in Argentina and Brazil was the belated entry of the US Big Three into car production in the sixties, with their emphasis on a strategy of product differentiation. At the same time locally owned firms, which had often produced a limited range of models were eliminated from the industry, accentuating the tendency for greater model diversity. Of the other Latin American countries Mexico, Peru and Venezuela were all characterized by a large and growing variety of models in the sixties. In Mexico the number of models increased from 34 in 1966 to 40 in 1972 (AMIA). In Venezuela there was an even more spectacular increase to 58 models in 1968 and 74 by 1972 (Fontanals and Porta, 1979, table 2). In Peru too as many as 32 models were produced for a very small market in 1970 (Fernandez-Baca, 1979). Significantly the two countries in which the variety of models on offer remained relatively limited throughout the sixties were Chile and Colombia. In both these countries there was considerable unsatisfied demand, as indicated by the low level of car density in relation to per capita income throughout the sixties. As a result realization did not become a problem and there was no need to adopt these types of competitive strategies to the same degree as in the rest of Latin America.

The introduction of new models as a competitive strategy in Latin America, as elsewhere in the motor industry, is supported by large-scale advertising. Although advertising accounts for only about 1 per cent of the total value of sales in the industry in Latin America (Jenkins, 1977, pp. 185–6, 194; Connor and Mueller, 1977, table 2.6; Guimaraes, 1980, p. 266), a level that was slightly lower than in the USA but higher than in the UK, in absolute terms the industry is an extremely important advertiser because of the value of sales. Moreover, because of the higher prices of cars in Latin America, a lower ratio of advertising to sales gives rise to quite similar levels of advertising expenditure per car sold to that of the United States.

Consumer credit has been another important element in the competitive strategies of the auto TNCs, providing a means of expanding the market for their product and also often being a profitable business in its own right. In 1973 it was reported that in Argentina sales on credit accounted for 85 per cent of total new car sales, while the corresponding figures in other Latin American countries were 96 per cent in Brazil, 45 per cent in Mexico and 70 per cent in Venezuela (AMDA, 1973). In Argentina the vehicle manufacturers were able to obtain access to bank credit at negative real rates of interest which were then used to provide financing for sales to the public which were always made at positive real rates of interest (Sourrouille, 1980, ch. V). There has been a massive growth in consumer credit in the Latin American countries since the sixties, the bulk of it directed to the financing of automotive sales (see de Oliveira *et al.*, 1979, pp. 257–66 for a discussion of the Brazilian case).

5 COSTS AND PRICES

Having reviewed the conditions of production in the Latin American motor industry in the last chapter and the sphere of circulation in the earlier parts of this chapter it is now possible to examine the way in which production and circulation interacted to create one of the fundamental characteristics of the Latin American industry in this period, namely the high level of costs and prices. It should be emphasized at the outset that it is only by understanding the complex interaction of production and realization that a complete analysis of this issue can be arrived at. The orthodox view which sees the problem primarily in technical terms, as the outcome of high levels of local content requirements in small protected markets in an industry subject to economies of scale is therefore inadequate (Baranson, 1969; Munk, 1969).

In 1970 production costs in Latin America were anything from a third higher than international levels in Brazil to more than two and a half times in Chile (see Table 6.4). While the exact difference in cost measured depends on the prevailing exchange rate, it provides some indication of the degree to which the various Latin American countries approached internationally competitive levels in the industry by the end of the sixties.

TABLE 6.4 Costs in the Latin American motor industry, 1970

		Argentina	Brazil	Colombia	Chile	Mexico	Peru	Venezuela
1	Cars produced	163 391	307 500	4798	20 684	136 712	10 273	57 295*
2	No. of firms	7	5	3	9	8	9	8
3	Cars per firm	23 342	61 500	1599	2298	17 089	1141	7162
4	Local integration (%)	91.6	98.3	23.6	58.8†	63.7	18.4	33.7
5	Costs (incl. import duties)‡	199.6	134.9	320.3	309.7	159.4	184.9	146.4
6	Import duties‡	4.7	0.3	126.5	45.8	6.8	21.1	1.4
6a	Contribution to total excess cost (%)§	4.7	0.9	57.4	21.8	11.4	24.9	3.0
7	Imports‡	10.2	2.2	110.0	56.7	47.0	106.0	88.0
7a	Excess costs (%)¶	121.4	129.4	144.0	137.6	129.5	129.9	132.7
7b	Contribution to total (%)‖	1.8	1.4	15.3	7.4	18.0	28.7	46.8
8	Local production‡	184.7	132.4	83.8	207.2	105.6	57.8	57.0
8a	Excess cost (%)**	201.6	134.7	355.1	352.4	165.8	314.1	169.1
8b	Contribution to total††	93.5	97.7	27.3	70.8	70.5	46.4	50.2

* 1971.
† Parts imported from LAFTA considered as part of local content.
‡ Taking the total cost of production in a developed country=100.
§ Calculated as Row 6÷(Row 5−100) expressed as a percentage.
¶ Calculated as Row 7÷(100−Row 4) expressed as a percentage.
‖ Calculated as [Row 7−(100−Row 4)]÷[Row 5−100] expressed as a percentage.
** Calculated as Row 8÷Row 4 expressed as a percentage.
†† Calculated as (Row 8−Row 4)÷(Row 5−100) expressed as a percentage.
SOURCE Own elaboration from ECLA, 1973, table 25.

In terms of accounting for the higher costs of Latin American vehicles it is useful first of all to distinguish between costs of production within Latin America and the cost of imports (including import duty). There is a clear distinction between the countries with highly integrated production (Brazil, Argentina and to a lesser extent Mexico) and the remaining Latin American countries. In the first group the greater part of the excess cost is accounted for by the extra cost of local production, whereas in the latter group imports are at least as great a source of excess cost. (The apparent exception here is Chile but this is due to the inclusion of compensated LAFTA imports as national production in the table.) The additional cost attributable to imports is partly a reflection of the high import duties especially in Colombia and Chile. It also arises out of the c.i.f. costs of imported parts and the earlier mentioned practice of applying deletion allowances to CKD packs when parts are replaced by local production. These factors appear particularly important in Peru and Venezuela where they account for over a quarter and almost a half of the total excess cost respectively.

Turning to the locally produced component of the vehicle it can be seen that costs ranged from one-third higher in Brazil to two and a half times higher than international levels in Colombia and Chile. It is the countries with very low levels of production per firm which have the highest costs relative to international levels for local production. These high costs can in turn be disaggregated between the high costs of locally produced parts and components and the high costs of the terminal firms themselves. Both these contribute to the high aggregate costs of car production in the region (cf. Jenkins, 1977, pp. 197–205).

The low level of labour productivity in the motor vehicle industry in the three main Latin American producing countries compared with European or North American standards was noted in the previous chapter. This was partly offset by the lower level of wages in the Latin American industry which were between one-fifth and one-third of US levels in the period under consideration (see Table 6.5). Although in the mid-sixties this was not sufficient to fully offset the productivity differential *vis-à-vis* the United States and wages were not much lower than in Western Europe, by the early seventies particularly Brazil and to a lesser extent Mexico compensated for lower productivity through lower wages. Other production costs must therefore have been significantly greater to give rise to the above mentioned differences in costs. The scale of production in the industry is generally recognized as a crucial factor in explaining these higher costs.[8]

In discussing economies of scale in the terminal industry, the relevant

TABLE 6.5   *International comparisons of wages and productivity in the motor industry* (US = 100)

	Mid-1960s		Early 1970s	
	Productivity	Wages	Productivity	Wages
US	100	100	100	100
Germany	51	36	49	64
Italy	53	31	46	36
France	45	32	46	37
UK	42	39	34	64
Japan	32	27	82	36
Brazil	10	22	21	19
Mexico	14	37	17	21
Argentina	21	26	15	25

SOURCES   Table 5.7; Baranson, 1969, annex table 22; Aguilar, 1982, table 13; de Oliveira *et al.*, 1979; Sourrouille, 1980; Eurostat; Japanese Economics Yearbook.

concept of scale relates to the size of individual plants. A rough approximation can be obtained by dividing the output of cars by the number of firms which produce them. When this is done it can be seen that the very low production runs in all the Latin American countries apart from Brazil is a result of the division of the market between seven, eight or nine firms (except in Colombia). As we argued earlier this fragmentation of the Latin American industry was a result of the international rivalry of the auto TNCs at the time when the industry was being developed and the failure of the local states to limit the entry of firms.

On top of this initial structure the competitive strategies employed in order to secure the realization of surplus value in the industry also contributes to an increase in the costs of production. The provision of a range of models results in shorter production runs for those parts that are not common to all models, more detailed planning of product flows within the plant, and large inventories of parts and components.[9] The cost penalty of model diversity will also reflect the level of local integration. The costs of producing a number of models are likely to be greater in Argentina and Brazil than in the other countries because the major body parts are stamped there. Nevertheless even in cases where there is only a limited local content costs will increase as a result of diversity (Sicard, 1970). Thus the competitive strategies applied which led to a proliferation of models, especially in Argentina, Brazil and to a lesser extent Mexico, is likely to have increased further the level of costs in those industries.

The length of life of models is a further important factor in determining production costs. Unlike model diversity, it has little effect on assembly costs, so that for plants with low levels of local content there is little incentive to keep models in production over a long time period. The period over which a model is kept in production becomes much more significant at high levels of integration, especially when the major body stampings are produced locally. It has been estimated that extending a model's life from two to ten years reduces the cost of the body by about 30 per cent at an output of 25 000 units a year. Other estimates suggest an even greater saving in body costs as a result of freezing models over a number of years. Savings can also be made in engine manufacture by spreading tooling costs over a longer time period. But because engines are changed less often than bodies and a lot of the machinery used can be adapted to produce different engines, these savings are likely to be less significant than those in stamping.

These same considerations can have an indirect effect on costs in the parts industry as well. In so far as the terminals attempt to ensure that they have their own captive suppliers then the fragmentation of the terminal industry is reproduced in the parts industry, thus making it difficult to achieve economies of scale there too. Similarly the diversity of models on offer and the frequency with which models are changed make it difficult for parts' suppliers to achieve the long production runs which are required to bring down costs for a number of components. With a few exceptions, particularly in Mexico, it has not been possible to achieve greater scale economies in the parts industry through the use of common components by different terminals.

Problems of realization, and the tendency of firms to build capacity ahead of demand as part of their competitive strategy, have led to considerable capacity under-utilization in the Latin American motor industry in the sixties (Jenkins, 1977, pp. 208–11; Mericle, 1984, pp. 8–9). This excess capacity further contributed to high costs particularly in those countries where major investments had been made in the industry. In Argentina it was estimated that full utilization of capacity in the late sixties could have reduced car prices by about 10 per cent (DNEI, 1969, p. 38), while in Mexico it was estimated that at 60 per cent utilization costs were 7 per cent higher than at full capacity and at 40 per cent utilization this increased to 16 per cent (Jenkins, 1977, p. 211).

Vehicle prices in Latin America are also considerably higher than for corresponding models in their countries of origin. In passing from costs to prices three main elements intervene, namely the profit margin of the manufacturer, the dealer's margin and sales or equivalent taxes. Data on manufacturers' profit margins is fragmentary and most of the studies comparing Latin American and international prices assume that the margin is the same (ADEFA, 1969; ECLA, 1973, table 25). While the basis for such an assumption is somewhat tenuous, the size of the profit margin in the overall price structure is sufficiently small for the final price not to be very sensitive to variations in its magnitude.

Dealers' margins are particularly high in Colombia, at almost one-third of the cost to the distributor. In the other Latin American countries they fall in the range of 15 to 20 per cent (ECLA, 1973, table 24). This is not exceptionally high by the standards of North America or Western Europe (the figure of 5 per cent used by ECLA in their international cost structure is a considerable underestimate ECLA, 1973, table 25). It should be remembered, however, that a similar margin involves a greater absolute amount in Latin America than in the advanced capitalist countries. This is partly attributable to the higher price of the cars sold which requires more working capital than if cars were cheaper. It also reflects economies of scale in distribution (cf. Pashigan, quoted in White, 1971).

Finally there is considerable variation in the levels of taxation on car sales in different countries, with Brazil where taxes account for almost 30 per cent of the price to the public at one extreme, and Venezuela where taxes are only 1 per cent of the price at the other (ECLA, 1973, table 25). As a result, although production costs are lower in Brazil than in any of the other Latin American countries, the lowest prices are found in Venezuela and Mexico.

6   CONCLUSION

This chapter has shown the conditions which contributed to the problems of realization in the Latin American motor industry in the sixties. The prevailing income distribution meant that the market for new cars was restricted to a small percentage of the total population. Once the initial deficit in the stock of cars was made up, a further expansion of sales came to depend on persuading existing owners to change their cars. The major TNCs therefore introduced the strategies which they had developed in North America and Europe of model competition. Given the restricted local markets and the fragmentation of these markets between a large number of producers, costs were well above international levels. This problem was further aggravated by the competitive strategies adopted. The oligopolistic market structure, together with the barriers to entry of new firms and high levels of protection from imports ensured that the major firms could pass on their high costs in the form of higher prices to the consumer.

NOTES

1. This approach is not without methodological problems. For a discussion of some of these see Jenkins, 1977, pp. 123–5.
2. In the case of Brazil the wide disparities in income levels and car density between different regions may make this average figure misleading. If it had been possible to use more disaggregated data this might have shown a shortfall in the stock of cars in each region which is hidden by the averaging procedure. As will be seen below there is some evidence to suggest that such a shortfall did exist in Brazil in the late fifties.
3. An alternative estimate by Sourrouille (1980), however, puts the date as late as 1972 on the basis of a more sophisticated model. In view of the changes occurring in market conditions in the Argentinian motor industry in the mid-sixties this seems much too late.
4. Milone finds that the desired real depreciated stock of cars is greater than the actual stock up to 1962 and inferior or equal to it from 1963 to 1967 (Guimaraes, 1981, p. 25).
5. Fox (n.d.) also reports that estimated price elasticities in Mexico and Brazil were not significantly different from zero.
6. In Brazil in 1972 the average price of a car was Cr.$20 092 (ANFAVEA). The average household income of the top decile was Cr.$53 035 but this fell to Cr.$16 138 in the ninth decile (Wells, 1977, table 1). In Mexico the average price of a car in 1969 was approximately $36 000 pesos (own elaboration from AMIA data and ECLA, 1973, table 25). The average income of the top decile was $140 000 pesos while that of the ninth decile was roughly $36 000 pesos (calculated from von Ginneken, 1980, table 2).
7. Given the observed discontinuities in income level at the top end of the income distribution a very large reduction in price would be necessary to bring new cars within the reach of a significantly greater percentage of the population while for many of those who were already in a position to buy cars their income was so high that they were able to do so virtually regardless of price.
8. The importance which has been attributed to economies of scale is disputed by Sourrouille (1980, pp. 112–24). However, he in turn underestimates the extent to which costs can be reduced at larger volumes because he only considers the capital cost (depreciation). In fact, however, larger scale production leads to a reduction in all costs per unit of output not just in the fixed capital cost.
9. Pratten (1971, tables 14.3 and 14.4) indicates that in Britain the costs of

production of a firm producing three basic bodies and five basic engines would be more than 25 per cent greater than that of a firm producing only one model, at a level of output of 100 000 vehicles a year. However, not all the additional costs would have to be borne by a subsidiary in an underdeveloped country since they include the initial research and development costs of developing a number of models.

7 Relations Between Terminals and Suppliers

1 INTRODUCTION

The profitability of the auto TNCs which dominate the terminal end of the Latin American motor industry reflects not only the ability of these firms to generate and realize surplus value, but also their success in appropriating surplus value produced elsewhere in the economy. It is possible to distinguish between transfers from other parts of the motor industry complex and those from the rest of the economy outside the complex. The terminals enjoy a hegemonic position within the motor vehicle complex, reflected in unequal relations between them and their suppliers (particularly parts producers) which supply them with parts and components at favourable prices. They are also able to draw on surplus from the economy as a whole through the financial system. The terminals are in a privileged position which enables them to raise capital both locally and internationally. This has favourable effects on their profitability particularly where (as has often been the case in Latin America) interest rates are negative in real terms.

2 TERMINAL–SUPPLIER RELATIONS IN THE ADVANCED CAPITALIST COUNTRIES

Because of the much greater empirical evidence available on the relationship between terminals and suppliers in the motor vehicle industries of the advanced capitalist countries, and the belief that the auto TNCs which control the terminal industry in Latin America will tend, with certain modifications, to try to reproduce the relationships which they enjoy with their suppliers in their countries of origin, this section considers the situation in North America, Western Europe and Japan. In the following section we analyse the structure of the Latin

American parts and components industry, before finally presenting some evidence of the relations of domination which exist within the Latin American motor vehicle industry.

Before discussing in detail the factors which contribute to the hegemonic position of the terminals within the motor vehicle industry, it will be useful first of all to clarify the factors which contribute to relations of dominance and dependence between capitals. Conventional analysis stresses the issue of market structure and market power reflected in such variables as the level of concentration in particular markets and the market shares of individual firms. Thus within a particular market, firms with large market shares enjoy considerable market power, those with low market shares have little or no market power. In vertical relations between suppliers and buyers the relative concentration of sellers and buyers is seen as the major factor determining the relationship between them. This concept of monopoly power based on market power is too narrow for the purpose of this analysis. It does not fully capture the extent of power of large units of capital (arising from the concentration and centralization of capital), which span many markets both geographically and in terms of products. 'This [corporate] power rarely has anything to do with market structure and the degree of concentration in the industries where they operate; it has more to do with aggregate concentration, absolute size and power over production processes' (Semmler, 1982, p. 110).

The significance of this distinction is immediately apparent in considering the relationships between terminals and suppliers in the advanced capitalist countries. If one considers the parts industry in aggregate it can be seen that it is much less concentrated than the terminal industry. In the terminal industry the four leading firms in all the major producing countries account for 80 per cent or even more of production, and there are usually no more than half a dozen mass producers in any one country. In the parts industry in contrast there are hundreds or even thousands of firms. For instance in the UK and the US there are over 2000 parts firms and in Japan as many as 7000 (EIU, 1977, p. 5; Bhaskar, 1979, pp. 303–4; Price Commission, 1979, p. 60). The majority of these are small or medium sized firms.

Aggregate concentration in the parts industry, however, is less relevant than concentration in the supply of specific parts and components. In many cases in Western Europe parts' suppliers are near monopolists in the products which they supply.[1] Other sectors of the industry are characterized by duopolies or near duopolies such as batteries and brakes in the UK, wheels in France and batteries and instruments in West Germany.

The tyre industry also has levels of concentration comparable with those found in the terminal industry with four firms accounting for over 70 per cent of production in the USA and West Germany and around 90 per cent in the UK, France, Italy and Japan (West, forthcoming, table 4). Thus for many parts and components it would be incorrect to view the situation as one in which a small number of oligopolistic terminal firms face a large number of competing suppliers.

In terms of absolute size, however, there is a marked difference between the terminals and even the largest parts producers which indicates the much greater *corporate* power of the former. This difference in size can be illustrated most readily by comparing the volume of sales and assets controlled by the terminal firms and their suppliers. In the USA the combined sales of 19 major independent suppliers of original equipment in 1976 came to over $8000 million, but this was only just one-half the sales of Chrysler, the third terminal in the industry. In the same year, the combined sales of all five US tyre transnationals was only slightly greater than those of Chrysler. In the UK despite the strength of the local components industry, only the four largest firms compare in size with the smaller terminals, Chrysler and Vauxhall. In West Germany only Bosch in the parts industry has a turnover greater than that of Opel, Ford or BMW and it is less than half the turnover of VW or Daimler-Benz. In France the largest parts manufacturer Ferodo has only one-third of the turnover of the smallest terminal Chrysler-France. In Japan the gap is even wider. Toyota's sales are almost four times and Nissan's more than three times the combined sales of a dozen leading parts manufacturers.

It is important to emphasize this difference in size between the terminals and the parts manufacturers because capital cost is an important barrier to entry in the motor industry. It is virtually inconceivable, therefore, for a parts producer to enter into production of vehicles in order to use his own parts. It is by no means inconceivable, however, for a terminal to integrate backwards into the production of a particular part or component, indeed the terminals are regularly making decisions over whether to buy-out or to produce parts themselves.[2] It is this asymmetry which makes it possible for the terminals to put pressure on suppliers in order to obtain favourable prices for original equipment. The situation for tyres is somewhat different from that for most other parts which are bought-in, because tyres are virtually never produced by the terminals themselves.[3] The threat of 'in-plant' production is therefore not really credible. Tyres also differ from a number of other parts in that the replacement market is more important than the original equipment market and that it is a visible part unlike most other parts which have to be replaced frequently which tend to be internal. In discussing the relationships between terminals and suppliers, the tyre industry will therefore be dealt with separately.

The unique relationship between the assemblers and their suppliers is manifested in a number of ways. The most important of these are the technological relationships which are established between the two types of firm, financial links and ownership of suppliers and the system of distribution of replacement parts. In each of these areas the terminals attempt to reproduce their privileged position *vis-à-vis* their suppliers in order to maintain their own profit rates above the average for the complex.

The technological relationship between the terminals and parts producers varies from one in which the latter acts as a simple subcontractor producing parts to the specification and design of the terminals to the more independent role of proprietary parts manufacturers who supply original equipment of their own design (e.g. clutches and sparking plugs) which may require modification in some cases to match the design of a specific car model. In the United States the assemblers have always insisted on owning all special tooling used by suppliers in manufacturing parts for them even if the tooling is produced by the supplier himself (Crandall, 1968, pp. 223–4). This permits the terminal to shift the tools from one firm to another if production is stopped by a strike. More importantly it means that the supplier is not able to utilize the tooling to enter the replacement market in competition with the vehicle producer.

The same tendency for the terminals to own all or part of the special tooling for the production of major parts which are bought from suppliers has been noted in the UK in recent years. Whilst this limits the capital expenditure and financial risk of the component manufacturer as in the United States it also limits the possibility of competition with the assemblers in the after-market. As a result this tendency has been resisted by the stronger proprietary parts manufacturers who see it as an attempt to reduce them to the position of subcontractors (Price Commission, 1979, pp. 40–1). A similar tendency has occurred regarding the design of parts whereby a parts manufacturer is subcontracted to design a part, but the ownership of the design is held by the terminal.

The terminal is then free to negotiate the production of the part with the supplier (Price Commission, 1979, pp. 40–1).

The tyre industry is at the most independent end of the spectrum in terms of the relationship between terminals and suppliers. The major innovations in the tyre industry have been made by the tyre companies themselves and they have also been involved in developing capital goods for the industry.[4] The tyre industry is also less closely tied to the terminals because the greater part of sales go to the replacement market and not as original equipment.

Financial and ownership links are also used by the terminals to control their suppliers. This is particularly common in Japan where many component companies are linked either financially or through their personnel to the terminals, especially Toyota and Nissan.[5] Toyota controls 12 major parts manufacturers with Nissan having an interest in as many as 29 firms (British Overseas Trade Board, 1974, pp. 13–14). A similar situation exists in Italy where Fiat has a majority shareholding in ten component firms and a minority holding in one case, not to mention its iron and steel subsidiaries (Fiat Annual Report, 1978). In the other major countries ownership of parts producers by the terminals is not so widespread although important cases do exist such as General Motors–AC/Delco.

In Japan the terminals not only exercise control of their suppliers through direct ownership but have also organized their main subcontractors into associations of parts suppliers. Each vehicle manufacturer has his own association with a hundred or more member companies. The vehicle manufacturers are described as having 'provided guidance in management techniques, assisted in raising loans and transferred staff to their subcontractors' (NEDO, 1971, p. 99). It is clear that the assemblers are able to exercise substantial control over their suppliers through these associations and have used them to coordinate and rationalize the operations of their suppliers (Altshuler *et al.*, 1984, pp. 146–9). It is the basis of the 'Kanban' (just-in-time) system whereby the terminal firms have been able to pass on the cost of holding stocks to their suppliers and minimize their own inventories which is often held to be an important competitive advantage of the Japanese manufacturers.

The third area in which the vehicle manufacturers reproduce their position of dominance *vis-à-vis* their suppliers is in the distribution of replacement parts. This they are able to do because of the role of franchised dealers in supplying the replacement market. The terminals and their franchised dealers account for between 40 per cent and 55 per cent of all replacement market sales in the USA, Western Europe and Japan (EIU, 1977, p. 98; Price Commission, 1979, pp. 45, 59–60; Commission des Communautes Europeennes, 1979, p. 12).

The way in which the role of the terminals in the replacement market creates a barrier to entry for the parts' producers and reinforces the former's favourable position in the commerical relation analysed above can be illustrated with the example of the United Kingdom.[6] As already indicated half the replacement market in the UK is supplied by the franchised dealers of the vehicle manufacturers. Two out of the four vehicle manufacturers operating in the UK and three of the five importers studied by the Price Commission had exclusive buying clauses in their contracts with franchisees which required them to buy components supplied by the terminal. Even where such exclusive contracts did not exist, a number of factors made it difficult for the franchisee to carry parts not supplied by the terminal. These included a requirement that warranty work should only be carried out with parts which they supplied; the direct monitoring of frenchisees stocks through computer-based inventory control systems which make it difficult to carry stocks not supplied by the terminal; the use of rebates tied to the growth of sales of parts supplied by the terminal. This situation makes it difficult for firms to produce parts only for the replacement market since if they do not sell original equipment to the terminals, their product is virtually excluded from that half of the replacement market supplied by franchised dealers. The situation in the other advanced capitalist countries is not very different from the one that has just been described.

In recent years the vehicle manufacturers have attempted to penetrate the replacement market further by producing 'all makes' programmes of spare parts which cover a number of the faster moving lines for both their own cars and other manufacturers. In the UK both Chrysler and Ford introduced their 'all makes' range of parts in 1970 and BL in 1974 (Price Commission, 1979, pp. 76–7). Ford and VW are both operating similar systems in West Germany (Price Commission, 1979, p. 64). The effect of this development is likely to be to put more pressure on independent part producers reducing the market for their products which is outside the control of the terminals. Moreover, the operation of the franchise system is such that it puts additional pressure on the parts producers to be an original equipment supplier and thus weakens his bargaining power *vis-à-vis* the terminal.

The situation in the tyre industry is rather different from that of parts generally. As already indicated, in terms of technological development and control over its own means of production, the industry is at the most independent end of the spectrum of relations between suppliers and assemblers. Moreover, the firms are themselves large organizations, although they are significantly smaller than the assemblers. In terms of distribution too, this sub-sector is not as dependent on the franchised dealers of the vehicle manufacturers as the parts producers, since only a small proportion of the tyres sold in the major producing countries go through vehicle dealers. Indeed, in most countries the tyre companies have their own distribution system of either company owned stores or franchised dealers. Nevertheless, despite these more favourable conditions, the tyre companies have still obtained significantly lower profit rates in the United States compared with the assemblers.

The terminals derive three main advantages from their relationships with independent suppliers in the motor industry. First of all wages tend to be lower in the parts industry than amongst the terminals (see Friedman, 1977, pp. 244–5 on the UK and Toder *et al.*, 1978, table 7.2 on the US). If the terminals decided to produce these parts 'in plant' they would have to pay workers the higher level of wages which prevail in the terminal industry. For many parts and components the lower labour cost achieved through buying out from a number of small suppliers outweigh any prospective gains from large scales of production which could be achieved through in-plant production. A major advantage of the Japanese system of controlling suppliers is that the terminals obtain the benefits of vertical integration in terms of close coordination without the cost of having to pay the higher wages found in the terminal sector (Altshuler *et al.*, 1984, p. 148).

Not only do the terminals benefit from lower prices of parts and components as a result of lower wages, but also from the lower profit margins in the parts industry. The case of the US motor industry provides clear evidence of this phenomenon. Over the period 1947–65 component firms earned a rate of return (after tax) on net worth of 13.8 per cent.[7] Over the same period vehicle assemblers earned a rate of return of 20.2 per cent the Big Three were earning an average of over 25 per cent (Crandall, 1968, p. 212). The recent success of the Japanese (terminal) motor firms is very much based on the special relationship which they enjoy *vis-à-vis* their suppliers, and this is reflected in the higher rates of return which the terminals earn even compared with the largest suppliers in the industry.

The average return earned by parts manufacturers is made up of the return which they earn on sales of original equipment to the terminal industry and the return on sales of parts to the replacement market. It is a common feature of the industry that the terminals pay significantly lower prices for original equipment than are charged in the after-market. The transfer of surplus to the terminals is therefore greater than a simple comparison of average rates of return would suggest.

In the case of tyres, prices of original equipment sold to the terminals in the United States and Western Europe are one-third or more lower than prices in the replacement market (FTC, 1966, p. 26; Commission of the European Communities, 1977; Commission des Communautes Europeenes, 1977, p. 24). Even greater differentials between original equipment and replacement market prices are found in some parts and components. Studies in the UK and the USA have shown many cases where parts are sold to the terminals either at a loss or at a very small profit, while the same parts are sold as spares at a healthy profit (see the case of sparking plug, electrical equipment and clutch mechanisms in Monopolies Commission, 1963 and 1968; *Motor Business*, 1960, p. 14).

Thus in addition to taking advantage of the lower wages of parts' suppliers, the terminals are also able to use their bargaining power, derived as was seen above from their control of technology, finance and markets in order to squeeze the profit margins on the parts which they buy. The third advantage which the terminals obtain from the use of outside suppliers is the greater flexibility which they achieve particularly in relation to fluctuations in the level of demand. In other words the existence of a significant bought-out component enables the terminals to pass on the effects of fluctuations to their suppliers and reduce the impact on their own production. It has been suggested that the extensive use of subcontracting is an important factor in the security of employment enjoyed by workers in large firms in Japan (Friedman, 1977, p. 126). It has also been argued that in the British motor industry the terminal firms squeezed their suppliers in times of falling demand.[8]

3   THE STRUCTURE OF THE PARTS AND COMPONENTS INDUSTRY IN LATIN AMERICA

The Latin American parts industry shows many of the structural characteristics that are found in the advanced capitalist countries. There are, however, two additional features which deserve to be mentioned. First, in a number of Latin American countries the truncated nature of the motor vehicle complex means that the development of the parts industry is incomplete with only certain parts and components being produced locally. Second, the industry is an important area of the economy in which foreign and local capital are found to coexist.

Argentina, Brazil and Mexico have all developed a relatively complete range of suppliers. In other Latin American countries, however, many complex parts are not produced locally. As a result the terminals obtain more of their parts from abroad than they do from the local parts industry. In Peru, for instance, the terminals import twice as much as they buy from the local parts industry, while in Venezuela imports are about 50 per cent greater (see table 5.2). Locally produced parts tend to be the technologically less complex parts and components and of course tyres which are produced mainly by TNC subsidiaries. [9] As will be seen below this continuing heavy reliance on imports gives the terminals an additional flexibility in their relationships with suppliers since they can choose between 'in house' production, buying locally or importing any specific part.

Whereas both the terminal industry and the tyre industry in Latin America are virtually totally dominated by TNCs, there is still a significant participation of local capital in the parts and components industry. In Peru, Colombia and Chile where the parts industry is composed mainly of the less complex parts, the bulk of production comes from locally owned firms. In Argentina, Brazil and Mexico there is a more even distribution with foreign capital accounting for between 40 per cent and 55 per cent of the output of the parts industry.

As in the case of the advanced capitalist countries, the parts industry in the Latin American countries, particularly those in which the highest level of local content has been achieved, is characterized by the existence of a large number of firms.[10] In Brazil there are around 1800 parts firms and in Argentina almost 1000. Mexico and Colombia each have around 500 such firms and Peru and Venezuela 150 and 200 respectively (data from country studies by ILET, Ronderos Tobon, 1981 and Aguilar, 1982).

Nevertheless a relatively small proportion of these firms are responsible for a large share of total sales in the industry. In Brazil 30 firms accounted for 70 per cent of the industry's sales (de Oliveira *et al.*, 1979, p. 105) while in Argentina 75 firms employing more than 300 workers accounted for two-thirds of sales (Sourrouille, 1980, p. 156). Concentration is less marked in those countries in which the parts industry is less developed. In the case of Peru which is representative of this situation, the 28 largest establishments accounted for just over half of total production in the industry (Fernandez-Baca *et al.*, 1979, table 78).

Sales to the terminals tend to be even more concentrated in a relatively small group of firms. In Argentina fifteen firms accounted for about half of all such sales while in Mexico the largest ten firms made up 45 per cent of sales (Sourrouille, 1980, p. 157; Lifschitz, 1979, table 38). What these figures emphasize is the extremely heterogeneous nature of the parts industry. On the one hand a relatively small number of firms producing complex parts in monopolistic markets, and on the other a large number of small or medium sized firms producing simple parts usually in competition with a considerable number of similar producers.

Within this heterogeneous structure the small firms tend to sell proportionately more of their output to the replacement market, while the larger firms sell mainly original equipment. This situation is illustrated for the Brazilian and Argentinian cases in tables 7.1 and 7.2. (Note, however, that even for the smallest firms a not insignificant part of their output is sold to the terminals.)

Foreign capital in the component industry tends to be concentrated

TABLE 7.1 *Argentinian parts industry: distribution of sales to terminals and replacement market (%), 1972*

	Terminals	Replacement
Up to 10 workers	27.0	73.0
11–50 workers	48.7	51.3
51–100 workers	63.0	37.0
101–300 workers	73.2	26.8
> 300 workers*	65.4	34.6

NOTE   Only sales to the terminals and to replacement market included.
* This category includes the tyre manufacturers who sell mainly in the replacement market.
SOURCE   Sourrouille, 1980, table 25.

TABLE 7.2 *Brazilian parts industry: distribution of sales to terminals and replacement market (%), 1975*

Sales	Terminals	Replacement
< Cr $5 m	49.1	50.9
Cr $5–20 m	58.6	41.4
Cr $20–100 m	76.0	24.0
> Cr $100 m	80.8	19.2

NOTE   Only sales to the terminals and the replacement market included.
SOURCE   de Oliveira *et al.*, 1979, table 61.

amongst the largest firms of the industry. In Brazil, for instance, 52 of the largest 100 firms were foreign owned, but only 55 of the remaining 352 members of SINDIPECAS (the parts producers' trade association) were foreign subsidiaries (de Oliveira *et al.*, 1979, p. 197). In Argentina and Mexico, the average sales of the foreign component producers were respectively 14 and 13 times those of local companies (Lifschitz, 1979, table 27; Sourrouille, 1980, table 21). Foreign firms, with the exception of the tyre manufacturers are likely therefore to sell proportionately more of their output as original equipment than locally owned firms. Major TNCs in the parts industry in Latin America such as Eaton, Bendix, Borg Warner, Lucas and Bosch in fact often followed their customers overseas establishing the same kind of relationships with the terminals as they had in their country of origin.

Not only are these foreign subsidiaries much bigger than local parts firms but they also tend to operate in the more highly concentrated sub-sectors of the parts industry. In Brazil, for example, the production of shock absorbers, ball bearings and sparking plugs are all concentrated in a small number of mainly foreign firms (de Oliveira *et al.*, 1979, p. 201–6). As in the advanced capitalist countries the industrial structure of the parts industry varies from sub-sector to sub-sector with some as, or more, highly concentrated than the terminal industry while others are characterized by a high degree of competition between a number of small and medium producers. In these latter sub-sector local capital tends to predominate and there is little foreign investment.

Not surprisingly, in view of the structure that has been described here, the average size of firms and plants in the parts industry is far smaller than in the terminal industry. It can be seen from table 7.3 that the average number of workers per establishment is anything from 10 to more than 100 times greater in the terminal industry than in the parts industry, although the size of tyre plants is much closer to that of the

TABLE 7.3 *Number of workers per establishment, terminals, parts, tyres*

	Terminals	Parts	Tyres
Argentina (1963)	1631	13	315
Brazil (1970)	2483	94	1270
Mexico (1970)	970	69	497
Peru (1974)	644	28	541
Venezuela (1977)	1143	58	869

SOURCES Lifschitz, 1978, tables 9, 12, 15; Fernandez-Baca *et al.*, 1979, table 59; Fontanals and Porta, 1979, tables 11 and 12.

terminals. Since the terminals are more likely to operate several plants, the difference in size of firm is likely to be even more pronounced. Given the heterogeneity of the parts industry it is also relevant to compare the size of the largest firms in the parts industry with that of the largest terminals. There is a considerable differential on this measure too, indicating that the difference in average size cannot be entirely attributed to the existence of a large number of marginal parts suppliers which affect the average size of firms disproportionately. In Brazil, for instance, the four largest terminal firms were five times as large as the four largest component firms in terms of capital invested, and almost ten times as large in terms of sales (de Oliveira *et al.*, 1979, tables 32, 33 and 34). In Mexico, the corresponding ratios were more than four times for total assets and almost six times for sales (AMIA, 1976, pp. 182–3). In Peru the four leading terminals were almost eight times larger in terms of sales and three and a half times larger in terms of the number of workers employed (Fernandez-Baca, 1979, p. 361). Thus the substantial difference in size between terminals and suppliers, which was shown in the last section to be a major factor in the unequal relationship between the two groups of firms in the advanced capitalist countries, also characterizes the motor vehicle complex in Latin America.

4   MECHANISMS OF DOMINATION

Technology

In many cases the relationship between the terminal firm and its supplier is not an 'arm's length' relationship where the terminal buys parts off the shelf. The nature of vehicle production makes it necessary for the parts which the terminals buy to meet detailed specifications in terms of dimensions, tolerances etc. Thus the supplier of original equipment is often more of a subcontractor than an independent enterprise. Whereas in the advanced capitalist countries the terminal may be able to provide its suppliers with technical specifications and leave production in the hands of the supplier, in the Third World generally it has been found that a much greater involvement in the suppliers' operations is required and terminals are engaged in providing technical assistance to their suppliers on an extensive scale.[11] These technical linkages between terminals and suppliers permit an even greater control over suppliers in the Third World than that observed in North America, Western Europe and Japan.

In Latin America too there is extensive involvement by the terminals in the production decisions of their suppliers. In Peru, for instance, the terminals were involved in assisting their suppliers to select machinery and other equipment, in guaranteeing productive efficiency in the plants of suppliers in order to keep down costs and in controlling the quality of the suppliers' output (UNCTC, 1981, p. 43). In Mexico in the early sixties a product engineer from the terminal was involved in the selection of suppliers, discussion of the specifications for parts, encouraging suppliers to apply industrial engineering techniques, selection of testing equipment and assistance with suppliers' specification to sub-suppliers. Interestingly the same product engineer also participated in price negotiations with suppliers and was responsible for looking for new potential sources of supply (Edelberg, 1976).

It is evident from these descriptions that technical assistance from terminals to suppliers is a two-edged sword. On the one hand it can create some technological capacity within the parts firm. On the other it ensures the dependence of the parts producer on the terminal and provides the detailed inside information on the supplier's production which strengthens the terminal's bargaining power in its negotiations over the prices to be paid for parts. As a UNCTC report points out:

A small and dependent supplier firm may be squeezed on price and payment schedules; it may be particularly hard hit during recessions; it may be dropped without due cause if the lead enterprise switches sources or decides to manufacture the relevant product itself; it may be required to bear an undue share of the cost of high inventories or frequent retooling to meet changing specifications; and it may suffer a skill drain to the lead enterprises if its trained workforce is tempted away by higher wages or better working conditions. At the worst, a small linked enterprise may end up being totally dependent on one buyer, experiencing heavy indebtedness and onerous terms and prices (UNCTC, 1981, p. 7).

As Sourrouille (1980, pp. 160–1) points out in the case of Argentina, the role of the parts supplier is even more circumscribed than in the countries of origin of the auto TNCs:

Its involvement is limited to carrying out the work required, under known procedures, restricted by strict controls on quality and costs, and threatened both by the possibility that the work could be transferred to other suppliers and that the product could be imported.

and as the Argentinian Consejo Coordinador de la Industria de Autopartes states:

> Its real scale, its present situation and future development are conditioned by the action of the terminal plants who really establish the parameters of all its operations.

Ownership

While the type of control discussed in the previous section implies that the supplier continues to operate under independent ownership, this is not necessarily the case and it is possible for the terminals to acquire a controlling interest in some of its suppliers. This is not unknown in Latin America. The most complete data available come from Argentina where it has been estimated that 12 per cent of the parts purchased by the terminals come from their own subsidiaries (Sourrouille, 1980, table 23). Unfortunately, comparable data is not available on other Latin American countries, but it seems likely that direct control by the terminals is less marked elsewhere. In Mexico ownership of suppliers by the terminals has been prohibited by law, apart from certain exceptional cases, since the initiation of manufacturing activities. In Brazil direct ownership also appears to be limited although it is known that VW, Ford, Fiat and Mercedes-Benz all have interests in the parts industry (de Oliveira *et al.*, 1979, p. 198). Similarly in Venezuela, GM, Ford, VW and Mercedes-Benz control some suppliers although the extent of this phenomenon is not known (Fontanals and Porta, 1979, p. 24). In Peru such ownership links seem to be of no significance (Fernandez-Baca, 1979).

Although direct ownership is limited in the Latin American parts industry, and certainly does not have the significance which it does in Japan, for instance, the size differential between terminals and suppliers makes both 'verticalization' (i.e. production of more parts 'in plant') and acquisition of parts firms by the terminals a very potent threat. It is therefore a further factor in the unequal bargaining power between terminals and suppliers.

Markets

A final form of dependence of suppliers on the terminals is in terms of the latter's control of the markets in which the parts industry sells. In the three countries which have achieved the highest level of local integration in the industry, Argentina, Brazil and Mexico, the bulk of parts sales (but not of tyre sales) are to the terminals. In each case over 70 per cent of such sales are to the terminals and less than 30 per cent to the replacement market (see table 7.4). This is much higher than in an advanced capitalist country such as the UK for instance where only 52 per cent of the parts industry's sales are to the terminals (CPRS, 1975, chart 1). In other words, the parts industry in these Latin American countries, because of the division between original equipment and replacement market sales, is more dependent on the terminals.

TABLE 7.4   *Parts industry: distribution of sales between terminals and replacement market (%)*

	Terminals	*Replacement*
Argentina (1972)	76.9	23.1
Brazil (1975)	78.5	21.5
Colombia (1975)	39.5	60.5
Mexico (1977)	72.7	27.3
Peru (1974)	54.9	45.1
Venezuela (1968)	44.0	56.0

SOURCES   Sourrouille, 1980, table 24; de Oliveira *et al.*, 1979, table 61; Ronderos Tobon, 1981, table 3.4; AMIA; Fernandez-Baca, 1979, p. 151; Fontanals and Porta, 1979, p. 7.

In the other Latin American countries, where imports of parts by the terminals continue to be much more significant and where only simple, low-technology parts are incorporated locally by the terminals, the replacement market is more significant, accounting for almost as much or even more of the industry's sales as the terminals. While the heavy dependence of the parts industry on the terminals in the first group of countries limits their bargaining power, it does not necessarily follow that the greater significance of the replacement market in the second group of countries leads to greater capacity for negotiation in these countries. The smaller size of suppliers, the highly competitive markets in which most of them operate, and the competition from imports all serve to weaken the position of capital in the parts industry in other ways.

As was seen in discussing the situation in the advanced capitalist countries, the replacement market is not necessarily free from the control of the terminals either, because of the role played by their franchised dealers in supplying spare parts. The terminals can, through the use of exclusive contracts or quotas for parts sales, require their dealers to buy 'genuine parts' from the terminals, and effectively bar them from acquiring spares directly from the parts industry. The pressure which can be put on the parts industry in this way depends on both the arrangements with dealers that are used by the terminals, and the extent to which their franchised dealers control the replacement market.

In Latin America, exclusive dealerships (i.e. selling only one firm's vehicles) are the norm although exceptions are sometimes made to accommodate two non-competing lines.[12] As far as replacement sales are concerned, it is the usual practice for the terminals to set quotas of spares which their dealers have to sell in a given time period. In Mexico dealers are only permitted to sell parts supplied to them by the terminals. In Argentina, Brazil and Venezuela quotas are set by the terminals, although dealers are permitted to sell parts from other sources (up to a maximum of 30 per cent of total sales of spare parts in the case of Argentina and Brazil). In all these countries therefore the greater proportion of sales of spare parts by dealers are supplied by the terminals. These represent an important source of profit to the terminals who charge considerably higher prices for parts (which they often buy from the parts industry) than are charged by parts producers when they sell directly to independent wholesalers. In Mexico, for instance, the prices charged by the parts industry are 20 per cent to 40 per cent lower than those charged by the terminals to their distributors. (See also de Oliveira *et al.*, 1979, p. 256 on Brazil.)

The existence of independent wholesalers, which buy directly, are an important source of competition for the franchised dealers in all these countries, and provide an alternative outlet to the replacement market for the parts industry. In Mexico, the only country for which we have an estimate of the quantitative share of the distributors in the after-market, it is less than 40 per cent of total sales. Nevertheless, taken together with the significance of original equipment sales, this gives the terminals control over a very high proportion of the parts industry's total market.

5 ADVANTAGES TO THE TERMINALS

The auto TNCs in Latin America are able to derive the same advantages from their asymmetric relations with their suppliers as they do in their countries of origin. First of all the average level of wages in the parts industry is considerably lower than that found in the terminal industry. As can be seen in table 7.5 wages can be anything from a third to a half lower in the parts industry compared with the terminals. This differential is particularly marked between the terminals and the small and medium sized suppliers, whereas the larger parts firms pay wages which are not that different from those found in the terminal industry.[13]

TABLE 7.5   *Average wage level in parts industry (terminal industry = 100)*

	Average wage
Argentina (1970)	55.6
Brazil (1970)	65.5
Mexico (1970)	58.3
Peru (1974)	51.8
Venezuela (1977)	66.7

SOURCES   Lifschitz, 1978, table 8; 1982, tables 5 and 6; Fernandez-Baca, 1979.

By using numerous small suppliers of standardized parts which are not subject to large scale economies, the terminals are able to keep down costs by taking advantage of the lower wages paid in such firms.

In view of the many advantages which the terminal firms enjoy in their relationship with their suppliers, it is to be expected that this enables them to obtain original equipment at favourable prices. Unfortunately detailed studies of the kind quoted above for the advanced capitalist countries, which would indicate the rate of return earned by Latin American suppliers on their sales to the terminals have not been made. There is no doubt that the terminals are able to obtain parts at a lower price than is charged when sales are made directly to the replacement market. In other words because of their weakness in negotiations with terminals and the need to supply original equipment in order to gain access to the replacement market, the parts producers are prepared to supply the terminals with parts at very low profit margins. The terminals may also postpone payments to suppliers which in an inflationary situation reduces the costs of local purchases (Nofal, 1983, pp. 71–2).

Finally, the parts industry provides the terminals with increased flexibility. One example of this occurred in Brazil in the seventies when the terminals faced with a slow-down in demand and consequent excess capacity began to produce more parts 'in plant' thus passing on the effects of fluctuations to the parts industry (de Oliveira, *et al.*, 1979, p. 180). In 1975 employment in the parts industry fell by some 17 000 (7.7 per cent of the work-force) compared with 1974. Over the same period employment in the terminal industry actually increased marginally (de Oliveira *et al.*, 1979, table 58, ANFAVEA).

6   TRANSFERS OF SURPLUS VALUE THROUGH THE FINANCIAL SYSTEM

For any given rate of profit on total capital advanced, a firm can raise the rate of return on its own invested capital by increasing the amount which it borrows provided it can do so on favourable terms. In other words the higher the debt-equity ratio of a firm, the higher will be its rate of return on its own capital, provided that outside sources of funds are available at a lower cost than the return on total capital.[14] Normally there is some upper limit beyond which consideration of risk or increasing difficulties of obtaining outside sources of funds at lower cost make it unadvisable to raise the debt–equity ratio. What the analysis does bring out, however, is the way in which access to external sources of funds on favourable terms can be used by firms to increase their return above that obtained by competitors who do not enjoy such favourable access.

In the case of the Latin American motor vehicle industry the terminal firms, particularly those controlled by the auto TNCs, are in such a favourable position, whereby they can if they so wish raise a considerable amount of capital from external sources. Because of their size and international reputation they have privileged access to local capital markets. It is a well known feature of TNCs in Latin America generally that they take advantage of this situation often avoiding new inflows of capital from the parent company. This is particularly advantageous where, as has often occurred in Latin America, high rates of inflation combined with controls on the level of interest have resulted in negative real rates of interest for those firms who are able to borrow. Similarly, TNC subsidiaries, because of the international contacts of their parent companies, are also in a much better position to borrow internationally than are local firms.

Table 7.6 indicates the high levels of the debt–equity ratio of the terminals in four Latin American countries. Not only are these levels much higher than the level found in the parts industry (see Fernandez-Baca *et al.*, 1979, table 14 on Peru), but they are also higher than the levels normally found in Latin American industry.[15] In the three countries with relatively low levels of local content included in the table, Chile, Peru and Uruguay, the extremely high debt–equity level reflects the ability of the TNCs to secure markets for their CKD packs with a minimal investment of their own capital. Although not so marked the levels of debt–equity in Argentina and Mexico are also high.

The ability of the auto TNCs to concentrate credit at the expense of other firms has been a source of criticism at times, particularly where money has been borrowed in order to offer credit facilities to car purchasers. In Argentina in the early 1960s, for example, a spokesman for local industrialists described the growth of finance companies providing consumer credit for car purchase as a 'cancer of the Argentine economy' (IKA, 1963, p. 61). In Brazil, the finance houses, the bulk of whose credits go to finance purchases of cars, increased their share of all private sector loans dramatically from 3.3 per cent to 15.1 per cent between 1963 and 1973 (de Oliveira *et al.*, 1979, table 86). This again is further evidence of the success of the terminal TNCs in attracting funds to activities directly related to their interests.

TABLE 7.6   *Debt–equity ratio of TNCs in terminal industry in Latin America*

	Debt–equity ratio
Argentina (1973)	3.1:1
Chile (1970)	7.5:1
Mexico (1973)	1.5:1
Peru (avge 1972–5)	7.7:1
Uruguay (1975)*	6.7 to 3.5:1

* Data on individual firms.
SOURCES   Sourrouille, 1980, table 33; Jenkins, 1977, p. 111; Lifschitz, 1979, table 40; Fernandez-Baca *et al.*, 1979, p. 291; Sarli, 1979, p. 124.

NOTES

1. Examples of near monopolies include electrical equipment, sparking plugs, transmission equipment, engine pistons, clutches and glass in the UK; clutches, carburettors, radiators, instruments, brakes and heating and air-

conditioning equipment in France; and clutches, sparking plugs, brakes, carburettors, radiators and glass in West Germany (Bhaskar, 1979, table 13; *Motor Business*, 1964; Commission des Communautes Europeenes, 1977; *Motor Business*, 1965a; Komission der Europaischen Gemein-schaften, 1979).

2. For a discussion of the 'pros and cons' of 'in-plant' manufacture, see EIU, 1978, pp. 74–6.

3. The major exception to this was Ford's production of tyres in the US for a short period from 1937.

4. See West, 1977, ch. 5 for a discussion of innovation in the tyre industry.

5. See NEDO, 1971, Appendix A5 for a list of the links between the motor vehicle producers and component suppliers in Japan.

6. The following description is drawn from Price Commission, 1979, pp. 45–9.

7. This may over-estimate the rate of return in component production in view of the degree of diversification of many of the largest producers. The rate of return for tyre producers was even lower, only 12 per cent in the period 1947–64 (FTC, 1966, table 27).

8. Friedman, 1977, pp. 114–29. See also Commission of the European Communities, 1977, p. 38 for a discussion of the way in which UK car manufacturers transfer the cost of variations in production to the tyre manufacturers.

9. See Fernandez-Baca *et al.*, 1979, table 39 for a list of locally produced parts incorporated by the terminals in Peru in 1970 which is representative of the types of parts produced in these countries at this time.

10. It has been suggested that the auto TNCs deliberately promoted the proliferation of suppliers in order to increase competition among part producers and thus increase their own bargaining power (Nofal, 1983, p. 71).

11. For interesting case studies in two non-Latin American countries, see the discussion of Ford's operations in South Africa and Taiwan in Behrman and Wallender, 1976, pp. 69–75, 112–120. In South Africa the authors cite examples in which Ford employees actually ran the operations of the parts supplier for a period.

12. What follows in the remainder of this section is based on information on Argentina, Brazil, Mexico and Venezuela provided in AMDA, 1973.

13. Sourrouille, 1980, p. 152; see also de Oliveira *et al.*, 1979, table 60 for evidence on the variation in wages with size of firm in the Brazilian parts industry.

14. This can be shown as follows. The total return on capital advanced is R/K. R is made up of P (profit after payment of interest) and I (interest payment). K is made up of D (debt) and E (equity plus reserves).

$R/K = (P + I)/(D + E)$

for total return $R/K = r$ and interest rate $I/D = i$
$r(D + E) = P + I$

$rD/E + r = P/E + I/E = P/E + iD/E$

$P/E = (r - i) D/E + r$

Thus if $r > i$, P/E (the return on own capital) increases with D/E (the debt–equity ratio).

15. See Quijano, 1979, table 1 for information on the relative importance of internal and external sources of funds for firms in Argentina, Brazil, Colombia and Mexico.

8 Profitability, Accumulation and the Balance of Payments

1 PROFITABILITY

In the last three chapters the conditions under which surplus value is produced and realized in the Latin American motor industry and the way in which surplus is transferred to the terminal firms, both from the parts industry and through the financial system, have been analysed. This analysis has clear implications for the profitability of vehicle production in the region and the pattern of capital accumulation in the industry. Both these aspects will be considered in this chapter.

First, however, before embarking on an empirical discussion of profitability in the industry, a number of problems concerning the definition and measurement of profitability must be mentioned. The first problem derives from the fact that the major enterprises with which we are concerned here, the terminal firms operating in Latin America, are not independent self-contained units of capital. They are almost all subsidiaries of auto TNCs with world-wide operations. As such the capital located in Latin America must be considered as an integral part of the total capital under the control of a single decision centre, namely the parent company. Consequently the relevant concept of profitability is the total contribution made by a Latin American subsidiary to the global profitability of the parent company and not the profit declared in any one country. That the two concepts may diverge is well known from the literature on TNCs (e.g. Vaitsos, 1974). In addition to the profits declared by the subsidiary, it is also necessary to take into account the return which the parent company obtains in the form of royalties and technical assistance payments, over-and-above the cost of supplying the technology, the profits earned in the supply of parts, components or capital equipment to the subsidiary, and the interest payments on loans from the parent company. It is often difficult or impossible to obtain the necessary information on these payments. Nevertheless they cannot be ignored. Technology payments may for example be a greater source of revenue to the parent company than profit repatriation as in the case of the Brazilian terminal firms (de Oliveira *et al.*, 1979, p. 144). Particularly in those countries with low levels of local integration, the scope for transfer pricing on imports of parts and components is extensive, and the practice of making deletion allowances on CKD packs which are less than the price of the part omitted is in effect a form of transfer price manipulation.

The other main problem in calculating profitability arises in the context of the rapid inflation rates characteristic of so many Latin American countries. Where accounting is carried out on the basis of historic cost, inflation leads to a tendency for the value of the firm's own capital to be underestimated, except in those years in which the capital is revalued. But even when such revaluations have taken place it is possible that the legal dispositions under which they are carried out tend to be arbitrary from an economic point of view. Unfortunately the available information rarely makes adjustments to take the effects of inflation into account in calculating profitability.[1] These difficulties imply that estimates of the rate of profit in the Latin American motor industry must be treated with some caution, particularly in those countries where the industry is heavily dependent on imports and where historically inflation rates have been high.

Countries with integrated production

There are strong reasons to suppose, on the basis of the analysis of the previous chapters, that vehicle production was highly profitable in the early years, particularly in those countries in which there was evidence of a considerable backlog of demand built up in a period when imports were restricted. The very favourable conditions for realizing surplus value in these years, together with the acquiescent nature of a new labour force, and the ability to continue to import many parts and components, meant high prices and low costs (low in relation to prices but not of course in relation to costs in the countries of origin of the vehicles produced).

Increasing difficulties of realization reflected in a decline in the rate of growth of production meant a decline in profitability in the industry. A situation in which both costs and prices remained high (by international standards) and profitability was declining, posed an objective need for restructuring from the point of view of both capital and the state. Thus an increase in the level of profitability and a renewed phase of capital accumulation required a restructuring of capital leading to concentration and centralization of capital, new mechanisms to dynamize the market, and increases in labour productivity while wages were kept under control. As will be seen below, after a period of stagnation in the early to mid-sixties such a restructuring was achieved in the Brazilian industry, while in Argentina it was never successfully carried through. The later development of the industry in Mexico meant that the effects of restructuring would only be seen in the post-1973 period.

Argentina

In 1960 and 1961 the terminal firms in Argentina enjoyed high profit margins and high returns on capital invested. The profit margin was 9.6 per cent in 1960 and 7.9 per cent in 1961, while the rate of profit was over 20 per cent in both years (Sourrouille, 1980, tables 34 and 35). This is certainly higher than the returns enjoyed by the terminals in their countries of origin in this period.[2] Moreover, the industry continued to be heavily reliant on imports of parts and components in this period with the direct foreign exchange cost of each vehicle produced coming to almost US $900. Total vehicle production increased by more than 100 000 units in these two years, and as was seen in Chapter 6 demand conditions were extremely favourable. This growth was interrupted by the 1962–3 recession. Commercial vehicle production fell sharply in 1962 and car production in the following year. Costs rose more rapidly than vehicle prices in 1962 and 1963 and profits fell. In 1963 the industry failed to return an overall profit (Sourrouille, 1980, table 34). With the recovery in 1964 car production renewed its upward trend, but with the elimination of the backlog of demand, there was little expansion during the remainder of the decade. Profitability also recovered but only to about half the levels of the early sixties.

The profitability crisis of the early sixties did give rise to a restructuring of capital in the industry. The number of firms producing vehicles in Argentina was reduced from 20 in 1961 to 13 by 1964, and the various indices of market concentration showed a sharp increase (Lenicov, 1973, table 11; Jenkins, 1977, table 7.1). This was accompanied by major changes in the ownership structure of the industry, with those locally owned firms which had initially produced under licence either being driven out of the industry, or being acquired by the foreign licensor. The inevitable consequence of restructuring through the operation of market forces was the elimination of the weak (local) firms and the concentration of production under the control of the strong (TNC) firms. A proposal for a state led restructuring, which would have involved merging the five remaining locally owned firms in the mid-sixties, was turned down by the government.

Thus by the time of the military coup of 1966 a major restructuring of the Argentinian motor industry had taken place. However, unlike the case of Brazil this restructuring did not result in a substantial increase in profitability and a renewed phase of rapid expansion. Despite concentration and centralization of capital in the mid-sixties the Argentinian industry continued to be highly fragmented betweeṅ a number of firms. As a result there was little rationalization of production. Labour productivity did not rise significantly in the second-half of the sixties, a result that was reinforced by the growing strength of workers' organization in the industry. Even the new competitive strategies of model changes and consumer credit did not lead to a dynamic expansion of the car market. Indeed as was seen above, by contributing to high costs and prices in the industry, these strategies further restricted the market to a small upper income group.

This should not be taken to imply that the Argentinian vehicle market was not a worthwhile sphere of operations for the auto TNCs. Despite high production costs and a slowly growing domestic market, the oligopolistic position of the TNCs within a highly protected market ensured them reasonable rates of return throughout the sixties (Sourrouille, 1980, figure 13). Moreover, these figures which are based solely on declared profits underestimate the total return to the TNCs in the ways indicated above. In 1970, for instance, it is estimated that seven terminal firms paid US $18 million in royalties (Raddavero, 1972, p. 369) and imported a further US $85 million (MacDonnell and Lascano, 1974, table 40). Transfer pricing on imports was not merely a theoretical possibility. A report prepared for the World Bank estimated that Ford earned US $1.2 million in this way in 1964 on top of the US $0.6 million which the subsidiary reported. Ten years later the Argentinian supreme court held that a part of the deferred payments made by Ford to the parent company for imported parts represented profit remissions (Jenkins, 1984, pp. 56–7. See also Nofal, 1983, pp. 382–4 for further evidence of transfer pricing).

   As will be seen below the prospects of future expansion of the market and the expected profit on new investment were not sufficiently high in Argentina in this period, in relation to alternative areas for investment, to lead to a major new phase of capital accumulation in the industry. In the early seventies, with productivity stagnant and wage costs rising faster than vehicle prices there was a further sharp decline in profitability, so that in 1972 the industry as a whole was declaring losses for the first time since 1963 (Sourrouille, 1980, table 34). By the end of the period under consideration in this part therefore there was growing evidence of a need for a major new restructuring of the Argentinian motor vehicle industry if it was to play a dynamic role in capital accumulation.

Brazil

There is evidence to indicate that in the early years of the industry's development in Brazil in the late fifties the terminals were able to earn relatively high profits. The consolidated accounts of the eight major terminals showed a return on invested capital of 16.5 per cent in 1956, 19.8 per cent in 1957, and 16.8 per cent in 1958 (ANFAVEA). Production grew rapidly in this period until 1962 when the backlog of demand was exhausted. Apart from the two dominant firms (VW in cars and Mercedes-Benz in commercial vehicles) profitability declined (Moore, 1969). In 1963 the rate of return of the terminals was 10.1 per cent and two years later it was down to 3.8 per cent (ANFAVEA).

   The initial period of establishment of the industry in which favourable market conditions ensured rapid growth of output without facing problems of realization, was followed by a five year period (1962–7) of stagnation, characterized by low profits or even substantial losses in the case of many firms. This was not, however, a period when things stood still. Rather it saw a major restructuring of the Brazilian motor industry which lay the basis for the restoration of profitability and a period of spectacular expansion in the late sixties and early seventies. It was also a period of major change in Brazil as a whole spanning the radicalization of political life under Goulart and the 1964 coup and its aftermath.

   Important changes took place in the structure of the industry. The number of producers was reduced from eleven to eight and concentration (in the car market) rose sharply (Guimaraes, 1981, table 11).

Centralization of capital played a crucial role in restructuring the Brazilian industry with two major producers of the early sixties, Willys and Vemag being acquired by Ford and VW respectively, as well as Chrysler which had re-entered the Brazilian industry through its acquisition of Simca in France, taking over International Harvester's loss-making operations. These ownership changes also brought about the elimination of Brazilian capital from the terminal industry to all extent and purpose, particularly when the state sold the nationalized vehicle producer FNM to Alfa Romeo in 1968.

It was on the car side of the industry and not commercial vehicles that the most significant changes took place (indeed it was not until 1972 that levels of production of CVs in Brazil exceeded that attained in 1962). In this context the entry of GM and Ford into car production in Brazil for the first time in this period was of particular significance. For a renewed phase of expansion in the industry to come about it was necessary to find ways of increasing the demand for cars. Given the exhaustion of the backlog demand by 1962 and the fact that consequently most new car sales were to consumers who already owned cars, accelerating the rate at which vehicles were replaced was obviously one way of achieving this objective. Three major factors contributed: first the product differentiation strategies of the US subsidiaries led to a rapid growth of the number of models on offer, particularly of medium and large cars which became the most rapidly growing segment of the car market in the late sixties as existing owners traded up from their small models (Guimaraes, 1981). Second, reforms of the financial system made consumer credit much easier to obtain in order to finance car purchases. Finally the concentration of income amongst the top income groups after the 1964 military coup increased the income of those who provided a potential market.

Expanding demand and production, as was seen in Chapter 5 was accompanied by significant increases in productivity, while wages were held down. (This of course was made possible by the anti-trade union policies of the military regime.) This was reflected in the increased rate of profit enjoyed by most of the major terminals in the late sixties and early seventies (Mericle, 1984, table 1.1). In contrast to the situation in Argentina, the Brazilian motor industry was so attractive in terms of its potential profitability that a number of European and Japanese auto TNCs were anxious to enter the industry. These included Renault, Peugeot, Citroen, British Leyland and Nissan, as well as Fiat and Volvo who did in fact enter.

Mexico

Mexico occupies an intermediate position between the high levels of local content found in Brazil and Argentina, and the much lower levels in the other Latin American countries. Imports by the terminals remained well above US $1000 per vehicle in the late sixties and early seventies, so that from the point of view of the auto TNCs, Mexico was of interest both as an area for producing surplus value and for realizing surplus value produced elsewhere, through the export of parts.

The characteristic pattern observed in Brazil and Argentina whereby an initial period of rapid growth while a backlog of demand was being eliminated, was followed by a period of much slower growth, was not so marked in Mexico for two reasons. First, there had not been a prolonged period of import restriction preceding the establishment of local manufacturing, so that the backlog was not as marked as in the two South American countries. Secondly, the Mexican government's quota policy effectively restricted the rate of growth of production in the early years to much more modest levels than in either Argentina or Brazil.

Because of the high level of import content in Mexico, data on profitability has to be treated with even more caution than in Brazil or Argentina, although the more modest inflation rate makes it easier in another respect. Although data on the average return on capital invested in the late sixties does not indicate a very high return there are reasons to believe that these figures are an underestimate. The combined internal rate of return of Ford and Automex (the two largest producers) was calculated as 34 per cent before tax and depreciation and 18.5 per cent after (Sanchez-Marco, 1968). Inclusion of royalty payments raised the profit rate of foreign firms by two or three percentage points, while assuming an average profit margin of 10 per cent on imports of parts gave foreign firms in Mexico a return of almost 20 per cent a year in this period (Jenkins, 1977, table 5.14).[3]

With buoyant demand, a significant increase in productivity in the late sixties, little problem with labour and wages successfully kept down, it is not surprising to find that the industry was reasonably profitable in this period, despite price controls on the industry's output. There is evidence, however, that by the early seventies the Mexican industry was entering a crisis similar (although less profound than) the ones experienced in Brazil and Argentina after 1962. The rate of growth of sales slowed down and there was increasing difficulty in finding new consumers. Productivity growth levelled off after 1970 and wages moved ahead of productivity. As was also seen in Chapter 5 there was increasing labour militancy in the industry from 1972 onwards. These trends are all reflected in a decline in the profit rate of the terminal industry in the early seventies.

There was a consequent limited restructuring of capital in the industry in the early seventies. The most significant aspect of this was the take-over of Automex, until then a majority Mexican owned firm, by Chrysler in 1971. This followed the closing down of another Mexican firm, FANASA, in the previous year. There was also a significant increase in concentration as measured by the Herfindhal Index in the period 1970–73 (Jenkins, 1977, table 7.3).

The scope for new methods of dynamizing car demand was rather more limited in Mexico than in Brazil. There already existed a wide variety of models and the US linked firms followed the US model changes. However, less than half of all car sales in the late sixties were made on credit (Jenkins, 1977, p. 139) and so there was some scope here for making more credit available to consumers. However, the particular geographical position of Mexico and the policy pursued by the Mexican government opened up another avenue for expansion for the industry, namely exports. Thus the early 1970s saw a reorientation of the Mexican motor industry towards international markets, as part of a process of international restructuring which became much more profound throughout Latin America in the subsequent period. Between 1970 and 1973 exports increased their share of total sales by the terminals from 5.3 per cent to 12.6 per cent, while the number of vehicles exported rose from negligible levels to around 7 per cent of total production over the same period (AMIA, 1982). A complete discussion of the restructuring of the Mexican motor industry in the 1970s must await until Part II of this study.

Countries with truncated production

As has already been indicated the remaining Latin American countries are viewed by the auto TNCs primarily as a market in which to realize the surplus value produced elsewhere through the export of CKD kits and parts and components. Production of surplus value locally is a secondary consideration. As has also been pointed out, it is extremely difficult to measure the contribution which one of these subsidiaries makes to the global profitability of its parent company because of the often arbitrary nature of the transfer prices which are charged on such imports. As a result the declared rate of profit by the subsidiaries of auto TNCs in these countries are often highly erratic and frequently losses are declared. Nevertheless despite prolonged periods of apparently unprofitable operations, these companies continue in the market. Even when the local state attempts to rationalize the industry and calls for bids from firms interested in producing locally, firms which have a history of losses are still anxious to participate. Such an apparent paradox can only be resolved when it is understood that the profits declared locally are in the first place arbitrarily determined as a result of the choice of transfer prices and alternative channels of remission, and in the second place of minor significance in relation to the profits which can be earned from the export of parts, components and CKD kits. Moreover, as was seen in the last chapter it is possible to ensure a position in the local market with a minimal investment of the firm's own capital.

These points can be readily illustrated with a few examples. In Peru for instance four of the five terminals made losses over the period 1972–5 (Fernandez-Baca, 1979, table 89). In Chile, Nissan which brought considerable pressure to bear on the Allende government to be allowed to continue in operation after initially being excluded as a result of the government's *licitacion*, declared losses in each year from 1967 to 1973. Indeed, foreign subsidiaries in the Chilean terminal sector as a group declared losses continuously between 1969 and 1972, and even in the pre-1969 period had earned lower profits than locally owned competitors assembling under licence (Baharona *et al.*, 1976, tables 25 and 27). Evidence from Uruguay for the 1970s shows General Motors making losses in three of the six years covered and the subsidiary's return on capital investment fluctuating wildly between a loss of 166 per cent and a profit of 78 per cent (Sarli, 1979, ch. F, table 3).

However, compared with the potential for transferring profits through over-pricing imported inputs these declared profits are quite marginal. In Peru in 1974 the terminals declared a modest profit of over 20 million soles which represented a return on their own capital of slightly over 3 per cent. However, in the same year these firms imported inputs valued at over 3500 million soles (Fernandez-Baca, 1979, tables 44, 87 and 91). Thus overpricing of only 10 per cent on these imports would have increased the subsidiaries' contribution to global profits more than fifteen-fold. A similar calculation made for Chile, referring to the year 1970, showed that assuming again overpricing of 10 per cent, a small loss declared by foreign terminal firms is turned into a profit in excess of 20 per cent (Jenkins, 1977, table 5.12).

In the case of Peru it has been suggested that in the period 1971–4 when the terminal industry as a whole showed a loss, the foreign owned firms were making increasing use of transfer pricing in order to remit profits (Fernandez-Baca, 1979, pp. 303–10). The most striking evidence in support of this is that in a period when the Peruvian exchange rate remained fixed, and local content requirements were increasing marginally, the prices of imported CKD kits increased by over 20 per cent per annum for some Chrysler and Toyota models and around 10 per cent for some Nissan models (Fernandez-Baca, 1979, table 88).[4]

2 ACCUMULATION OF CAPITAL

In discussing the activities of TNCs a distinction has been drawn between those subsidiaries which are oriented to re-investment of profit and those which are oriented to repatriation. It has also been widely held that the subsidiaries of TNCs in Latin America were predominantly oriented towards repatriation (Chudnovsky, 1981). In this section therefore we shall consider the extent to which the auto TNCs have utilized their profits to further local accumulation, or alternatively have repatriated the bulk of their profits.

A first indication of behaviour can be obtained, where the data is available by comparing re-invested profits with total remittances, not only of profits but also of technology payments. Unfortunately in the absence of detailed information on the level of transfer pricing, this can only be a rough approximation and is likely to be wildly inaccurate where the main channel for remitting profits is through overpricing intermediate inputs. In Argentina the terminal firms were clearly very heavily oriented towards remittances throughout the 1960s (see Table 8.1). This reflected the very limited opportunities for new investment in

TABLE 8.1 *Argentina: remittances and re-investment in the motor industry* (m$)

	Profits remitted	Royalties	Profits re-invested	Remittance ratio
	(1)	(2)	(3)	$\dfrac{(1)+(2)}{(1)+(2)+(3)}$ %
1959–64	108.8	22.7	4.3	96.9
1965–70	203.3	52.2	8.7	96.7
1971–5	0.5	55.5	26.0	60.9

SOURCE Sourrouille, 1980, tables 30 and 31.

the industry once it had been established, given the slow growth of the market after 1964 and the considerable excess capacity which had been created.

It is also in line with the general pattern in Argentina where a high level of remittances by US subsidiaries has been attributed to the generally unfavourable (from the point of view of capital) economic and political situation in the country (Chudnovsky, 1982, p. 751). In the seventies, although a greater share of profits and royalties was re-invested locally, remissions remained of far greater importance, and the increased share of re-investment owed as much to the decline in profits as it did to the increase in accumulation.

Although not as marked as in Argentina, taking the entire period 1966–74 remittances of profits, royalties and technical assistance payments from Brazil have outweighed re-investment (see Table 8.2). The much higher level of re-investment in the Brazilian terminal motor vehicle industry compared with Argentina is consistent with the preceding analysis of the industry in the two countries. It is also consistent with the pattern observed for US foreign investment in Latin America whereby Brazil has had the lowest ratio of remittances in the region (Chudnovsky, 1982, p. 751). It should be noted, however, that the ratio of remittances in the terminal industry is higher than either that of US manufacturing subsidiaries as a whole, or that found in the parts industry.

There is only very fragmentary data available for the other Latin American countries. In Peru remittance of profits and royalties by the

TABLE 8.2 *Brazil: remittances and re-investment in the motor industry* (m$)

	Profits, dividends and technology imports	Re-invested profits	Remittance rates
	(1)	(2)	(1)/(1) + (2) %
1966	16.5	0	100.0
1967	11.9	28.0	29.8
1968	15.0	2.7	84.5
1969	48.6	28.6	62.9
1970	42.1	38.0	52.5
1971	46.1	16.4	73.7
1972	40.6	67.8	37.5
1973	37.5	30.5	55.2
1974	47.8	3.5	93.1

SOURCE   de Oliveira *et al.*, 1979, tables 44 and 46.

terminals averaged 56.6 per cent of remittances plus re-invested profits in the period 1972–5 (Fernandez-Baca *et al.*, 1979, table 87). However, given that most firms declared losses in this period, and as was argued above the over-pricing of CKD packs was used as a mechanism to remit profits, this figure is not very meaningful and considerably overestimates the extent to which profits were re-invested in the period. The only data available for Mexico, covering only the US firms for one year (1970) shows that re-investment was negligible while remittances of profits, royalties and other payments came to US $23 million (Sepulveda and Chumacero, 1973, pp. 246–7).

The above analysis gives no indication of the use to which re-invested profits are put, in other words whether they contribute to a real process of capital formation through increases in the firms' fixed assets, or whether they are invested in other ways (see Trajtenberg, 1977, pp. 29–30 for a discussion of the alternative possible uses). It also takes no account of new investments made in the industry as opposed to re-investment. An alternative approach which will be used here is to compare the net investment in fixed assets made by the terminals with their profits.

A common pattern emerges in all three major producing countries. In an initial period when a manufacturing base is being built up, investment levels are in excess of the internal capacity for accumulation of the firms. This period seems to have lasted for anything up to five years (see Table 8.3). Subsequently, however, the rate of capital accumulation fell off sharply and the level of local profits is more than enough to finance any new investment in fixed assets. Profits can therefore be remitted or reinvested in other ways. When the rate of profit falls, however, particularly if this is accompanied by a new wave of investment as part of a process of restructuring in the industry, re-invested profits may again prove insufficient for the needs of accumulation. This suggests that while subsidiaries may normally be primarily oriented towards remittances, in a particular conjuncture they may change to being oriented towards re-investment.

In the other Latin American countries it seems likely that the accumulation requirements of the subsidiaries fall well short of the profits generated. It is impossible to show this accurately because of the lack of hard data on the degree of transfer pricing. The relatively limited investment in fixed assets by the terminals in these countries contributes to this situation. In both Chile and Peru fixed assets constituted less than 20 per cent of the total assets of the terminal firms (Baharona *et al.*, 1976, table 28B; Fernandez-Baca *et al.*, 1979, tables

TABLE 8.3 *Net investment and profits in the initial stages of developing the motor industry. Brazil, Argentina and Mexico*
(m US $)

(a) *Brazil*

	Fixed assets	Change in fixed assets	Profits	Investment − profit
1956	32.0			
1957	46.3	14.3	21.8	− 7.5
1958	133.2	86.9	29.8	57.1
1959	177.0	43.7	25.6	18.1
1960	214.0	37.0	n.a.	n.a.
1961	186.0	−28.0	n.a.	neg.
1962	168.4	−17.6	n.a.	neg.
1963	182.2	13.8	31.0	−17.2
1964	194.1	11.9	n.a.	n.a.
1965	224.2	30.1	20.6	9.5

(b) *Argentina*

	Gross investment	Net investment	Profits	Net investment − profit
1959	26.4	24.6	20.0	4.6
1960	50.7	45.6	32.0	13.6
1961	67.6	58.0	45.6	12.4
1962	94.9	78.9	14.6	64.3
1963	64.9	44.6	− 4.7	49.3
1964	34.5	11.9	24.7	−12.8
1965	32.5	7.7	26.3	−18.6
1966	41.9	14.3	47.0	−32.7
1967	28.5	− 1.0	17.7	−18.7
1968	33.8	2.1	31.5	−29.4

(c) *Mexico*

	Fixed assets	Change in fixed assets	Profits	Investment − profit
1965	105.8	—	—	—
1966	118.1	12.3	9.4	2.9
1967	129.8	11.7	− 0.1	11.8
1968	140.5	10.7	9.0	1.7
1969	147.0	6.5	17.2	−10.7
1970	148.4	1.4	16.9	−15.5
1971	149.0	0.6	0.8	− 0.2
1972	177.7	29.7	1.5	28.2
1973	252.4	73.7	22.0	51.7

NOTE For Brazil and Mexico the annual increase in the value of fixed assets has been used as an indicator of net fixed investment. All values have been converted to US $.
SOURCES ANFAVEA; Sourrouille, 1980, table 29; AMIA.

52, 83 and 84). If the return on CKD kits and parts supplied to the subsidiaries were computed together with declared profits, there is little doubt that they would far exceed the low levels of net investment in fixed capital found in these countries.

3   BALANCE OF PAYMENTS

As was seen in Chapter 3 one of the main factors which led many Latin American states to promote the development of a local motor vehicle industry in the late fifties and sixties was the weight of vehicles, parts and components in total imports. It is therefore highly relevant to consider the extent to which the industry still contributed to the balance of payments deficit by the early seventies. It is also an important question in the broader context of capital accumulation in the region, because the external sector has continued to be a major overall constraint on capital accumulation, particularly since a significant proportion of capital goods must be imported.

Capital flows

Since the issue of profit remittances has already been raised in the context of capital accumulation, we shall begin this section by looking at capital flows, before then turning to imports and exports of goods. Implicit in the distinction between subsidiaries oriented towards re-investment and those oriented towards remittances is the notion that whereas for the latter locally generated profits are more than sufficient for the opportunities for new investment which exist so that there is a net outflow of capital, in the former case, additional inflows of new capital may be required to supplement the re-investment of profits, so that there may be a net inflow of capital.

The evidence in Table 8.4 indicates that in Argentina and Brazil remittances have considerably outweighed new inflows of capital, at least since the mid-sixties. This is most marked in Argentina, particularly in the late sixties when the industry was still reasonably profitable. In Brazil, as was seen above, remittances have been a lower share of total profits and royalties than in Argentina, and consequently the outflow of capital has been less marked, with some years even showing a net inflow.

When the major investments to set up the industry are first made,

TABLE 8.4   *Capital inflows and outflows in the Argentinian and Brazilian motor industries* (m $)

	Argentina			Brazil		
	Inflows*	Outflows†	Balance	Inflows*	Outflows†	Balance
1959–64	106.0	131.5	− 25.5	n.a.	n.a.	n.a.
1965–70	72.5	255.5	− 183.0	59.4	151.1	− 91.7
1971–5‡	25.4	56.0	− 30.6	151.3	172.0	− 20.7

* Direct foreign investment.
† Profits, dividends, royalties and technology payments.
‡ 1971–4 for Brazil.
SOURCE   Sourrouille, 1980, table 31; de Oliveira, 1979, tables 46, 48 and 49.

there must be a period in which there is a net inflow of capital to the host country. Judging from the net outflow of capital from Argentina in the period 1959–64, this period must have been shortlived. This is also borne out by some fragmentary evidence from Mexico. Although the data refers to foreign investment in the transport equipment industry (of which motor vehicles are an important, but by no means the only part), it shows a sharp reversal from a net inflow of US $16.7 million in 1967, when the investments to establish the industry were being made, to a net outflow of US $16.6 million three years later (Sepulveda and Chumacero, 1973, p. 241).

It is possible to conclude therefore that in the three major vehicle producing countries in the region in this period, after an initial period which lasted only a few years, in which there was a net inflow of foreign capital, the predominant pattern was for capital to flow out of the region in the form of profits, royalties and technical assistance payments.

In the smaller Latin American countries the situation is rather different. In Chile, for instance, between 1961 and 1974, there was an estimated net inflow of capital (new investment minus profit remittances) of US $33.3 million (Barahona *et al.*, 1976, table 8C). With royalty payments amounting to only US $0.4 million between 1966 and 1974 (Barahona *et al.*, 1976, table 26) this seems to indicate a substantial net inflow of capital to the Chilean terminal industry over a prolonged period. Such a conclusion, however, ignores the role which countries like Chile play in the global strategies of the auto TNCs. Remittances are of relatively little significance because the main purpose of the local subsidiary is as an outlet for the CKD packs, parts and components supplied by the parent company. Or to put it another way, the main channel for remittances are not those which are open to public inspection but the hidden mechanisms of transfer pricing.

The trade balance

There are two alternative ways of looking at the impact of the motor vehicle industry on the balance of trade. The first, and simplest in terms of the ready availability of data, is to derive from international trade statistics the value of exports and imports of motor vehicle products. The second on which it is not always so easy to obtain data, is to estimate the total exports and imports of a specific group of firms, usually in this case the terminals. Both of these measurements fail to capture the total effect of the industry on a country's trade. The first approach ('trade approach') only includes those products whose origin or destination can clearly be identified as the motor vehicle industry. This is particularly likely to lead to an underestimation of the total value of imports because imported raw materials such as steel, as well as capital equipment destined for the industry will not be included. The second approach ('firm approach') also fails to give a complete picture because it only includes the direct imports of the firms' concerned and not the import content of locally purchased parts and components. If, as will be done here in order to narrow the number of firms that need be considered, only the trade of the terminals is considered, both exports and imports will be undervalued by the amount of exports and imports by the parts' industry. Furthermore, if imports of complete vehicles are made by firms other than the terminals, these will also not be included in the total.

Table 8.5 presents data on motor vehicle imports and exports in the early seventies for seven Latin American countries using the trade approach. At this time all the countries registered substantial deficits in their trade in automotive products. In Colombia, Mexico and Venezuela imports of such products accounted for more than 10 per cent of all imports, while it was only in Brazil that imports had been reduced to relatively low levels. Exports were minimal in the three Andean Pact countries, and although much greater in absolute terms, in Argentina, Brazil and Mexico, they accounted for a small proportion of total exports.

Table 8.6 summarizes the position of the TNCs in the terminal industry in four countries for which it was possible to obtain information. Because unlike trade data this type of information is not

TABLE 8.5   *Trade in vehicles and parts of selected Latin American countries, 1972*

	Auto imports (m $)	Percent total imports	Auto exports (m $)	Percent total exports	Trade balance (m $)
Argentina	85.2	4.5	34.5	1.8	− 50.7
Brazil	117.4	2.4	59.4	1.5	− 58.0
Chile	88.0	9.3	2.6	0.3	− 85.4
Colombia	108.7	12.7	1.2	0.1	− 107.5
Mexico	278.2	10.2	52.6	2.9	− 225.6
Peru	59.4	7.5	—	—	− 59.4
Venezuela	289.1	11.6	1.8	0.1	− 287.3

SOURCES   UNCTC, 1982; Junta del Acuerdo de Cortagena; AMIA; UN *Yearbook of International Trade Statistics*.

TABLE 8.6   *Exports, imports and trade balance of TNCs in terminal industry* (m$)

	Imports	Exports	Trade balance
Argentina (1971)	91.3	21.5	− 69.8
Brazil (1972–3)	214.1	83.2	− 130.9
Mexico (1972)	156.1	40.9	− 115.2
Peru (1972)	51.3	—	− 51.3

SOURCES   MacDonnell and Lascano, 1974, table 40; Müller and Moore, 1978, table 2; SIC. Direccion General del Registro de Inversiones Estranjeras, 1974, table V; Fernandez-Baca *et al.*, 1979, table 51a.

published on a regular basis, there are slight differences in the exact period covered, but in all cases the figures refer to the situation in the early 1970s. In all four countries, the terminals showed large trade deficits in this period, in excess of US $50 million in Peru and Argentina, and over US $100 million in Brazil and Mexico. Apart from the case of Mexico it would seem (although because of differences in the reference year the figures are not comparable in some cases) that the deficit of the terminals is even greater than that calculated using the 'trade approach'. The reason probably lies in the substantial imports of raw materials and machinery and equipment by the terminals which are not included in the trade data. In 1973, for instance, it is reported that the motor industry accounted for 29 per cent of all machinery imports in Brazil and about a quarter of all the steel imported (Open University, 1983, p. 22).[5]

Taking Tables 8.5 and 8.6 together the indications are that in the early seventies all the Latin American countries showed substantial trade deficits in their motor industries. Taking account of all auto industry related imports and exports this negative balance can be roughly estimated as follows:

Venezuela	> US$300 million
Mexico	> US$200 million
Argentina ⎫ Brazil ⎬	− US $150–200 million
Colombia	> US $100 million
Chile ⎫ Peru ⎬	− US $50–100 million

In addition to the trade deficit the outflow of capital in the form of royalties and profit remittances (minus new investment) also needs to be included in order to calculate the total balance of payments effects. With remittances exceeding new capital inflows by about US $10 million a year in Brazil and Argentina (see Table 8.4), and possibly a similar figure in Mexico, it can be seen that although substantial in absolute terms, the net capital outflow is far less of a burden on the balance of payments than the sector's trade deficit.[6] However, in relation to the outflow of profits, royalties and technical assistance payments from the countries concerned the terminal firms in particular account for a high proportion of the total. In Argentina they account for 9.8 per cent of all such payments in the period 1971–5 (Sourrouille, 1980, table 30) and in Brazil for 10.7 per cent between 1971 and 1974 (de Oliveira *et al.*, 1979, tables 46 and 47).

Thus despite the import substitution policies of the 1960s, it can be seen that the motor vehicle industry in all the Latin American countries represented a considerable drain on the balance of payments. The reasons varied from country to country. In all cases the level of exports was low despite early attempts to stimulate exports. On the other hand in Brazil despite the high level of local content set by government legislation, the industry continued to rely on imports for key raw materials such as steel as well as for capital goods. Similarly in Argentina imports of raw materials, capital goods and materials used by the parts industry were the major causes of the foreign exchange outflow. Mexico with much lower levels of integration had substantial imports of parts and components for both the terminal and the parts industries as well as imports of built up units to the *perimetros libre*. Elsewhere in Latin America imported CKD packs for the terminal industry were the main cost although in some cases imports of built up vehicles were also important.

CONCLUSION

The Latin American motor industry in the early seventies was in many respects ripe for restructuring. Particularly in Argentina and Mexico the industry experienced a crisis of profitability in the early seventies. In the Andean Pact countries, despite efforts by national governments to increase local content, the limited size of local markets made it difficult to effect a transition to full manufacturing. In all the Latin American countries as we have just seen the industry accounted for a substantial outflow of foreign exchange. As was seen in Chapter 6 production costs and vehicle prices in the region were considerably higher than in the advanced capitalist countries despite the growth of production in the sixties. Only Brazil seemed to stand out as an exception to this gloomy picture, with the industry growing rapidly, making high profits and costs if not prices much more in line with international standards than elsewhere in the region. However, as the decade of the seventies unfolded, with the OPEC price rises of 1973 and the deepening world recession, the Brazilian motor vehicle industry too entered a period of major restructuring. In the next part we turn to the transformations which occurred in the international motor industry in the 1970s and the way in which these converged with the contradictions of the industry's development in Latin America to bring about radical transformations in the industry in the region and the forms of its integration into the emerging world industry.

NOTES

1. An exception is Sourrouille, 1980, ch. VI, where the profitability of the terminal firms in Argentina is recalculated in dollar terms in order to adjust for inflation.
2. In the USA the average annual rate of return of the terminals was 13.6 per cent in the period 1956–61 (White, 1971, table 15.2).
3. It should also be noted that the average rate of profit is significantly reduced by the large losses shown by VW in the years before 1969. This was in large part the result of a deliberate strategy by the company of keeping prices low

(only 30 per cent above West German prices) in order to expand its share of the market (Sanchez-Marco, 1968a).

4. For circumstantial evidence on the use of transfer pricing in the Chilean motor vehicle industry, see Jenkins, 1977, pp. 106–8.

5. The apparent anomaly in the case of Mexico is difficult to explain and may be the result of some deficiency in the data. AMIA data shows much higher levels of imports by the terminals than that recorded in Table 8.6.

6. As has already been seen in other Latin American countries profit remittances and royalty payments are much less significant as a source of capital outflow because of the use of other mechanisms for remittances.

Part II

9 The Creation of the World Automobile Industry

The period since the early seventies has been a time of profound change in the international motor industry. It has of course been a period of severe crisis in the industry. It has also been a period of significant advance in the internationalization of capital which has led to the creation of a truly global industry. Whereas the sixties were characterized by the development of three major blocs within the motor industry in North America, Western Europe and Japan, the seventies have been characterized by the increasing unification of these three blocs to create a single world industry. This development can be seen in the increasing similarity of motor industry markets and production techniques in the three centres, the increasing interpenetration of capitals and the reorganization of the operations of the major multinationals on a global scale integrating production operations not only in different countries within regions but also in different continents. This development in the internationalization of the motor industry has further intensified competition in the industry giving rise to centralization of capital both at the national and the international levels. The tendency towards greater internationalization of capital in the industry is a further development of the process analysed in Chapter 3. However, the process has been accelerated in the seventies by the general economic crisis and the effects of the increased price of petrol on the motor industry.

1 THE CRISIS IN THE INTERNATIONAL MOTOR INDUSTRY

The crisis which has beset the motor industry since the early seventies is often attributed to the oil price rises of 1973 and 1979. However, at a more fundamental level it can be seen as a result of uneven accumulation internationally in the industry and the effects of the world recession.

The rapid growth of the Japanese motor industry in the sixties and early seventies was accompanied by a substantial increase in labour productivity, so that by 1973 Japanese productivity levels were considerably higher than those of Western Europe and the gap continued to widen in the seventies (Jones, 1981, table 14). One estimate made in 1974 suggested that Japanese costs were 17 per cent lower than in the United States and 24 per cent less than in West Germany (Toder, *et al.*, 1978, table 6.1). A more recent estimate suggests that in the early 1980s Japanese cars landed in the United States enjoyed a cost advantage of $1500 to $2000 even after paying freight costs of $450 (Sinclair, 1983, p. 68). Thus the Japanese advantage in production costs is in the region of 20 per cent to 25 per cent).[1] This set the scene for the intensification of competition in the international motor industry which has characterized the seventies and early eighties. The six leading Japanese companies increased their share of vehicle production in the capitalist world from 19.5 per cent in 1971 to 30.3 per cent in 1983. Between 1971 and 1983 Japan's share of world vehicle exports increased from 24 per cent to 45 per cent in volume terms (*International Automotive Review*, 1984, p. 85). This reflected increased Japanese penetration of the US market, the Western European market and the traditional export markets of the major European producers.

Increased competition from Japan came at a time when the domestic markets of the major producing countries were already showing signs of saturation. The North American market for cars had been growing slowly since the fifties. By the late sixties there were signs that the Western European market for cars was also approaching saturation as ownership became more widespread. Moreover, as the demand for vehicles became increasingly a replacement demand rather than demand from new buyers, the market tended to become increasingly volatile as consumers could postpone replacing their cars when times were bad.

These long-term developments had placed the industry in a very vulnerable position even before the world recession and the increases in oil prices. As a result vehicle production and sales dropped sharply in the major producing countries in the mid-seventies. In 1974 it was estimated that the West European car industry was working at only 65 per cent of capacity and despite subsequent reductions in capacity there was still considerable excess capacity in the industry in the late seventies (CPRS, 1975, table 7; Bhaskar, 1980, pp. 185–7).

The decline in demand for vehicles had a knock-on effect on parts suppliers and tyre producers. In the case of tyres the situation was particularly serious because declining replacement demand as a result of the growing use of longer life radial tyres came on top of the contraction of the original equipment market. Moreover, the oil price rise also led to a squeeze on the cost side because of the increasing cost of synthetic rubber, a petrochemical product.[2]

The immediate impact of these developments was a sharp decline in profitability in the motor industry generally. Many firms found themselves in severe financial difficulties in the seventies including Chrysler, British Leyland, Volkswagen, Renault, Fiat and more recently Ford. In the tyre industry a number of the smaller companies including Avon in the UK, Kleber-Colombes in France, Phoenix and Metzler in West Germany as well as the smaller US companies came under pressure in the mid-seventies. By the late seventies and early eighties these problems extended to the major tyre TNCs such as Dunlop (which abandoned tyre production) and Michelin.

2   CRISIS AND RESTRUCTURING IN THE MOTOR INDUSTRY

The crisis of the industry in the early seventies has also been a period of restructuring of capital. Economic crises always pose the need for restructuring in order to recreate conditions for renewed profitability and accumulation. The specific characteristics of the crisis in the motor industry in the seventies has meant that restructuring has required massive new investment at a time of low profitability. Concretely restructuring has led to two major developments within the motor industry. The first has been the further internationalization of capital which has laid the basis for the establishment of an integrated world motor industry. The second has been the increased involvement of the State in the promotion and support of the industry.[3]

A major objective of capital in the industry in the seventies and eighties has been to match Japanese standards in terms of productivity levels and costs. Ford has laid out an 'After Japan' strategy for its European operations which explicitly aims to 'ensure that productivity improvements at least equal those expected to be made by the Japanese manufacturers' and to 'utilize, where appropriate and socially achievable, those Japanese practices which will result in productivity and quality gains in Europe' (Cohen, 1982a).

Attempts to match Japanese levels of productivity and costs have led to significant changes in the labour process in the motor industry in the seventies and eighties. A major feature has been automation through the increasing use of robots, particularly in the body-shop and the paint-shop. It has been estimated that up to 60 per cent of the world's robots are used in the motor industry (UNIDO, 1984, p. 52). Their use increases the proportion of welding spots which are automated from about 50 per cent to 80 per cent, and in the most modern factories such as Fiat's Miafiori plant, Nissan's Zama plant and BL's new Longbridge plant it is claimed that as much as 95 per cent of welding is carried out automatically. In future it is expected that the use of robots will be extended to other areas of vehicle production.

Automation and the use of robots gives rise to several advantages. There is a considerable saving in labour costs since for every ten workers displaced only three new jobs are created (Coriat quoted in TIE, 1983, p. 21). It has moreover been estimated that the 'economic wage' of a robot is only about £2.20 an hour, making them considerably cheaper than workers in either the UK (£4 an hour) or the US (£7 an hour) (OECD, 1983). Robots can not only be used to replace labour but also to increase the intensity of labour for those workers which remain. GM is reported to use robots alongside humans in bench assembly in order to dictate work-speeds (CSE Microelectronics Group, 1980, p. 85). Alongside other forms of automation and new technology, they considerably increase the control and surveillance powers of management over the labour process. Robots are also a new method of expropriating workers' knowledge where this has resisted Taylorist methods. Thus a robot can be programmed to record and automatically reproduce the movements of the worker. It is not only unskilled workers who are threatened by the new technology. For instance, in the United States draughtsmen's work is being hit by the use of computers to design dies (CSE Microelectronics Group, 1980, p. 85). Finally, the use of robots and computerized control systems has given rise to greater flexibility enabling different models to be produced simultaneously and as in the case of the Fiat Robocarriers, the re-routing of production. It has been estimated that the use of robots will reduce capital expenditure in assembly plants by about 60 per cent to 80 per cent because it ceases to be necessary to radically change transfer lines and other equipment for each new model (Bhaskar, 1980, p. 79). It may also reduce the minimum efficient scale of production in assembly plants (OECD, 1983).

While the introduction of new technology can take place within the conventional framework of assembly line production, simply replacing workers by robots, several companies have attempted more radical change in the organization of work. Faced with problems of high absenteeism and labour turnover firms such as Volvo, Saab-Scania and Renault have experimented with unit working, whereby a small group of workers are responsible for a particular stage in the manufacturing process. This method has been used in the assembly of engines and of complete cars in order to improve both productivity and working conditions. It leads to longer work-cycles – 15 to 20 minutes at Volvo's Kalmar plant – compared with the frequent repetition of simple tasks characteristic of the conventional assembly line (Hermele, 1982, p. 30). The group has considerable autonomy in determining the organization of tasks within the group. However, overall production levels are still determined by management so that the autonomy of the groups is severely circumscribed. As Coriat observes '"Autonomy" thus becomes a tool of self-discipline' (Coriat, 1980, p. 40). Improvements in working conditions associated with such changes in the labour process have also been used by management as a tool with which to obtain concessions from workers. In the case of Volvo, the company was able to secure trade union acquiescence in redundancies, avoiding unrest and any damage to Volvo's image (Hermele, 1982, p. 29). For Fiat the introduction of the new Digitron system at the Miafiori plant was a way of breaking trade union control in the plant and removing the unions from their position of mediators between management and workers (CSE Microelectronics Group, 1980, ch. 9). The key point to note is that the main examples of 'humanizing the assembly line' do in fact contribute to increased productivity, greater flexibility and reduced costs.

Substantial increases in productivity, in a situation in which market growth is slow and new competitors (particularly the Japanese) are making significant inroads into existing markets, can only be achieved through a large scale shedding of labour. Redundancies and long-term layoffs have therefore been a characteristic feature of the motor industry in North America and Western Europe since the early seventies. Total employment in the industry fell by more than 250 000 in the United States between 1973 and 1981 and over 150 000 in the major Western European countries over the same period (Altshuler *et al.*, 1984, table 9.1). Most of the major European and North American TNCs employ significantly fewer workers today than they did in 1973 (see Table 9.1).

Growing unemployment in the industry and increasing international competition has enabled management to put pressure on workers to make wage concessions. The US producers have been particularly successful in this respect. GM hived off its Hyatt Bearing Plant to the workers in the early 1980s. As a result the average level of wages (including benefits) was cut by almost one-third, and the work-force was substantially reduced. In 1982 Ford workers in the United States accepted a $2 an hour reduction in wages over the life of the contract (Cohen, 1982b). Both GM and Ford are also reported to be actively trying to reduce costs by sourcing from US plants which do not have UAW wage agreements (UNIDO, 1984, p. 163). The troubled Chrysler corporation has also obtained considerable concessions from its work-force in recent years. Similarly in Britain, particularly at BL, little or no wage increases were accepted by the unions at a time of rapid inflation.

A further aspect of restructuring in the car industry has been the need to adjust to new demand conditions and specifically to introduce smaller and more economic (in fuel terms) models. This has led to intensified competition in the small car sector of the market which was least affected by the drop in demand. VW introduced the Golf as a replacement for the Beetle in 1974 and Ford went ahead with the development of the Fiesta, building a new assembly plant in Valencia,

TABLE 9.1 *World-wide employment in leading automotive TNCs, 1973–82 ('000s)*

	1973	1982
GM	811	657
Ford	474	404*
VW	215	239
Renault	98‡	132†
Peugeot	229¶	208
Fiat	201	124*
Toyota	43	56
Nissan	53	59

* 1981.
† Data for vehicle production and not the whole Renault group.
‡ Domestic employment only.
¶ Including estimated 78 000 employees in Chrysler's European subsidiaries.
SOURCES Company reports; UNIDO (1984), table 6.

despite the high level of excess capacity in the European motor industry in the mid-seventies.

The need for greater fuel economy has had a major influence on the development of cars in this period. In the United States a major aspect of this process has been the 'down-sizing' of cars in order to meet US government fuel requirements (CAFE). However, this has only been the most obvious response to the need for fuel economy. Other measures to improve fuel economy have been a more aerodynamic design of cars, more economic engine design and the use of lighter materials to reduce vehicle weight (see OECD, 1983, ch. 3 for details). These measures require considerable investment both in research and development and in new plant and equipment. All the major TNCs engaged in massive investment programmes in the late seventies and early eighties (UNIDO, 1984, p. 4). General Motors describe theirs as the 'largest investment programme in the firm's 71 years in operation'.

Not surprisingly these changes, combined with government safety and emission controls have resulted in a substantial increase in the costs of developing new cars in the seventies. R & D expenditure in the automobile industry of the major producing countries almost doubled between 1967 and 1977 (OECD, 1983, table 25). It is now estimated that even the simplest new cars cost $500 to $700 million to develop, and the new generation of 'world cars' being developed by GM and Ford cost well over $1 billion a piece. These increases are astronomical when compared with an estimated $40 million spent by Ford in introducing the Mustang in the sixties (White, 1971, p. 37). The result of increasing development and tooling costs is the need to amortize these expenses over ever-increasing volumes of output in order to remain competitive at a time when demand in the major markets is stagnant.

In trucks too, the shift in demand in favour of diesel engines requires new investment in the United States. The industry is also investing in the introduction of weight saving innovations such as independent suspension which would make it possible to have lighter axles and a simple rigid platform for the chassis. Development costs have not reached the levels indicated for the car industry but even so it is estimated that the introduction of a new truck model in Europe would cost around $300 million.

These developments in the terminal industry also have implications for the parts industry. One area in which there is potential both for a direct increase in fuel economy through better control systems and an indirect increase through a reduction in vehicle weight is through increasing use of electronics in vehicles. Replacement of mechanical systems by electronic systems is on the increase. Other foreseeable developments are computer control of the throttle replacing the direct link from the floor pedal. The other major area where the parts industry is involved in major new investments is in the development of light-weight mechanical components. The Japanese have for several years been applying high pressure die casting techniques for the production of parts and components for engines and transmissions (CPRS, 1975, p. 20), while the GKN automotive components group is involved in redesigning all the components of a truck in order to make it possible to build a lighter series of super-trucks capable of carrying heavier loads (*The Economist*, 1979, p. 18).

The need for new investment to increase productivity to Japanese levels, as well as the research and development expenditures required to introduce new models and the cost of converting existing plants to produce smaller models (particularly in the US), all combined to give rise to massive capital requirements on the part of the major auto TNCs in the seventies and early eighties. Thus at a time when the slow growth of demand, high levels of excess capacity and intensified international competition were all having adverse effects on profitability, the motor manufacturers needed to maintain and even increase the level of investment. Not surprisingly the squeeze between falling profits and increasing investment requirements created major problems for the weaker manufacturers. It has even affected the leading TNCs compelling them to go to the money market to raise capital. As a result 'the Triple A credit rating in the public debt market, which the large motor corporations once held as a matter of course, has now been withdrawn even from GM' (quoted in UNIDO, 1984, p. 43).

3   RESTRUCTURING AND INTERNATIONALIZATION OF CAPITAL

The crisis of the seventies has led to major changes in the structure of the motor industry at the international level and it is now possible to see the emergence of a single world industry. As with the development of the Western European motor industry discussed in Chapter 3, this has a number of aspects. The three major blocs in North America, Europe and Japan are becoming much more closely integrated. This is reflected both in increasing trade flows particularly Japanese exports to North America and Europe, and increasing cross investments as well as joint production agreements. The major transnationals are also increasingly treating their global operations as an integrated whole and developing 'world component supply strategies'. Finally the tendency towards increasing homogenization of vehicle markets has been extended to include all the major producing areas.

Figure 9.1 shows the pattern of international trade in cars in 1983. Comparing it with Figure 3.2 it shows the major changes which have taken place since the early seventies (note difference in scale used). While the growth of intra-regional trade in North America and Western Europe which characterized the 1960s has continued, the most significant change has been the growth of inter-regional trade particularly Japanese exports to North America and Western Europe. Western European exports to North America and the rest of the world have declined, partly reflecting the increased competition of Japan and partly increasing overseas production.

Japan, which did not export more than 100 000 cars a year until the mid-sixties was by the early eighties exporting over half of its total production. Japanese imports accounted for about 21 per cent of the United States car market in 1983. In the EEC about 9 per cent of all cars sold were Japanese despite the restrictions on imports from Japan applied by both France and Italy. Even the West German car industry was feeling the effects of competition with Japanese firms taking 10 per cent of the market. Japanese parts firms have also been increasing exports rapidly initially to the replacement market.

Although as Figure 9.1 shows, the trade links between Japan and the other major producing regions are virtually one-way, in other respects the pattern of internationalization has been more balanced. The growth of Japanese car exports to the United States in the late sixties led to pressure being put on the Japanese government to open up the motor industry to foreign capital. After a period of intense negotiation, a partial liberalization was permitted in 1971 and this resulted in Chrysler acquiring a 35 per cent shareholding in Mitsubishi and General Motors entering a similar arrangement with Isuzu. After a number of abortive attempts, Ford eventually took a 24 per cent shareholding in Toyo-Kogyo in 1979. Finally GM obtained a 5 per cent share in Suzuki in 1981 to complete the US penetration of the Japanese industry. VW has also entered Japan through an agreement with Nissan to produce a VW model for the Japanese market.

Intensified competition in the seventies has led to further centralization of capital. Although there have been important examples of national mergers such as the acquisition of Citroen by Peugeot in 1975

172

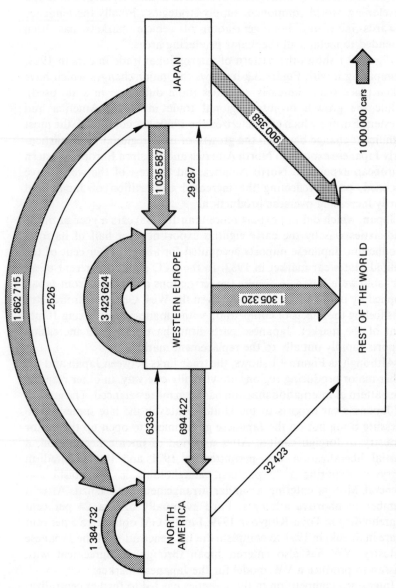

FIGURE 9.1 *Major international trade flows in cars, 1983*

JAPAN

WESTERN EUROPE

NORTH AMERICA

REST OF THE WORLD

1 000 000 cars

900 358

1 035 587

29 287

1 862 715

2526

3 423 624

1 305 320

6339

694 422

1 384 732

32 423

and the SEV-Marchal/Paris-Rhone Cibie merger in the French electrical components industry two years later, a new feature of the seventies have been important examples of international mergers within Europe. The mergers of the sixties had in many countries virtually exhausted the possibilities of centralization on a national basis. The Dunlop–Pirelli union in 1971 was the first of the major international mergers, but others include the formation of IVECO by Fiat and Magirus-Deutz in 1975 and Volvo's acquisition of the Dutch firm DAF's car operations. In the late seventies Peugeot-Citroen acquired Chrysler's European operations with plants in Britain and Spain as well as in France. These developments have further integrated the European motor industry along the lines described in Chapter 3.

Another aspect which has also qualitatively changed in the seventies has been the interpenetration of capitals between the different regional blocs. This has involved an extension of US ownership in the European motor industry in the commercial vehicle and parts sector. International Harvester acquired the specialist truck producer Seddon-Atkinson in Britain and a 33 per cent share of DAF's truck operations. In the parts industry in Britain Turner Manufacturing making transmissions for commercial vehicles has been acquired by Dana and Wilmot Breedon producing a variety of parts (bumpers, door handles, locks etc.), has been taken over by Rockwell. ITT has been active in Europe taking over a group of component manufacturers in Italy, Alfred Teves in West Germany and Koni in Holland, and together with TRW is one of the largest parts companies in Europe.

Unlike the fifties and sixties when there was also substantial US investment in Europe a novel feature of the seventies has been the two way flow with a number of European companies investing in the United States or acquiring US companies. This has been part of the rapid growth of foreign investment in the USA generally in the seventies. The total foreign investment stock has increased from $25 billion in 1974 to $41 billion five years later. This has been attributed to the loss of US technological advantage in certain industries in the late sixties and early seventies with the collapse of the Bretton Woods System, the rising price of oil and decline of the dollar acting as a final catalyst after 1973 (Young and Hood, 1980, pp. 21–3).

In the motor industry the most commented upon instance has been the Volkswagen assembly plant which began production in 1978. However, it is by no means an isolated case. Daimler-Benz has opened a truck plant in Virginia where it assembles components imported from Brazil. Renault has acquired control of American Motors, which is now producing the Renault 9 in the United States and the independent truck company, Mack, while Volvo acquired the White Motor Corporation. The West German commercial vehicle firm MAN is starting to assemble buses and considering local production of diesel trucks. Michelin has already built four new plants in the United States and has a fifth under construction and the company aims to triple its existing 5 per cent share of the US market. In the components industry too a number of firms are showing interest in starting production in the US (EIU, 1977, p. 37). SKF has brought a division of the Eaton Corporation, Thyssen has taken over Budd – one of the leading US component producers – while Chloride acquired the Connrex Corporation.

Although European firms have taken the lead in entering the US motor industry, there has been increasing pressure on the Japanese to do so as well as their share of the US market increased. Honda has already begun production in the United States and Nissan has opened a plant for light commercial vehicles in Tennessee. The other major Japanese exporter to the United States, Toyota, has formed a joint venture with GM to produce a small Japanese derived car in the United States. A number of Japanese parts producers have followed the Japanese assemblers in investing in the US (EIU, 1983a, pp. 70–71). The increase in European and Japanese investment in the US motor industry and the interpenetration of capital that this represents is a result of the growing homogenization of conditions in the motor industry. The United States is no longer a high labour cost area for European producers particularly German capital. There was also an increase in the US market for European and Japanese type cars as a result of the shift in demand towards smaller cars in the seventies and the slowness of the major US firms in adjusting their production. Finally, increasing political pressure was brought to bear on the Japanese either to restrain exports or invest locally as their share of the US market rose. Japanese capital is also becoming more directly involved in Europe as its growing market penetration there meets increasing resistance. Nissan is the first Japanese manufacturer to acquire a significant manufacturing foothold in Europe with the purchase of Massey-Ferguson's minority holding in the Spanish firm Motor Iberica in 1979. It is also involved in a joint venture with Alfa Romeo to produce cars in Italy and is building an assembly plant in Britain. Honda is also expanding into Europe through its agreement with BL to assemble a Honda model in the UK.

The increasing interpenetration of capital within and between the three major producing areas has led to a much more complex structure of interrelations as Figure 9.2 illustrates. Comparison with Figure 3.3 brings out the extent to which the structure of the international industry has changed during the seventies. Links between the major regions are much more frequent while within Europe international links through ownership have increased in significance as a result of the extension of centralization of capital to the international level.

In addition to the interpenetration of capital through trade and investment, a third crucial factor in the development of a world motor industry in the seventies has been the tendency for the major regional markets to become increasingly alike. Three aspects of the homogenization of the motor industry within the three major blocs appear to be of particular significance in this context. The first is the trend towards increasingly similar cars in terms of size in the three major production centres.[4] The most obvious manifestation of this is the 'downsizing' programme forced on the US manufacturers by the government's fuel economy requirements. While this trend has been accentuated by the increase in oil prices, it is clear that even before 1973 there was a move in this direction reflected in the increasing share of imports in the US market and the introduction of the sub-compacts by GM, Ford and American Motors in 1969 and 1970. By the early 1980s compact cars or smaller models accounted for over 60 per cent of the US market (EIU, 1983a, p. 4).

The 'downsizing' of US cars in the seventies has been accompanied by another kind of Europeanization of the car market, namely the growing importance of front-wheel drive models. Traditionally the US car has been very conventional in terms of engineering. GM took the lead in introducing front-wheel drive in the United States. It was first used in the 1966 Oldsmobile but its growth came with the introduction of the new generation of small cars in the late seventies. By 1980 only a fifth of GM cars had front-wheel drive but this is expected to increase to nine out of every ten cars produced within five years. Ford and Chrysler have followed suit with the introduction of their new models.

While the most clear evidence of the homogenization of the car industry has been the growth of the market for European type cars in the US, the Japanese market has also been showing a similar trend. In particular the share of very small cars in total Japanese production has dropped very sharply since 1970 when cars of less than 360 cc accounted for 24 per cent of local output. By the late seventies cars of less than 550 cc were only about 3 per cent of all cars being produced. At the same time cars of over 2000 cc have significantly increased their share of production.

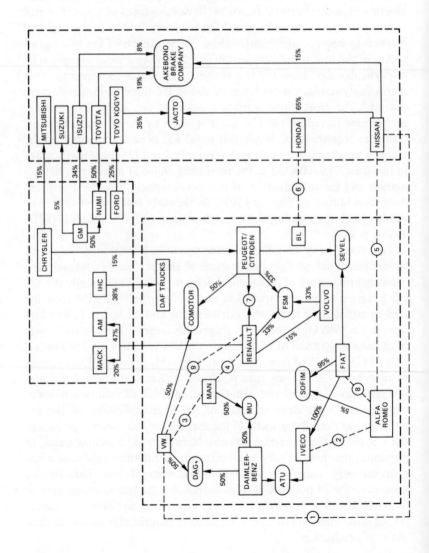

Terminal firm

Other firm

→ Ownership link with percentage shareholding indicated

---- Other link

1 Nissan and VW cooperation to produce a VW car in Japan.

2 IVECO and Alfa Romeo have a jointly developed and produced van.

3 VW and MAN jointly produce and market a range of medium trucks.

4 Renault and MAN have an agreement for cooperation in production and marketing of trucks.

5 Alfa Romeo is to assemble a Nissan car in Italy.

6 BL is to assemble a Honda car in UK.

7 Peugeot-Citroen and Renault share a number of joint ventures, e.g. Française du Mecanique, Société des Transmission Automatiques as well as undertaking joint research in certain areas.

8 Alfa Romeo and Fiat are to jointly manufacture and make joint purchases from third parties of large components.

9 Renault and VW are jointly developing a new type of automatic gearbox.

FIGURE 9.2 Links between major motor manufacturers, c. 1984

A second aspect of the homogenization of the motor industry has been the growing importance of diesel-powered trucks as compared with petrol engined vehicles. While most of the CVs produced in Western Europe and Japan used diesel engines those in the United States have been predominantly petrol driven. By the late seventies there was a swing towards diesel-engined trucks because of their greater fuel economy. In 1979 only 10 per cent of medium duty (9–15 tonnes) trucks in the United States were diesel powered, but this was expected to increase rapidly to reach 50 per cent by 1982 and 85 per cent by 1984 (*The Economist*, 1979). While the 'downsizing' of US cars has given a competitive advantage to US manufacturers, the 'dieselization' of the US truck market may benefit European manufacturers with their greater experience of diesel technology. But while US truck manufacturers are likely to meet increased competition from European firms such as Mercedes-Benz, IVECO, Volvo and Renault, it should be remembered that one of the leading US truck makers, International Harvester, is an important producer of diesel engines for its tractors. European firms in the component industry are also well placed to benefit, especially firms such as Bosch and Lucas with their fuel injection equipment.

While the growth of diesel trucks is clearly related to the oil crisis and the 'downsizing' of US cars has been accelerated by government measures in the aftermath of the oil price rise, the main development in the tyre industry, the generalization of the steel radial has been quite independent of it. The radial tyre had become widely used in Western Europe by the early seventies. In the United States, however, the major manufacturers had resisted the introduction of radials, partly because this would have made much of their existing equipment obsolete and would have reduced the demand for replacement tyres by giving them a longer life. In the sixties the companies introduced the bias-ply, a modified form of cross-ply tyre. It was not until after 1969 that Goodrich, General Tyre and Uniroyal all began producing radials, finally followed by Firestone in 1971 and Goodyear at the end of 1972. This reluctant adoption of the radial in the United States was prompted first by the growth of imports from Europe and later by Michelin setting up a radial plant in Canada in 1971. In 1972 only 5.6 per cent of all the tyres sold in the United States were radials but five years later their share had reached almost a half. In Japan too the growth of the radial tyre was a phenomenon of the seventies. The generalization of the radial tyre has been accompanied by an intensification of competition in the international tyre industry, particularly reflected in Michelin's challenge to the major US companies, Goodyear and Firestone.

Again, although less evident than changes in the final product, changes in production processes appear to be giving rise to increasingly similar techniques in car factories around the world. Unitized body construction[5] began to be introduced in Europe in the late forties but in North America the large size of cars militated against its use. New techniques developed during the sixties enabled unitized construction to be successfully applied in the United States and this was given further impetus by the increasing importance of small cars. In the seventies the major change in production techniques has been automation through the introduction of automated welding equipment in body assembly. As already indicated there is a growing similarity in terms of production technology as other manufacturers attempt to match Japan's productivity levels.

The trend towards increasing homogenization of individual vehicle markets that is an essential aspect of the internationalization of capital in the industry in the seventies gives rise to the possibility of an international integration of the operations of the major transnationals on a world-wide basis similar to that pioneered by Ford within Europe. The much heralded 'world cars' of the US companies appear as the realization of such a concept. On closer analysis, however, much of this turns out to be corporate rhetoric attempting to present an industry in crisis as being in the vanguard of international capitalist development. Nevertheless even when this rhetoric has been discounted a significant degree of international integration remains and is a further manifestation of the tendency towards developing a world industry.

The 'world car' concept has been interpreted in different ways. In 1976 Ford executives were predicting that

> The day is not far off when manufacturers – and especially auto manufacturers – will be producing the same line of products for sale everywhere in the world, with only the most minor variations among countries (W. O. Burke, Vice-President of Ford, quoted in NACLA, 1979, p. 26).

This conception of the world car sees it as being essentially the same vehicle produced by the transnational all over the world. While the homogenization of markets has certainly made this increasingly feasible it has still not been fully realized. Nevertheless the previous situation in which each major producing centre had its own separate set of models, and in which subsidiaries in less developed countries were integrated into corporate operations as simply a market for a greater or smaller number of parts depending on local content requirements, is being replaced by increasingly integrated international production strategies. More recently Ford has redefined its concept of the world car. It now involves

> The design, engineering and development of a product by international teams of technical talent inherent in a worldwide corporation.   The end result should be a car with a uniform engineering philosophy and sufficient commonality in component design to permit optimum use of the productive resources of the company (*Financial Times Survey*, 26/9/80, p. 1).

The essential feature of this modified view, which serves to classify the Ford Escort as a world car (despite being produced in different versions in the United States, Europe and Australasia) is the saving in pre-production costs which common design permits. In view of the rapidly increasing costs of design and development in the seventies, this has become an increasingly important element in international competitiveness. Ford estimates that it saved $150 million and 15 000 man-years in engineering time through its worldwide approach to developing the Escort. GM adopted a similar approach in developing the Chevette which involved the parent company, its British, German and Brazilian subsidiaries and Isuzu in Japan. Both Ford and GM are planning to develop further the world car concept in the eighties with a range of standardized models being introduced which have been designed internationally. GM intends to use only seven basic bodies for all its cars worldwide of which the three largest will be reserved for the US market. At the same time the company will be using only four or five petrol engines and two diesel engines. This will give the companies enormous potential economies of scale with the most popular models having annual runs of over 2 million units and the others averaging around a million.

Another concept of the world car is summed up by Renault President Vernier-Palliez when he says that:

> There are no world cars, only world components to be made on a vast scale (*Financial Times*, 26/9/80, p. 11).

On this interpretation the use of common components in models produced in different countries giving rise to a truly international vehicle is the essential feature of a world car. Again within Europe, as was described in the previous chapter, this concept was pioneered by Ford. Its further development on an inter-continental level is still limited however. The Ford Escort produced in the United States will have a 95 per cent local content. Attempts to develop international sourcing in the United States in the past have met considerable union resistance.

Nevertheless a number of countries are increasingly becoming involved in world sourcing of components. Although sourcing of components outside the United States accounts for only 5 per cent or 6 per cent of the value of components used by US companies in the early 1980s (Sinclair, 1983, table 8.5), this is expected to increase. Plans have been made which involve as many as 4.5 million engines and 2.9 million transmissions being imported into the United States by the mid-1980s, although it is unlikely that these levels will in fact be attained (EIU, 1983a, pp. 36–7). It has also been estimated that overall foreign parts sourcing would rise to 25 per cent by 1985 and 35 per cent by 1990 (Cohen, 1982b). Currently the main sources of imported automotive parts to the United States (excluding Canada) are, in order of importance, Japan, Mexico, West Germany and Brazil (EIU, 1983a, table 18). In the late seventies and early eighties imports of engines from Mexico, Japan and Brazil grew rapidly while imports from Canada and West Germany fell sharply (EIU, 1983a, table 17) and imports of transmissions from Japan and Mexico increased at the expense of France and West Germany (EIU, 1983a, table 21).

European manufacturers have also used internationally sourced components in their vehicles. Renault, for instance, used engine blocks from Spain, wheels from Mexico and gearboxes from Romania in its vehicles. Fiat is using Brazilian engines in the 127 and VW imports engines and gearings from Brazil and Mexico. BL and Alfa Romeo will import a high proportion of the parts and components for their models produced in association with Honda and Nissan respectively from Japan. This international sourcing together with the increasing number of imported vehicles in use in the major producing countries, has been a major factor in the rapid growth in international trade in parts and components during the seventies and early eighties.[6]

4 RESTRUCTURING AND STATE SUPPORT FOR CAPITAL

Faced with increasingly competitive conditions in the international motor industry in the seventies and the need to make major new investment in order to survive, capital has in many cases sought support from the state. In the case of the weaker firms, state support has been seen as a means of survival, in some cases as with British Leyland requiring the state to take over the firm. But the phenomenon of increasing reliance on the state for finance has not been confined to weaker capitals. Even the strongest firms have sought to take advantage of fiscal incentives and subsidies on an unprecedented scale in order to maintain their rhythm of accumulation.

Three major examples of the way in which the state has intervened directly to support weaker firms in the industry are provided by the cases of BL and Chrysler UK in 1975 and more recently the US government's rescue of the Chrysler parent company. In all three cases the ailing company would almost certainly have been forced to close down if the state had not stepped in. In the case of BL the British government took control of the company in 1975 after attempts to raise money from the banks and the Saudi Arabian government had failed. The two Chrysler rescue operations did not involve the British or US government acquiring a shareholding in the company, but simply a financial injection through a government loan in the case of Chrysler UK and a loan guarantee for the Chrysler parent company. In all three cases the survival of the firm was in question because of their inability to raise capital privately for the massive investment required in order to remain viable in an increasingly competitive international environment. All three cases described above have arisen where companies have been in serious financial difficulties as a result of the crisis in the industry and where there has been a threat of closure of a major enterprise.

However, the squeeze on profitability in the industry has affected not only the weakest firms but also the more successful companies. In a number of countries major auto companies have sought the support of their home governments. As well as Britain and the United States, government financial support of this kind has been particularly forthcoming in France and Italy (Bhaskar *et al.*, 1984).

The international operations of the auto TNCs also puts them in an extremely good position to shop around for incentives by offering to locate new plants in different foreign locations. Intense competition among states to attract new investment has meant that the TNCs best placed to do this have been able to socialize a significant proportion of the cost of new plant. A pioneering example was Ford's decision to locate its new engine plant at Bridgend in South Wales following negotiations with a number of European governments over the incentives which they were prepared to offer to the company. The eventual agreement arrived at with the British government was extremely favourable to Ford. Table 9.2 summarizes a number of major new investments undertaken in recent years in which auto TNCs have obtained substantial financial assistance from overseas governments. It is clear that even the world's largest motor manufacturers faced with the need for large new investments in a period of reduced profits, and

TABLE 9.2   *Subsidies granted for major new investments by auto TNCs*

Company	Country	Project	Investment	Government contribution
Ford	UK	Bridgend engine plant	£180 m	£73 m under regional aid £75 m interest relief grant.
Nissan	UK	Washington assembly plant	£350 m	£112 m
Ford	Spain	Valencia plant	n.a.	$100 m tax and other benefits.
GM	Spain	Zaragosa plant	n.a.	$150 m; grant for 10 per cent of investment, 20 per cent cheap loan and free land
Ford	Portugal	Offer to build a plant	n.a.	Fifty per cent of investment plus part of a new industrial complex.
GM	Austria	Vienna engine plant	$350 m	$110 m; tax concessions and infrastructure
Ford	Mexico	Hermosillo assembly plant	$500 m	$200 m
Ford	Canada	Windsor engine plant	$535 m	$68 m
GM	Canada	Quebec aluminium casting plant	$400 m	$86
VW	USA	Pennsylvania assembly plant	n.a.	> $100 m

SOURCES   Bhaskar *et al.* (1984); Sinclair and Walker (1982); Wong Gonzalez (1984); Leyton-Brown (1980).

with the opportunities which increasing internationalization has given them, are seeking state subsidies on a massive scale.

5   THE CHANGING ROLE OF PERIPHERAL ECONOMIES IN THE WORLD MOTOR INDUSTRY

The restructuring of capital in the major producing countries and certain developments in the peripheral economies themselves during the seventies have led to important changes in the role assigned to the motor industry in these countries in the international division of labour. This is most clearly seen in those countries where manufacturing developed on an import substitution basis and which have emerged as exporters of parts and vehicles in the seventies. As will be seen below, however, this is not primarily a consequence of a cheap labour strategy of the kind that has characterized the electronics industry.

The intensified competition from Japanese capital, which as was noted earlier was faced in North America and Western Europe, has also extended to the Third World and the new producing countries. Japan's share of car exports from the major producing countries to the Third World almost doubled from 31 per cent in 1971 to 57 per cent in 1981, while in commercial vehicles its position is even more dominant, accounting for three-quarters of all exports in 1981, up from 47 per cent in 1971 (*International Automotive Review*, 1982/3, p. 11). There have also been significant Japanese inroads in three of the seven semi-industrialized countries discussed in Chapter 3 since the late sixties. By the early eighties Japanese vehicles comprised around half the vehicles produced in Australia and South Africa and 15 per cent in Mexico.

The stagnation of demand and production in the major developed country markets in the seventies has given a new significance to peripheral markets from the point of view of the transnationals. Between 1973 and 1981 when world production of vehicles fell from 39.2 million to 37.6 million, production in Third World countries rose from 1.5 million to 1.8 million. The growing importance of the Third World is even more striking in terms of exports from the major producing countries. These rose from 1.0 million vehicles in 1971 to 2.7 million a decade later. This represented 45 per cent of the total increase in vehicle exports from the major producing countries over this period. In 1981 exports to Third World areas accounted for 15 per cent of car exports and 40 per cent of commercial vehicle exports worldwide, despite the increase in domestic production in this period

(*International Automotive Review*, 1982/3, tables 3 and 4). By the early eighties the total demand for vehicles in the Third World was probably in excess of 5 million units, making it comparable with Japan as a market and about half the size of the US or Western European market. The shift to the Third World is even more marked if one looks at areas where new demand for vehicles is being created. Increasingly the demand for vehicles in the advanced capitalist countries is a replacement demand as these markets mature. Growth in the stock of cars and commercial vehicles on the roads will come to be increasingly concentrated on the LDCs. Between 1950 and 1976 only 12 per cent of the increase in the world's car stock and 19 per cent of the increase in CVs was in LDCs (including those of Southern Europe). Projections to the year 2000 indicate that 44 per cent of the increase in car stock and 48 per cent of the increase in the number of CVs will be in these countries.

The growth of demand in the Third World has been accompanied by a further extension of assembly activities. The number of vehicles assembled in the underdeveloped countries increased from 224 000 in 1967 to 1 041 000 in 1979 or from 20 per cent to 37 per cent of world assemblies (UNCTC, 1982, p. 28). By 1981 the number of vehicles produced by the leading Third World assembling countries had increased further to 1 132 500 (*International Automotive Review*, 1982/ 3, table 9). This reflects the increasing number of countries which are restricting imports and imposing local content requirements on locally assembled vehicles (see Table 3.3).

Given the importance of the markets of the Third World and the less developed countries of Southern Europe in terms of future expansion, it is not surprising that there is still considerable competition among capitals for privileged access through the creation of local subsidiaries. This is by no means limited to the Japanese penetration mentioned earlier. In Brazil, for example, Fiat entered the car market in direct competition with Volkswagen in 1976 and Volvo entered the commercial vehicle industry. Ford began production at its new Fiesta plant in Spain in 1976 and more recently GM have also built a factory to produce small cars in Spain. There has also been intense competition to enter into new areas such as the Andean Pact countries and Algeria which embarked on substantial development programmes in the seventies.

Host countries have in the seventies become increasingly aware of the problems which emerged with the development of highly protected import substituting industries in the sixties generally with very liberal foreign investment regimes. Government negotiators have attempted to exploit inter-capitalist rivalry in order to change the terms on which foreign firms are permitted access to the local market. A major objective has been a greater contribution to foreign exchange earnings through increased exports. Both Fiat in Brazil and Ford in Spain had to undertake substantial export commitments in order to begin local production. Also the terms of access of existing producers have in many cases been renegotiated, taking advantage of the firms' interest in the local market, to increase exports.

While these exports have thus largely been the result of government pressures (and not primarily an initiative of the companies to take advantage of lower labour costs) it is important to remember that these changes are also congruent with the international strategies of the major transnationals. The companies have on the whole been quite willing to increase exports but have sought as a *quid pro quo* a reduction in the level of local content required in the production of vehicles for the domestic market. In the words of *The Economist*

> Now Ford and GM are saying: if you continue to insist on a very high local content, we shall continue to build costly, outdated models; but if you lower your requirements, in exchange for a compensatory rise in exports, we will build cheap modern vehicles – and the change will create at least as many jobs as it kills (*The Economist*, 22/12/79).

A number of countries have already reduced their local content requirements in return for export commitments and the companies are pressurizing for further reductions. Australia is held up by the car companies as an example to other countries. There the government agreed to increase the permitted import content from 15 per cent to 20 per cent in 1982 in return for a new GM engine plant two-thirds of whose output will be exported. Further increases in import content may then be granted if the new arrangement is successful. This type of arrangement is particularly attractive, especially to Ford and GM and it is not surprising that they have been its most active proponents. Despite the internationalization of the industry in the seventies, the two firms still have the widest spread of international operations giving them more scope and flexibility than their competitors. Moreover, the scale of their world-wide operations makes it possible for them to meet export requirements with a minimum of dislocation to their home country operations. Relocation of production of a few parts or components for the US market enables them to meet export commitments which may appear large in relation to a particular less developed country's motor industry.

The role of the Soviet Union and the Eastern European countries within the international division of labour has also been changing during the 1970s. One aspect of this change has been the substantial growth of exports from the socialist countries especially the Soviet Union and Czechoslovakia. Eastern European imports have begun to make their presence felt in Western Europe running at about 140 000 cars a year in the late seventies. It is possible that such imports will increase considerably during the 1980s intensifying further the competitive struggle in Europe.[7] Already in the tyre industry, Eastern European manufacturers have made considerable inroads into certain markets selling at well below the price of locally manufactured tyres. Imports of cheap Eastern European tyres have caused considerable concern in the United Kingdom in the late 1970s.

In some cases the Eastern European motor industries are being inserted into the world industry in a rather similar way to the semi-industrialized peripheral countries. The case of Romania supplying gearboxes to Renault in France in return for imported components has already been mentioned. Citroen has agreed to import transaxles from East Germany and under an agreement signed in 1979 Fiat is bringing Poland into the company's global production plans, phasing out Italian production of the Fiat 126 (Maxcy, 1981, ch. 9). Thus it is possible that the 1980s will see a further integration of the world industry with a growing incorporation of the socialist countries.

6 CONCLUSION

The last decade or more has seen major changes in the international motor industry. In the long term the most significant of these changes has been the emergence of a truly global industry. The internationalization of capital has tended to eliminate the characteristic features of vehicles produced in the different major producing regions. Increasingly vehicles have come to be designed for a world market and production to be organized on an international basis. There has been growing interpenetration of capitals as firms seek to participate in all the major centres of production in order to spread their rapidly rising design and development costs.

This process has been accelerated by the world recession and the sharp increases in oil prices in the seventies which intensified the need for restructuring of capital in the industry. The need for major new investments at a time of declining profits led most of the major auto TNCs to resort to state support, either to stave off bankruptcy or to construct new plants. The increasingly international nature of vehicle production, intensified competition and the growing importance of new markets outside the traditional industrial centres, has enabled a number of semi-industrialized countries to emerge as important exporters of vehicles and parts. In the next chapter the policies pursued by certain Latin American states in the seventies and early eighties will be considered.

NOTES

1. The average price of an imported car in the US in 1981 was $9318 (Sinclair, 1983, chart 8). For a similar estimate of the Japanese cost advantage see Altshuler *et al.*, 1984, pp. 155–62.
2. The average direct costs of producing styrene-butadiene rubber (SBR 1500) increased by over 70 per cent in the major developed countries between 1973 and 1975 (IBRD, 1978, table 12).
3. Another aspect of restructuring which will not be considered here is the diversification of certain firms out of the industry. Both Fiat and Renault have announced plans to reduce their dependence on car production while Volkswagen has acquired an office equipment and small computer company. Some of the major tyre companies are also reducing their dependence on the motor industry.
4. It should be stressed that this is only a trend and regional differences have by no means been entirely eliminated. For further evidence on this see Altshuler *et al.*, 1984, especially Figures 6.1 and 6.3.
5. Unitized body construction involves building up the body to serve as both chassis and body so that there is no separate chassis.
6. World trade in auto parts grew by 121 per cent between 1975 and 1979 (UNIDO, 1984, p. 27).
7. Some car firms believe that East European imports could account for as much as 7 per cent of the West European market by the mid-1980s (Sinclair, 1983, p. 31).

10 The State and the Restructuring of Capital in Latin America in the World Recession

1 INTRODUCTION

It was seen in Part I that the motor industry throughout Latin America was ripe for a major restructuring by the early 1970s. In most countries the industry continued to represent a considerable cost in terms of foreign exchange, despite the pursuit of import substitution policies. In all countries, but particularly the Andean Pact countries with relatively small markets (Chile, Colombia and Peru) and Argentina, production costs and vehicle prices were well above international standards. The industry was not playing a major role in dynamizing the accumulation process. In the countries where the terminals were engaged primarily in assembly, investment in fixed assets was extremely limited. Of the countries with more integrated production both Argentina and Mexico were experiencing a crisis of profitability and accumulation was stagnating.

The only apparent exception to this gloomy picture was Brazil where production grew rapidly in the late sixties and early seventies and where production costs were considerably lower than elsewhere in Latin America. Indeed, Brazil in the early seventies appeared to be one of the best areas anywhere in the world for investment by the auto TNCs. This situation was, however, to change suddenly as a result of events totally outside the Brazilian state's control. The sharp increase in oil prices in 1973 highlighted the vulnerability of the Brazilian economy generally and the motor vehicle industry in particular because of their heavy dependence on imported petroleum. Over 90 per cent of Brazil's petroleum is imported. As a result of the 1973 oil price increase the proportion of Brazil's export earnings needed to cover oil imports rose from one-tenth to one-third (and following the 1979 price rises it rose again to almost a half) (Open University, 1983, p. 34). The use of motor vehicles has been estimated to account for 60 per cent of Brazil's petroleum consumption, much of which is used in private cars (Mericle, 1984, p. 26). Thus the very 'success' of the development of the Brazilian motor industry in the period up to 1973 served to store up problems which became acute after that date. Thus the Brazilian industry also required the state to intervene to restructure capital in the mid-seventies.

As was seen in the last chapter the internationalization of capital in the motor industry in this period created a new context within which such a restructuring would have to take place. This both created new opportunities for Latin American states and new constraints in terms of the options available. It is possible to discern three major strategies of restructuring within the region. The first followed by the larger countries (Brazil, Mexico and Argentina up to 1976) was based on a renegotiation of the insertion of the local industry into the world industry involving a strengthening of the international links of the industry to take advantage of the emerging global strategies of the auto TNCs. The second pursued by Chile and Argentina (after 1976) was characterized by a different form of integration through the liberalization of imports of CBU vehicles (taking advantage of new sources of competition particularly Japan) in order to reduce domestic prices and rationalize the existing industry. Finally, the Andean Pact countries proposed further import substitution on a regional basis within a planned framework allocating the production of particular models and components to member countries. This strategy attempted to take advantage of intensified international competition in the industry to obtain new investment proposals on the best possible terms. In the remainder of this chapter we shall describe the main features of the policies pursued in each country.

2 PRODUCTION FOR GLOBAL MARKETS

The main feature of the state sponsored restructuring of the motor vehicle industry in Brazil, Mexico and Argentina (up to 1976) in the seventies was an attempt to orient production away from exclusive reliance on the domestic market to become an important participant in the world auto market. If successful such a strategy implies a much closer integration into the world motor industry and a move away from the relatively self-contained auto industries which characterized Brazil and Argentina in the sixties. Such a strategy was consistent with the emerging trends in development strategies and international economic advice which had increasingly emphasized the promotion of manufactured exports since the late sixties.[1]

Given the high cost of production in Latin America in the early seventies, the control of the auto TNCs over the terminal industry in the region and over production facilities in the major world markets, it was highly unlikely that the motor industry in these countries would generate significant exports of its own accord. If the industry in Latin America was to become a source of supply for international markets, this would only come about as a result of active state intervention. In each of the three countries, therefore, an element of compulsion was involved in getting the auto TNCs to export. This was supplemented by certain fiscal incentives which also made exporting more attractive and helped offset any over-valuation of the local currency.

The first important steps were taken in Mexico as early as 1969 with the introduction of an export requirement. The Mexican state had in fact provided a certain incentive to the auto companies to export from the inception of a manufacturing industry in the early 1960s. The 1962 Decree which set a local content of 60 per cent for the industry, also provided for increases in the quota which firms could produce locally in return for either a higher level of national integration or exports. In the 1960s, a number of firms, especially Ford, Automex (Chrysler) and Volkswagen made use of this system in order to increase their share of the Mexican market. In 1969 the government began to require vehicle producers to cover an increasing proportion of their imports aiming to have 100 per cent compensation of imports within ten years. The new Decree introduced in 1972, on the expiry of the initial 1962 Decree, required at least 40 per cent of the total value of exports by the vehicle producers to be provided by firms in the parts industry with at least 60 per cent Mexican ownership. In this way the government attempted to ensure that some of the benefits of the export promotion policy would accrue to local firms. The main fiscal incentive received by exporters were the Certificados de Devolucion de Impuestos (CEDI) introduced in 1971. These took the form of a tax credit which could be set against a company's tax liabilities. They were set at 11 per cent of the value of exports and applied to most manufactured products.

In 1977 the Mexican government introduced a new Decree which redefined the system for calculating the import content of locally produced vehicles[2] and established a new system of 'foreign exchange budgets' to replace the previous quota system.[3] Again the aim was to achieve a balance between imports and exports. It was left up to the terminals themselves to determine whether to achieve this through increased exports or higher levels of local content. The proportion of exports provided by the parts industry was increased to 50 per cent. In 1978 export promotion was given a further boost when the government permitted duty free imports of any new and completely modern machinery and equipment, raw materials and components which could not be produced locally. Components and raw materials considered to be indispensable to uninterrupted production for export could be imported at 25 per cent of the normal tariff levels, which themselves were reduced by 25 per cent from existing levels (NACLA, 1979, p. 28).

The Argentinian policy towards promoting exports in the early 1970s was in many ways similar to that used in Mexico. In 1973, car manufacturers were required to meet certain export targets if they were to expand production for the domestic market. Firms which had exports equal to a certain proportion of their domestic sales (which would increase from 15 per cent in 1974 to 100 per cent by 1978) would be allowed to expand their domestic sales by 8 per cent per annum. Failure to meet these export targets would result in domestic sales being reduced accordingly. These export requirements applied only to the passenger car industry and not to commercial vehicle production.

In addition, the industry in Argentina had benefited from a variety of fiscal incentives from the early 1970s. The Ley de la Reconversión de la Industria Automotriz of 1971 had increased tax rebates on exported vehicles and parts by 50 per cent and these incentives were further extended in 1972. A subsidy of 35 per cent of the f.o.b. value for cars and 40 per cent for commercial vehicles was introduced and tax rebates were granted whose value was estimated at about 11 per cent of the f.o.b. price for cars and over 18 per cent for heavy trucks. Taken together with a number of other smaller incentives such as those for exporting tyres, the repayment of freight and insurance charges and the incentives for exports to new markets, the total incentive received by an exporting company by 1973 could amount to almost 60 per cent of the export price for cars and 75 per cent for heavy trucks. In addition the Central Bank provided credit on favourable terms which could amount to a subsidy of more than 5 per cent of the vehicle price.

The Brazilian government began to require export commitments from the terminals in 1972 with the negotiation of the first of the Special Fiscal Benefits for Exports (BEFIEX) programmes with Ford.

The local content requirements for firms signing BEFIEX agreements was reduced to 85 per cent for cars and between 78 per cent and 82 per cent for commercial vehicles. This was considerably less than had been required by GEIA and firms not undertaking export commitments were required to show a level of integration of 95 per cent. The products exported could have an even lower local content subject to the value added in Brazil being at least three times the f.o.b. value of imports (Guimaraes, 1981, p. 50). Under BEFIEX exporters were eligible for a number of special tax incentives and exemptions from restrictions on imports. Reductions of between 70 per cent and 90 per cent of the Industrial Products Tax on imported equipment and up to 50 per cent of the tax on imported raw materials, components and intermediate products were offered. Companies were also allowed to amortize pre-operational expenses related to exports over a ten-year period. The pressure which forced firms to take up the BEFIEX programme was the control of the Brazilian Council for Industrial Development (CDI) over the authorization of investment and its ability to offer attractive incentives to the manufacturers. The initial agreement with Ford was signed when the company wished to expand in Brazil through the introduction of the Maverick. In 1973 Volkswagen, worried about the impact of the Maverick on its market share, entered the BEFIEX programme in order to introduce a new model. By 1978 all the TNCs in the Brazilian terminal industry, with the exception of Toyota, had signed BEFIEX agreements. These involved export commitments of between $300 million and $1350 million over a period of ten years or less. The agreements with Mercedes-Benz, Saab-Scania, Fabrica Nacional de Motores, Fiat and GM all involved a positive effect on the balance of trade of $100 million or more over the ten years of the programme (de Oliveira *et al.*, 1979).

In addition firms were able to benefit from the general fiscal incentives for manufactured exports introduced in the late 1960s and early 1970s. The most important of these were the exemption from the state sales tax (ICM) in 1967 extended to include a tax credit in the 1970s, and the introduction of a tax credit for the industrial products tax (IPI) in 1969. These were particularly beneficial to the automotive industry which in 1971 received exemptions equivalent to 17 per cent of the value of exports from the ICM and 13 per cent from the IPI and tax credits of 13 per cent for ICM and 14 per cent for IPI (de Oliveira *et al.*, 1979, table 53). The total value of incentives received by the industry was 62 per cent of the value of exports in 1971 and 67 per cent in 1975.

The measures applied in each of these three countries have a number of common features. The state attempted to exploit the international competition between TNCs in order to force increased exports. In return the TNCs were granted privileged access to a protected domestic market and a whole range of export incentives. In Brazil and Mexico they were also given a wider margin of flexibility in integrating their subsidiaries into the world motor industry. In the case of Brazil this was achieved through reducing the very high levels of local content that had been achieved by the early 1970s. In Mexico it took the form of successful pressure from the TNCs for efforts to improve the industry's balance of payments to be focused on increasing exports rather than reducing imports (in the 1972 Decree) and on maintaining their options open through the use of the foreign exchange budget (in the 1977 Decree).

Although other measures were also taken by the state to restructure the local motor industry in these countries in the seventies the main thrust of policy was to renegotiate the form of insertion of the local industry into the global motor industry. Other government measures were either likely to have a minimal effect because they attacked the symptoms and not the causes of the industry's problems or were themselves linked to the promotion of exports and became subordinated to that end.

Both the Ley de la Reconversión de la Industria Automotriz of 1971 in Argentina and the 1972 and 1977 automotive Decrees in Mexico attempted to rationalize the industry in various ways. However, since they were not prepared to countenance the closure of existing firms, such measures were limited in scope. In Argentina the entry of new firms was prohibited while in the case of Mexico firms producing popular models were not permitted to produce other types of cars and the US firms were excluded from the popular car sector. Neither measure of course did anything to improve the existing situation. Measures to improve the situation focused on reducing the number of models produced. However, these measures were so permissive as to have little real effect on the situation.

In Mexico particularly, many other measures were subordinated to the goal of increasing exports. Thus firms could produce more than one basic engine provided that 60 per cent of the output was exported and terminals were permitted to produce parts and components (normally reserved for the parts industry) provided that these met export requirements. Exports were also exempted from the minimum local content required for production for the domestic market.

In Brazil after the 1973 oil price rises the government took a number of steps to restrain the growth of the industry. These included sharp increases in the price of petrol, tighter control on credit and in 1979 increased taxation. The traditional investment incentives available to the car industry, apart from those related to an export commitment, were all withdrawn in 1974. As Mericle (1984, p. 28), notes 'The message to the automobile producers was clear; any major future expansion was contingent on a commitment to export'.

In addition to promoting exports, however, the Brazilian state attempted to restructure the industry in two further ways to meet the external sector crisis. One was to give greater emphasis to commercial vehicle production as opposed to passenger cars. The other was to attempt to force the companies to develop and produce in growing proportions, alcohol-fuelled vehicles. The first involved reorienting the system of fiscal incentives towards the production of commercial vehicles, and, as was mentioned above, withdrawing incentives, other than those related to an export commitment, for the car industry. The alcohol programme was designed to enable the country to continue to rely heavily on private road transport while reducing the import cost by substituting alcohol (ethanol) produced from locally available biomass for imported petroleum.

The Comisión Nacional del Alcohol was set up in 1975 to coordinate the alcohol programme which would increase production of alcohol to over 2.5 billion litres per annum by 1983. This would be used in two ways: mixed with petrol in the proportion 1 to 4 to produce 'gasohol' which could be used to fuel conventional petrol engines with minimal conversion, and to fuel specially modified cars which would run on 100 per cent alcohol. Following the second oil price 'shock' of 1979 the programme was expanded with a target of 10.5 billion litres in 1985. The state provided finance for an extensive programme of distillery construction to be undertaken by the private sector. It also obtained an agreement from the motor manufacturers to produce an increasing number of alcohol-powered cars, production of which began in 1977. Thus by a combination of incentives to alcohol producers and pressures on the auto TNCs, the state hoped to bring about a major change in the pattern of energy consumption in road transport.

3 LIBERALIZATION – CHILE AND ARGENTINA

As was seen above the import substituting policies pursued by most Latin American countries in the sixties, whether for the development of full scale manufacturing or only assembly of vehicles with some incorporation of local parts, involved high levels of tariff protection and often virtually a complete ban on imports of built-up vehicles, at the same time as local content requirements were progressively increased. Two countries which followed this type of policy in the sixties and early seventies, Chile and Argentina, totally reversed these policies in the mid-seventies. These policy reversals followed military coups in both countries which brought to power authoritarian regimes committed to liberal economic policies.

The most radical liberalization policy has been pursued by the Pinochet regime which has virtually dismantled the Chilean motor industry. Following the military take-over in 1973, the bidding which had taken place previously was declared null and void and a debate began over whether vehicles should be produced in Chile or imported.

In 1975, Chile opened up the industry to tender from the TNCs once more. This differed from the previous tender in that firms set up would have to be foreign subsidiaries (whereas earlier they were to be majority government owned joint ventures). No limitations were set on the number and range of models produced and the required level of local content was much reduced. New legislation reduced the local content requirement to 35 per cent for cars and 30 per cent for trucks, half their level in the early 1970s. Local content would be increased slightly to 50 per cent for cars and 40 per cent for trucks by 1979. Import duties were set initially at 115 per cent for cars and 80 per cent for trucks but would be gradually reduced to 55 per cent for both categories by 1983. Tariffs on imports of parts ranged from 10 per cent to 35 per cent. Three firms, Peugeot-Renault, Fiat and GM were selected to produce in Chile while the state-owned CORFO-Citroen company was subsequently also allowed to continue production. Early in 1976 Chile opened the national market to imports of new vehicles. In 1977 the government announced that there would be a 10 per cent uniform tariff on all imports, with the exception of motor vehicles over 850 cc, by mid-1979. Application of the 10 per cent tariff for the motor vehicle industry was delayed until 1986.

The aim of the strategy, which has to a significant degree already been achieved as will be seen below, is to subject the local motor industry to rigorous international competition. In accordance with the precepts of comparative advantage, if the industry cannot survive in these conditions then Chile would be better off without it.

The policy pursued in Argentina is in some ways a less extreme form of that followed in Chile, reflecting the more qualified adoption of liberal economic policies by the post-1976 military regime and the greater development and economic significance of the motor vehicle industry in that country. In 1978 the Ley de la Reconversión de la Industria Automotriz was repealed freeing the industry from the restrictions that had been introduced in 1971 on the production of new parts and models, vertical integration and ownership by foreign capital.

As in Chile imports of CBUs were liberalized and local content requirements for locally produced vehicles reduced, although in both cases the policy was far less drastic. The ban on imports of vehicles was lifted and a programme for reducing import duties from 95 per cent to 55 per cent for cars and 65 per cent to 45 per cent for lorries within three years was announced. However, the duty on finished vehicles was based on a minimum price of US $3.50 per cubic centimetre of engine capacity for cars, and US $3.50 per kilogramme for commercial vehicles plus 15 per cent of the base price to cover transport costs. This was some way from the extremes of liberalization which characterized the Chilean policy, since the minimum price of an imported 1500 cc car in Argentina (including the import duty) would be over US $9000 on this basis. Even if the actual price charged was less than the base price for calculating the import duty, the importer would still have to pay over US $3000 in duty. In 1979, it was calculated that the effective rate of protection for domestic vehicle production was between 260 per cent and 340 per cent (Nofal, 1983, p. 355).

The reductions in local content were also less drastic than those applied in Chile. Between 1979 and 1982 the import content of vehicles was permitted to rise from 4 per cent to 12 per cent for cars and car derivatives and from 10 per cent to 25 per cent for commercial vehicles over 1500 kg. These applied to all vehicles in the category produced by a manufacturer and not on a model-by-model basis giving some scope for flexibility. Higher levels of imports were permitted when undertaken under bilateral agreements, provided that at least three times as much was exported as imported and that imports under such agreements did not constitute more than half the total parts imports permitted to the firm. The obligation to incorporate locally produced parts where available was also relaxed.

The liberalization policy in Argentina has therefore been much less extreme than that followed in Chile and is more of an intermediate case between full scale liberalization and an attempt to negotiate a reinsertion of Argentina in the world motor industry à la Brazil or Mexico. The reduction of tariffs on imports of CBU vehicles has not been so extreme that local producers are faced with ruinous international competition although as will be seen below, import penetration has increased markedly. Nor has the reduction in import content been so great that firms which wish to continue to produce locally can become mere assemblers. The greater permitted margin for imports and the provisions for bilateral agreements can indeed be seen as measures which permit those TNCs which continue to manufacture in Argentina a greater margin of flexibility in organizing regional and global component sourcing networks.

4   THE ANDEAN PACT AND THE EXTENSION OF IMPORT SUBSTITUTION

The Andean Pact countries have regarded the development of a regional motor industry programme as a high priority since 1971. In contrast to the strategies discussed in the previous two sections the approach adopted by the Andean Pact countries during the 1970s, both on a national and a regional basis, has been to deepen the process of import substitution. Furthermore, whereas the previously discussed strategies have attempted to restructure the motor industry in an indirect way, by changing the rules of the game in terms of the incentives and constraints applied to the industry while letting the market determine the outcome in terms of the new structure which emerges, the Andean Pact countries have used the state much more directly in an attempt to bring about a rationalization of the industry.

The problems of the motor industry discussed in Part I were particularly acute in the case of the Andean Pact countries. Levels of production were extremely low because of the small size of the internal market, and the problem was accentuated by the extreme fragmentation between a large number of firms and models in production. As a result the highest vehicle prices in Latin America were to be found amongst these countries. The level of local content was extremely low – less than 40 per cent in 1970 – in all countries (ECLA, 1973, table 23).[4] This meant that the industry had created few backward linkages locally and that there was virtually no local production of the more technologically sophisticated parts and components. It also meant that the industry imposed a considerable drain on the balance of payments in terms of imported parts and components.

The strategy of rationalization proposed by the Junta del Acuerdo de Cartagena for the Andean Pact motor industry had its antecedents at a national level amongst the member countries, particularly Peru and

Chile. The strategy of state imposed rationalization of the motor industry was first applied by the Peruvian military regime which overthrew Belaunde in 1968. The Peruvian motor industry at that time was composed of 13 terminal firms sharing a market of 10 000 vehicles produced with a local content of around 10 to 15 per cent (Fernandez-Baca, *et al.*, 1979, ch. 3). In other words the firms were simply assemblers buying a few simple parts from local suppliers and importing virtually complete CKD kits from abroad. In 1969 the government issued a decree the main features of which were an increase in local content to 70 per cent by 1973 and a reduction in the number of firms and models in the market. Bids to remain in the Peruvian market were received from ten firms of which four were selected to produce cars and one to produce trucks. Although the local content targets were reduced subsequently as were the high tariffs that had been imposed on CKD kits, the Peruvian policy set an important precedent as the first attempt to rationalize the motor industry in Latin America through deliberate government action taking advantage of the interest of a number of producers in remaining in the market, rather than hoping that competition in an oligopolistic industry would achieve the necessary reduction in the number of firms.

Two years later (in 1971) the Popular Unity government in Chile attempted a similar restructing of the local industry. The proposed restructuring was even more drastic than that attempted in Peru. The number of models produced locally was to be reduced to two cars and one commercial vehicle chassis and engine. The successful firms were required to enter a joint venture in which the Chilean state (through CORFO) would have a majority share-holding. Despite the restrictive terms imposed four firms participated in the bidding for each of the three categories of vehicles and the eventual winners were Citroen, Peugeot and Pegaso of Spain.[5] Again the policy adopted involved a concerted attempt to take advantage of inter-capitalist rivalries in order to develop a more effective industry structure.

Both these cases imply a substantial departure from the approach adopted in Brazil, Argentina and Mexico in the late fifties and early sixties when these countries' governments made the transition from local assembly to manufacture. They also represent a very different approach from that taken by previous Peruvian and Chilean governments. As was discussed above in Chapter 4, certain groups within the Mexican government did argue for a limit on the number of firms which would be allowed to operate in Mexico, but were defeated by the pressures which the auto TNCs were able to mobilize on their own behalf. Why then were the Peruvian and Chilean governments able to secure the compliance of a significant number of auto TNCs with this type of policy in the late sixties/early seventies? One crucial difference between the two situations is the nature of the regimes in power in these countries at the time. In Mexico in 1962 (as indeed in Brazil and Argentina in the late fifties) the regime was essentially developmentalist (*desarrollista*) in orientation, and the attraction of new foreign investment into manufacturing was a crucial aspect of its economic strategy. The fear of alienating foreign capital was therefore a potent restraint on the pursuit of a more restrictive policy in Mexico. Both the Velasco regime in Peru and the Allende government in Chile took a far more critical view of foreign capital and did not allocate it a central role in the model of economic development which it wished to implement. There were also other areas of the economy where these governments' policies were far more threatening to foreign capital than the motor industry, particularly in mining and petroleum extraction. Thus the policy pursued towards the motor industry was not the major consideration in defining foreign capital's view of the country. To stress the nature of the regime in power is not to neglect the general change in attitude that had taken place in Latin America towards foreign capital in the 1960s. A much more critical approach towards the benefits of direct foreign investment was now being taken by governments and academics (Vaitsos, 1973). In the case of the motor industry the pitfalls of the liberal strategies pursued in the larger Latin American countries were all too clear and the arguments that had been used to justify such policies totally bankrupt.

The motor industry programme was one of several sectoral programmes which were a keystone of the Andean Pact's policy of promoting industrialization for the regional market. The original Proposal 45 outlining the automotive programme was presented in 1974 and was subsequently changed five times before its final approval as Decision 120 in 1977. These changes were in part a result of the withdrawal of Chile from the Pact, but also arose because of prolonged negotiations over the terms of the proposal.

The basic feature of Proposal 45 and Decision 120 was the allocation of production of different categories and classes of vehicles and parts and components to the various member countries. Cars are divided into four size categories and commercial vehicles into six groups, with a further category for four-wheel drive vehicles. Plans are for the production of seven different car models, nine CV models and two four-wheel drive vehicles. These models will be distributed among the member countries as indicated in Table 10.1. In some cases, in order to reduce the transport costs incurred in shipping built-up vehicles, assembly agreements have been signed whereby cars or trucks assigned to one country can be assembled in another. Thus Bolivia and Colombia will assemble the A3 and A4 car categories produced by Venezuela; Colombia and Venezuela will assemble the B1.1 truck from Bolivia; Bolivia and Colombia will assemble the Peruvian B2.1 truck; Colombia and Ecuador will assemble the Venezuelan B.4 truck. In addition, there are a series of bilateral agreements for the joint production of certain models with each country making different components and sub-assemblies.

As well as allocating production among member countries, Decision 120 sets a common External Tariff for the industry to protect it from competition from outside the region. This varies from between 40 per cent and 65 per cent for parts and between 115 per cent and 155 per cent

TABLE 10.1   *Allocations and assembly agreements within the Andean Pact auto programme*

	Bolivia	*Colombia*	*Ecuador*	*Peru*	*Venezuela*
Cars					
A1 (< 1050 cc)		X			
A2 (1050–1500 cc)		X	X		
A3 (1500–2000 cc)	A	A		X(2)	X
A4 (> 2000 cc)	A	A			X(2)
Commercial vehicles					
B1.1 (< 3 m.t. GVW)	X	A			A
B1.2 (3–4.6 m.t. GVW)			X		C
B2.1 (4.6–6.2 m.t. GVW)	A	A		X	
B2.2 (6.2–9.3 m.t. GVW)	X				
B3 (9.3–17 m.t. GVW)	X	X	A	X	X
B4 (>17 m.t. GVW)		A	A	X	X
C(4-wheel drive)	A	X	A	C	X

KEY   X, allocation of 1 basic model; X(2), allocation of 2 basic models; A, assembly agreement; C, co-production agreement.
SOURCES   Junta de Cartagena; R. N. Gwynne, 'The Andean Group Automobile Programme: An Interim Assessment', *Bank of London and South America Review*, August 1980.

for vehicles. Unlike the import substitution strategies followed on a national level described above, the Andean Pact automotive programme does not set an explicit minimum level of local content for the vehicle industry, choosing instead the obligatory incorporation of certain components.[6] It has been estimated that the implicit local content achieved in this way would on average be 53 per cent of the value of the vehicle, but it would be possible for any country to increase integration above this level.[7] A further Decision (No. 131) provides for compensated foreign trade with countries outside the Andean Pact. This permits imports of parts from third countries on preferential terms provided that imports in any two years do not exceed exports over the same period.

The existence of a large number of assembly plants in the Andean region prior to the implementation of the automotive programme made it necessary to adopt a mechanism for the rationalization of the industry. This has been done by member countries calling tenders for each of the vehicle categories which they had been allocated, in order to select the firm prepared to offer the most favourable terms.

Despite considerable competition to remain in the Andean Pact motor industry, the results of the programme have been disappointing. While firms were anxious not to be excluded from the industry, and therefore competed vigorously in order to be selected to produce locally, they also had a common interest in maintaining a situation in which production in the Andean Pact countries was an extension of their international operations, providing an important market for CKD packs, and were by no means committed to the goals of the sectoral programme. This is reflected in the fact that while the bidding for model allocations was hotly contested, implementation of projects once allocated has been extremely slow. By 1983 the motor industry programme was grinding to a halt. This was explicitly recognized by the Junta del Acuerdo de Cartagena which proposed revisions of Decision 120 involving a more gradual development of the industry and the postponing of production of the more complex components requiring large-scale investment (Acuerdo de Cartagena, 1983, pp. 64–6).

There are a number of factors which account for the failure to implement the automotive programme. The developments in the international motor industry during the past decade have served to undermine the original conception. The industry has become much more technologically dynamic so that the long drawn out process of negotiation has run the risk of leaving the Andean Pact countries with obsolete models. The main thrust of the auto TNCs' strategy has been directed to international integration on a far wider scale than the regional market constituted by the Andean Pact. The motor industry programme was conceived before these international developments and changes in strategy were apparent and was largely based on the experience of the larger Latin American countries in the fifties and sixties. It was therefore not adjusted to the new global environment of the motor industry in the seventies and eighties.

While the creation of the Andean Pact may appear to have involved a strengthening of the member states' capacity in negotiation with the auto TNCs, in practice it has been a source of weakness and division as well. Thus Ford was able to persuade the Ecuadorian government to object to Venezuela granting the six-cylinder engine to GM because it was not sufficiently powerful to run Ecuador's B1.2 truck which was to be produced by Ford. Although in this instance Ecuador and Venezuela eventually got together to negotiate jointly with the companies, the potential for conflict between member countries is clearly a source of weakness.

In some cases member countries have chosen to disregard Decision 120 in pursuit of their own automotive policy. The requirements of basic models have been ignored and countries have permitted the assembly of models which have not been allocated to them. In other cases legislative norms which contradict those laid down in Decision 120 (for example, for the formula for measuring local content) have been adopted. Conflicts between member countries of course add to the conflicts which arise within countries between different groups which are often reflected within the state apparatus itself in conflicts between different branches and inconsistencies in policy.

When one looks at the policies pursued by individual Andean Pact countries in this period, the trend away from further import substitution towards more liberal policies and the promotion of exports is clear. In Venezuela the 1975 auto legislation proposed increasing local content from existing levels of 45 per cent for cars and light CVs and 23 per cent for heavy lorries and buses to 78 per cent by 1981 and 90 per cent by 1985 (Fontanals and Porta, 1979, p. 8). This would involve local production of the drive-train by 1981. It was also proposed to reduce the number of models in production from 59 to 11 by 1985 and existing producers were forbidden from manufacturing in new classes of vehicles. Imports were to be compensated for by exports by 1979 and exports would no longer be counted towards the fulfillment of local content requirements (Coronil and Skurski, 1982, p. 76). This policy was significantly altered in 1980 by the Social Christian government. The rate of increase of local content was reduced from 3 per cent a year to 1 per cent a year, and the maximum local content aimed at was reduced from 90 per cent to 75 per cent. A year later the policy was further changed, dropping the obligation of compensating imports with exports and permitting 30 per cent of the required local content to be met through parts exports (Coronil and Skurski, 1982, p. 87).

A similar trend can be observed in Colombia. The contract signed with Renault in 1969 required the construction of an engine plant in Colombia, representing a significant step forward in the integration of the Colombian motor industry. Local content in the car industry increased from an average of less than 25 per cent in 1970 (see Table 6.4) to between 35 per cent and 55 per cent by 1976 (Ronderos Tobon, 1981, table 5.7). New contracts signed with Fiat, GM and Renault in 1979–80 gave more emphasis to production for export. Both GM and Fiat undertook to export parts to cover 20 per cent of the value of their CKD imports, while Renault plans to export 120 000 gearboxes to American Motors in the United States and to France which will cover about half the cost of the Colombian subsidiary's imports of CKD packs. At the same time reductions in the tariff on cars to 150 per cent in 1979 has led to a sharp increase in imports of CBU vehicles in 1980.

Peru too, which abandoned its ambitious local integration plans of the early seventies, has followed the same path. In 1980 the Peruvian market was opened to imported vehicles and the earlier emphasis on import substitution reversed (Hermele, 1982a).

By the early 1980s the pattern of development of the motor industry in the Andean Pact countries seemed to be evolving in the direction taken by other Latin American countries. In other words the emphasis had moved away from a process of programmed integration on a regional basis towards an attempt to integrate more closely into the international motor industry as a supplier of certain parts and components and as a market for CKD kits and complete units. This is exactly the view taken by the auto TNCs themselves, Ford for instance arguing that the Andean Pact countries should for the moment only assemble vehicles and engines and compensate by exporting parts from the region, e.g. aluminium dies from Venezuela (Coronil And Skurski, 1982, p. 87).[8]

NOTES

1. See the various case studies in Baer and Samuelson (1977).
2. This was changed from 60 per cent of the direct cost of the vehicle to 50 per cent of the total value of parts which make up the vehicle.
3. See Lifschitz, 1979, p. 79 for the exact formula used.
4. Although the level of local content was apparently higher than this in Chile, this was merely because compensated (by exports) imports were regarded as local content. Parts produced within Chile accounted for around 40 per cent of the total value in the country of origin in the late sixties.
5. In 1973, shortly before the Popular Unity government was overthrown, a fourth company, Nissan, was added to the list.
6. Components and parts must have a local content of at least 70 per cent.
7. Venezuela set a local content level of 90 per cent to be achieved by 1985.
8. See also the advocacy of the 'Australian model' by John F. Beck, Vice-President of GM at a meeting of the Andean Pact in October 1980, where he criticized the Pact's plans for local integration. Quoted in Sotelo and Artega, 1981.

11 Changing Patterns in the Latin American Automobile Industry

1 LATIN AMERICA'S INTEGRATION INTO THE WORLD MOTOR INDUSTRY

The new trends in the internationalization of capital in the motor industry in the 1970s described in Chapter 9 and the new strategies pursued by different Latin American states in the same period have given rise to distinctive patterns of capital accumulation in the region in the past decade. This new phase in the development of the Latin American motor industry offers a number of contrasts with respect to the earlier period of import substitution in the industry discussed in Part I. The most significant change is that the industry in the region has become a much more integrated part of the world motor industry. In the late fifties and sixties the trend was for a weakening of the links between the motor industry in the Latin American countries and the rest of the world. This was particularly marked in those countries in which manufacturing operations were established in this period, but it was also true of the countries in which the terminal industry remained largely an assembly industry, because of the increased incorporation of certain locally produced parts and components in the assembled vehicles and the reduction in imports of CBU vehicles. As will be seen below, the exact form taken by the reintegration of the Latin American motor industries into the world industry differs from country to country, but the general trend is the same throughout the region.

The new pattern of accumulation in the Latin American motor industry in the seventies is reflected in a number of significant changes. It has been associated with the concentration and centralization of capital at both the regional and the national level. In certain countries, particularly Brazil and Mexico, it has involved massive investments in new plants radically different in terms of the technology applied from those of the import substituting period. This in turn has implications for workers in the region because of the new types of labour processes involved, while the internationalization of capital itself also poses new problems and the need for new responses from labour in the region. It is not only labour but also other capitals which are affected by the new patterns of capital accumulation in the industry. This is particularly true of those sections of capital which are engaged in the parts industry. In this chapter therefore we shall first of all document the growing integration of the Latin American motor industry with the world industry and then discuss some of the major consequences of this integration.

Both the policies of export promotion and liberalization discussed in the last chapter have as an explicit goal a greater degree of integration into the world industry. In the case of Brazil in the early seventies, the motor industry was to a large degree autarchic.[1] In order to improve the balance of payments situation of the industry the Brazilian government reduced local content requirements and pushed exports both of which implied a move away from autarchy. In the case of Mexico, there was a clear and explicit choice between moving towards greater autarchy through higher local content requirements and greater integration into the world industry through the promotion of exports. The latter avenue was chosen by the government in the seventies. Liberalization offers an alternative route to greater integration in the world industry. Here the primary effect is on the import side where both reduced content requirements and reduced tariffs on imports of CBU vehicles represent a reversal of the earlier trend towards autarchy.

A useful measure of the degree of integration of an industry into the world industry is the ratio of imports and exports to local production. In this case we have chosen to include imports and exports of vehicles and parts, partly because this is the form in which data is readily available (because as indicated earlier trade data does not include imports of capital goods and raw materials by industry of destination) and partly because both the extent to which an industry relies on imported inputs and the extent to which it faces competition from imports are relevant factors in analysing the degree to which it is integrated into the international industry.

The availability of more recent data led to the choice of the number of vehicles produced as the indicator for local production, rather than the value of production. Consequently it was necessary to deflate the value obtained by dividing imports plus exports by vehicle production to make the 1982 figure comparable with 1972. The deflator used was the purchasing power of the US dollar at producer prices. Table 11.1 shows that between 1972 and 1982 the ratio of imports plus exports to production increased substantially both in the countries which emphasized export promotion and those which pursued trade liberalization. Perhaps more surprisingly the same is also true of the Andean Pact countries which continued to pursue import substitution policies during this period.[2] Thus the entire Latin American motor industry became progressively more integrated into the world industry during the course of the 1970s.

The exact form of increased integration varied from country to country. In the case of Brazil, it was mainly as a supplier of vehicles and parts to international markets. Although imports also grew during this period, they did so at a much slower rate than exports. The same was also true of Argentina in the early seventies, but following the military coup in 1976 and the move towards liberalization, growth focused on the import side. In the case of Mexico, despite the more rapid growth of exports, the higher initial level of imports meant that both contributed in roughly equal proportions to the increased openness of the industry. In Chile and the Andean Pact countries exports remained low throughout the period and the major factor was the increasing level of imports.

2 PRODUCTION FOR GLOBAL MARKETS

Growth of exports

Even amongst the countries which have emphasized export promotion a more detailed analysis reveals considerable differences in the exact form of integration into the world industry. The most rapid growth of exports has been achieved by Brazil where exports rose from less than US $100 million in 1972 to almost US $2 billion in the early 1980s. Mexican exports also increased substantially to over US $500 million by 1982, but in Argentina exports never reached as much as US $200 million mark and declined from the late seventies with the change in government policy. The success of the Brazilian export drive has been primarily based on the growth of exports of vehicles in both CBU and CKD form, which accounted for 58 per cent of total auto exports between 1972 and 1982 (Table 11.2). Mexico on the other hand, has

TABLE 11.1   Openness of Latin American motor industry, 1972–82

	1972			1982			
	Vehicles produced (1)	Imports and exports (2) (m $)	(2) ÷ (1) (3) ($)	Vehicles produced (4)	Imports and exports (5) (m $)	(5) ÷ (4) (6) ($)	(6) in 1972 price* (7) ($)
Argentina	268 593	119.7	446	132 117	365.1	2 763	1 153
Brazil	609 470	176.8	290	859 295	1 834.5	2 135	891
Chile	26 228	90.6	3 454	29 259†	623.6†	21 313†	10 119†
Colombia	24 015	109.9	4 576	35 567	730.9	20 550	8 577
Mexico	229 848	330.8	1 439	472 637	1 878.5	3 975	1 659
Peru	23 796	59.4	2 496	21 977	412.5	18 769	7 833
Venezuela	88 674	290.9	3 281	155 108	1 573	10 141	4 232

* Deflated by the US purchasing power of the dollar in terms of producer prices.
† 1980.
Sources   UN, *Yearbook of International Trade Statistics*; and MUMA, *World Motor Vehicle Data*.

TABLE 11.2 Automotive exports from Argentina, Brazil and Mexico, 1972–82 (M $)

	Argentina			Brazil			Mexico		
	Vehicles	Parts	Total	Vehicles	Parts	Total	Vehicles	Parts	Total
1972	22.4	12.1	34.5	37.4	22.0	59.4	5.7	46.8	52.5
1973	73.8	23.8	97.6	41.0	29.3	70.3	40.4	80.2	120.6
1974	107.9	28.5	136.4	119.4	75.5	194.9	44.7	104.2	148.9
1975	99.2	22.1	121.3	227.5	156.6	384.1	8.7	113.3	122.0
1976	114.3	22.3	136.6	244.0	163.4	407.4	18.4	173.9	192.3
1977	118.3	37.0	155.3	275.1	302.7	577.8	30.0	223.5	253.5
1978	95.6	71.0	166.6	421.3	405.0	826.3	67.9	266.0	333.9
1979	68.4	83.8	152.2	527.3	466.2	993.5	116.8	260.0	376.8
1980	74.3	77.3	151.6	819.8	615.7	1435.5	128.6	275.8	404.4
1981	21.7	49.6	70.7	1227.0	706.7	1933.7	107.3	263.0	370.3
1982	54.4	39.5	93.9	886.9	615.3	1502.2	81.2	449.8	531.0
Total 1972–82	838.3	475.3	1317.2	4826.7	3558.4	8385.1	649.7	2256.5	2906.2
Per cent	63.6	36.4	100.0	57.6	42.4	100.0	22.4	77.6	100.0

SOURCES UN, *Yearbook of International Trade Statistics*; AMIA; Larriva and Vega, 1982, table 3.

been used by the TNCs primarily as a source for parts and components, particularly engines and gearboxes. Up to the mid-seventies a growing proportion of Argentinian exports of automotive products were vehicles, reflecting the requirements of the government's legislation. In the late seventies, however, parts exports accounted for a growing share of the industry's exports.

These different patterns are also reflected in the evolution of the number of vehicles exported in the three countries. In Brazil both the number of vehicles exported and the share of total production going to external markets has increased considerably, so that by 1981 (admittedly a year in which the domestic market was extremely depressed) more than 200 000 vehicles were exported, representing over a quarter of all those produced locally (Table 11.3). In Mexico in contrast the pattern of vehicle exports has been highly erratic, reaching a peak in terms of the proportion of output in 1973 and 1983 and in absolute terms in 1978. This is largely a reflection of the behaviour of Volkswagen, consistently the largest exporter of vehicles from Mexico. The peak in the early seventies came when Mexico was allocated production of the Safari model for world markets, and this model was enjoying some success in the United States before being excluded for failing to comply with US safety regulations. In the late seventies exports of the 'Beetle',

TABLE 11.3   *Number of vehicles exported. Argentina, Brazil, Mexico, 1972–83*

	Argentina		Brazil		Mexico	
	Exports no.	*Share of production (%)*	*Exports no.*	*Share of production (%)*	*Exports no.*	*Share of production (%)*
1972	3 493	1.3	13 528	2.2	2 212	1.0
1973	11 214	3.8	24 506	3.3	20 141	7.0
1974	15 443	5.4	64 678	7.1	19 117	5.4
1975	13 741	5.7	72 935	7.8	2 938	0.9
1976	13 442	6.5	80 407	8.1	4 172	1.3
1977	8 013	3.4	70 026	7.6	11 743	4.2
1978	3 988	0.2	96 172	9.0	25 828	6.7
1979	2 262	0.9	105 648	9.4	24 756	5.5
1980	3 607	1.3	157 085	13.5	18 245	3.7
1981	285	0.2	213 266	27.3	14 428	2.4
1982	3 234	2.4	173 254	20.0	15 819	3.3
1983	5 202	3.2	168 700	18.8	22 426	7.9

SOURCES   ADEFA; ANFAVEA, AMIA.

particularly to West Germany, increased considerably when production of this model was terminated in Europe. In Argentina exports of
vehicles increased in the early seventies, only to decline again from the
mid-seventies with the change in government policy.

The differences between the forms of integration of Brazil and
Mexico into the international motor industry reflect not only different
national conditions but also the strategies of different groups of foreign
capital. Generally speaking US capital with its wide network of foreign
subsidiaries in Latin America and elsewhere and the geographical
proximity of its home market has tended to export parts and components for incorporation in vehicles built elsewhere. European and
Japanese capital on the other hand, have tended to stress exports of
finished vehicles both through the allocation of particular models to
their Latin American susidiaries and through a geographical division of
markets. However, the internationalization of capital and the growing
homogenization that this brings with it is already tending to undermine
these differences. The fact that all the non-US firms operating in
Mexico now have substantial investments in the US (VW and Nissan
through direct investment and Renault through its link with American
Motors) means that they are also in a position to use Mexico as a base
for sourcing parts and components for their US plants in the same way
as the US firms. This is reflected in the new plants built in Mexico by
VW, Renault and Nissan with exports of parts (particularly engines) to
the United States specifically in mind.

While the form of export expansion which characterizes the Mexican
motor industry is likely to be increasing integration with the US motor
industry along the pattern which has occurred in Canada since the mid-
sixties, the Brazilian pattern has been described more generally as one
of 'sub-imperialism' whereby the country becomes an export base for
foreign capital with markets in less developed Third World countries.
The most clear example of this type of strategy in Brazil is that of VW
which exports not only to other Latin American countries, but also to
North Africa and the Middle East and to sub-Saharan Africa (Guimaraes, 1981, p. 54).

A crucial question that must how be considered is whether the
growth of exports from Latin America reflect the achievement of
international competitiveness by the industry in the 1970s. In other
words have price and cost conditions changed significantly in Brazil,
Mexico and Argentina compared with the situation which prevailed in
1970 (see above Chapter 6). A number of indicators suggest that, taken
as a whole, the motor industry in these countries has not become

significantly more competitive in this period. Direct comparisons of local prices with international levels in the early 1980s indicate that these are still much higher in Argentina and Mexico. In Argentina these reached 4 to 5.5 times international levels in 1980 and even with a more favourable exchange rate in subsequent years, they were still probably double international levels (Nofal, 1983, p. 144). In Mexico prices of vehicles and parts were between 30 per cent and 100 per cent above international levels (Islas, 1983, p. 993).

The evolution of productivity in the Latin American motor industry since the early seventies also suggests that there has been no major gain in international competitiveness either. Particularly in Brazil and Mexico where productivity increased rapidly in the sixties and early seventies, the crude index of productivity (vehicles produced per person employed in the terminal industry) stagnated in the mid- and late-seventies (see Table 11.4). The only exception was in Argentina where there was a sharp increase in productivity in 1979 and 1980. The significance of this increase is, however, questionable since it coincided with a sharp rise in production from very low levels in the mid-seventies and the moves to liberalize the industry which led to greater reliance on imported parts.

Although the existing production facilities in Latin America may not be internationally competitive because of the continued existence of the problems analysed in Chapter 6, some Latin American countries might nevertheless prove to be attractive locations for purpose built new plants. In other words, although lower labour productivity in the

TABLE 11.4   *Index of labour productivity in Argentina, Brazil and Mexico*

	Argentina	Brazil	Mexico
1974	100.0	100.0	100.0
1975	88.2	102.4	106.0
1976	77.6	101.4	95.7
1977	96.8	94.0	87.5
1978	93.6	102.3	106.3
1979	123.2	101.3	107.0
1980	145.3	100.6	102.2
1981	123.9	81.7*	104.6
1982	14.8	n.a.	90.8
1983	137.6	102.1	78.7

* Estimate
SOURCES   ADEFA; ANFAVEA; AMIA.

industry as a whole might offset the advantage of lower wages, new export-oriented plants might be built which can approach international productivity levels and thus enjoy a considerable labour cost advantage.

Recent estimates on this basis suggest that labour productivity in Mexico and Brazil is 15 per cent to 20 per cent lower than in the United States, and 40 per cent to 45 per cent lower than in Japan (Table 11.5a). This gives the two Latin American countries substantially lower labour costs than in the United States and marginally lower costs than Japan. When transport costs are taken into account this makes Mexico and to a lesser extent Brazil low cost areas for US TNCs to source certain parts and components (engines, transmissions and starter motors) (see Table 11.5b).

The problem with this analysis is that is focuses on only one aspect of cost, namely labour costs and does not take into account possible differences in other costs. However, it is not unlikely that non-labour costs may be higher in Mexico and Brazil than in the United States or

TABLE 11.5 *Comparative costs in USA, Japan, Mexico and Brazil (1982)*

(a) Labour rates, productivity and labour cost

	Labour rate ($ per hour)	Productivity ratio	Relative labour cost
USA	19.37	1.00	1.00
Japan	7.24	1.40	0.27
Mexico	3.53	0.85	0.22
Brazil	3.66	0.80	0.24

(b) *Cost savings in production of selected components compared with US production ($ per unit)*

	Engines			Transmission			Starter motor		
	Labour cost*	Shipping cost	Net saving†	Labour cost*	Shipping cost	Net saving†	Labour cost*	Shipping cost	Net saving†
USA	96.0	—	—	59.0	—	—	3.26	—	—
Japan	26.0	44.0	26.0	16.0	21.0	22.0	0.88	1.65	0.73
Mexico	21.0	22.0	53.0	13.0	8.0	38.0	0.72	0.97	1.57
Brazil	23.0	48.0	25.0	14.0	23.0	22.0	0.78	1.87	0.61

* Calculated by applying the relative labour cost figure from Table 11.5(a)
† Calculated as US labour cost minus local labour cost minus shipping cost.

SOURCE EIU (1983a), tables 31, 32, 33, 34, 35 and 36.

Japan. In Europe, for instance, it was found that although labour costs in Spain were considerably lower than in other parts of Europe this was offset by higher material costs (Cohen, 1982a). When these factors are taken into account it is by no means clear that Mexico and Brazil enjoy significantly lower production costs than the United States. This is borne out by Table 11.6 which compares the total cost of importing an engine from Mexico with the cost of producing in the United States and shows only a very marginal gain from outsourcing, when fiscal benefits are not considered. Indeed, it has been argued that without such incentives it would have made little sense for 'Ford management to accept the risks of longer supply lines, less assured Mexican government policies, and the inevitable criticism from US politicians and union leaders' (William Johnston quoted in Cohen, 1982b, p. 4).

TABLE 11.6 *Cost of Ford engine, US versus Mexico*

	US	Ex-benefits	Mexico With benefits†
Landed cost (CIF	$1235	$1221	$821
Detroit)*	$1062	$1078	$738
Petrol	$1556	$1487	$975
Diesel			
Additional annual profit (cf. US)	—	$25 m	$220 m

* Weighted average of 65 per cent petrol and 35 per cent diesel.
† Mexican export incentives include rights to increase imports into Mexico (which increase Ford earnings by $0.37 per dollar), and tax reductions equal to 8 per cent of export volume.
SOURCE Cohen, 1982a, table 1.

In fact of course in all three Latin American countries which have stressed export promotion, the auto TNCs have received substantial subsidies. In Brazil export incentives to the motor industry were equivalent to two-thirds of the value of exports in 1975, twice the level for other products which benefited from such incentives (de Oliveira *et al.*, 1979, table 53). The total cost of these incentives in terms of government revenue foregone came to almost US $200 million in that year. Even higher levels of incentives were found in Argentina in the seventies with one estimate putting the cost of promoting passenger car exports at 80 cents for each dollar exported. Had export targets for the period up to 1978 been met, the total cost to the exchequer would have been of the order of US $1000 million (Nofal, 1983, p. 110). Although direct incentives to exports were at a more modest level in Mexico with the main incentive for much of the 1970s (the CEDIs) running at 11 per cent of the value of exports, the benefits from increased quotas in the domestic market were considerable. As indicated in Table 11.6 it is estimated that the right to increase imports is worth US $0.37 in additional earnings, for each dollar exported. Thus the total incentive effect here is equivalent to almost half the value of exports, not far short of those found in Brazil and Argentina. The high cost of these export promotion programmes must of course be met either by increased taxation, reduced government expenditure in other areas or an increase in the government deficit.

Balance of payments effects[3]

Although the strategy of increasing integration with the world industry has led to notable increases in exports, particularly in Brazil and Mexico, it does not necessarily follow that they have been so successful in terms of the objective of improving the balance of payments. As was seen in Chapter 10, an integral part of the strategy of production for global markets was a reduction in local content requirements and greater freedom for the auto TNCs to import in order to optimize their global production. In all three countries therefore it is not surprising to find that motor industry imports increased substantially in the 1970s.

Table 11.7 shows three very different patterns in the three countries which have pursued this strategy. In Brazil the industry's deficit has been turned into a large trade surplus. This was so large by the late seventies and early eighties that even if imports not included here (such as machinery and steel) and profit remittances, technology payments etc. had been included the motor industry would still have been in surplus. Thus within less than a decade, the Brazilian motor industry has turned from being a drain on foreign exchange earnings to a net contributor.[4]

In Argentina the table shows the motor industry having a small surplus in the mid-seventies when the government pursued its policy of export expansion. However, it is doubtful whether the sector as a whole did show a surplus if other imports not shown here were included. For the period 1971–5 it has been estimated that the Argentinian motor industry had a total trade deficit of US $237.4 million to which should

TABLE 11.7   *Trade balance of the motor industry. Argentina, Brazil,*
Mexico, 1972–82 (M $)

	Argentina	Brazil	Mexico
1972	− 50.7	− 58.0	− 225.7
1973	6.9	− 61.1	− 231.3
1974	23.2	− 45.8	− 356.1
1975	11.9	111.5	− 628.3
1976	23.3	90.1	− 526.4
1977	− 16.9	287.4	− 385.4
1978	0.2	538.4	− 559.1
1979	− 187.8	693.9	1 049.5
1980	− 678.1	1 064.6	− 1 498.8
1981	− 708.6	1 521.3	− 2 148.3
1982	− 160.1	1 169.9	− 816.5

SOURCES   UN *Yearbook of International Trade Statistics*; AMIA; Larriva and
Vega, 1982, table 1.

be added a further US $55.5 million in royalty payments (Sourrouille,
1980, table 31). Since this covers the period in which most of the growth
in exports took place and predates the expansion of imports in the late
seventies it seems that despite intense promotional efforts the Argentinian motor industry never became a net earner of foreign exchange.

Finally in Mexico despite a more successful export drive than in
Argentina, this has not succeeded in reducing the trade deficit which
grew from less than US $250 million in 1972 and 1973 to over US $2
billion by 1981. The growth in the deficit has only been interrupted in
1976, 1977 and 1982, when the domestic market contracted and there
was a consequent fall in imports. Otherwise imports have tended to rise
as local production grew reflecting the continuing high import content
of locally produced vehicles. Indeed, since 1976 the rate of growth of
imports has exceeded the growth of exports further contributing to the
sector's deficit. By the early 1980s the motor industry accounted for
half of Mexico's total trade deficit, compared with just over one-fifth in
1970 (Larriva and Vega, 1982, table 5).

New labour processes and implications for labour

The initial expansion of automotive exports from Latin America was
based on the utilization of existing excess capacity. As exports

expanded during the seventies, however, a new strategy of building capacity with the export market as the main outlet for production came to be adopted, particularly in Mexico and Brazil. Whereas the plants set up during the import substitution phase of the industry's development, and those assembly plants which dated from an even earlier period, were characterized by low scales of production, less mechanized production techniques and often used second-hand machinery, the new generation of export-oriented plants were radically different in nature.

First, since they were constructed with a view to producing for the world market from the outset they were not constrained by the limited size of the domestic market. It was thus possible to take advantage of economies of scale and construct plant at or above the minimum efficient scale. The most clear examples are the new engine plants which have been built in Mexico and Brazil with capacity of between 250 000 and 500 000 engines a year (Table 11.8). This compares favourably with most estimates of the scale of plant necessary to take advantage of scale economies (cf. Table 5.1).

Secondly these plants are equipped with modern technology and new machinery. The General Motors engine plant in Ramos Arizpe (Mexico) uses automatic transfer machines, and is comparable in terms of its technological level to equivalent plants in the United States (the neighbouring assembly plant, which will produce primarily for the domestic market is more labour-intensive, however, and robots have not been installed) (Davila Flores, 1982). Labour productivity in the new General Motors and Chrysler engine plants in Ramos Arizpe is three times as high as the average productivity in previously existing engine plants in Mexico (Davila Flores, 1982, p. 47). The Nissan aluminium foundry at Aguascalientes (Mexico) also employs the latest technology with the incorporation of advanced low pressure casting methods. Similarly in Brazil a newly built assembly plant of one of the US TNCs was virtually identical to the same company's UK plant in terms of its technological level, although the body-shop was more labour intensive in Brazil (Humphrey, 1984). Even in Argentina, where the TNCs have not built new export oriented plants, there has been a partial modernization by the firms most committed to Argentinian production and in some cases the most advanced equipment has been installed (Nofal, 1983, pp. 178–84).

The rationale for this is clear. In order to be internationally competitive and acceptable in the United States or other markets in which these parts and components might be used, they must conform with the standards of quality control and productivity obtained in the plants set

TABLE 11.8   *New investments in Mexico and Brazil by major TNCs*

Company	Location	Product	Capacity	Investment	Employment
Ford	Chihuahua, Mexico	4-cyl. engine	500 000	$445 m	—
Ford	Hermosillo, Mexico	Assembly	130 000	$500 m	—
Ford	Saltillo, Mexico	Aluminium cylinder heads	860 000	—	—
General Motors	Ramos Arizpe, Mexico	V-6 engine	400 000 ⎫ $300 m		6000
General Motors	Ramos Arizpe, Mexico	Assembly	100 000 ⎭		2500
Chrysler	Ramos Arizpe, Mexico	4-cyl. engine	270 000 rising to 400 000	$125 m	800 rising to 1300
Volkswagen	Puebla, Mexico	4-cyl. engine	400 000	$250 m	1600
Nissan	Aguascalientes, Mexico	4-cyl. engines and stampings	350 000 engines	$150 m	1500
Renault	Gomez Palacio, Mexico	4-cyl. engine	200–250 000	$100 m	—
Renault	Gomez Palacio	Suspensions	300–340 000	—	—
Ford	Brazil	Assembly	200 000	$300–$400m	—
Ford	Brazil	4-cyl. engine	255 000	$200 m	—
General Motors	Brazil*	Multi-fuel engines	330 000	$500 m	—

* Conversion of existing diesel engine plant.

SOURCES   AMIA; Mericle (1984); Maxcy (1981); *Motor Business*; EIU (1983); *Comercio Exterior*, March 1983.

up in the advanced capitalist countries. The best way of ensuring this is to construct essentially similar plants irrespective of local conditions. As a result the plants themselves are highly capital intensive and create limited additional employment. The new VW engine plant in Mexico involved an investment of around US $250 million and generated 1600 new jobs at a cost of over US $150 000 each. The cost per person employed at the new Chrysler plant in Mexico appears to be roughly similar (Table 11.8).

The advance in the internationalization of capital represented by the construction of new export-oriented plants in Brazil and Mexico and the emergence of these two countries as suppliers of vehicles and parts to the world industry poses a direct challenge to labour in the industry. The internationalization of labour in the form of international labour solidarity has historically tended to lag behind the internationalization of capital. Unless international links are built up between workers in different countries then capital is able to take advantage of its international extension and mobility in order to divide the working class. Such divisions serve to weaken labour and reinforce the domination of capital.

It did not take long for workers in Europe to recognize the implications of the European-wide coordination of production pioneered by Ford in the sixties. The result was a growing cooperation between workers in different countries and international support for strikes in the form of refusal to increase production in other countries and so forth. The widening of the scale of international integration from the regional to the world level poses new challenges for labour. These arise from the greater geographical distances to be bridged, the greater divergences in wages and working conditions and the very different historical experiences of the working class in different parts of the world.

Although there are a number of isolated examples of international solidarity with auto workers in Latin America these links are still weak (Wurtele, 1977). Despite some contacts being established in the phase when manufacturing plants were constructed in the region, the seventies saw changes which tended to weaken such links. As Wurtele notes 'Today international trade union policies are largely carried out apart from the membership'. Attempts to develop links at the shop-floor level, such as the International Auto Workers' Consultations sponsored by Transnational Information Exchange have tended to be European based although the second consultation held in 1983 did include representatives from Brazil and Malaysia for the first time.

The difficulties of creating international solidarity among auto workers are not simply the result of organizational problems such as distance or language. The new forms of integration in the world motor industry creates certain antagonisms between workers of different countries. In the early phase of the development of the Latin American motor industry, this was not a problem. Since access to the local market required local assembly or production, and the local subsidiary continued to depend on the import of some parts and components, there was no direct competition for jobs between workers in different countries. With the promotion of exports, expansion in Latin America represents a direct threat to the jobs of workers in the country of origin, either because Latin American parts and components will now be used in the vehicles which they assemble, or because export markets will be served from Brazil or Mexico rather than from the home country. The plans of the US manufacturers to import large quantities of engines from Mexico and Brazil aggravates the decline in employment in the industry in the United States. Volvo, in order to meet its export commitments from Brazil, has begun to supply Saudi Arabia from Brazil instead of from Sweden as was formerly the case (Hermele, 1982a). These objective difficulties in no way alter the need for labour to build international links in order to prevent capital taking advantage of its greater international mobility. Moreover, in so far as plants are being built to increasingly similar specifications in different parts of the world, and production techniques are being homogenized, the dissimilarities in the conditions of different national groups of workers are partly attenuated, and this in turn could provide a basis for closer cooperation.

The new type of export-oriented plants being constructed in Latin America are changing the nature of the labour force in the motor industry. The plants of the import-substitution phase, because of their outmoded production methods and the advanced age of much of the machinery and equipment, relied heavily on the knowledge of the workers. As one Mercedes-Benz worker in Argentina commented noting the age of the firm's machinery 'It all comes from Germany. In Argentina it must have 20 to 25 years and a bit more from Germany. Its all from the war. Its only because of the skill of the Argentine worker that they don't all fall to pieces' (Evans *et al.*, 1979). The highly automated production processes of the new plants and the use of new machinery and equipment reduces the need to rely on the individual capacity of the worker and changes the nature of the labour force employed.[5] Thus the element of control which the worker was able to exercise over his labour process in the traditional plants is increasingly removed with the introduction of advanced technology associated with production for world markets.

The new plants also tend to be built away from the previous centres of auto production where working class organization has achieved a certain degree of strength. In Brazil, Volvo built its plant in the mid-seventies in Curitiba, state of Parana, and not in the Sao Paulo area because it believed that workers and trade unions were more orderly and disciplined there (Hermele, 1982a). In Argentina, Saab Scania, the company which is most clearly oriented towards the international integration of its local vehicle production and component exports, built its plant in Tucuman in 1975 away from the two existing centres of auto production, Buenos Aires and Cordoba (Nofal, 1983, pp. 208–9, 323). Similarly Nissan in Mexico has expanded by building new plants in Lerma, state of Mexico and Aguascalientes, rather than expand at its existing location in Cuernavaca which has a history of labour militancy (Quiroz, 1981), while GM, Chrysler and Ford have built plants in the north of Mexico. In the latter case proximity to the US market is of course an important consideration, but this does not negate the importance of control over labour as a factor. In 1980 a major industrial dispute broke out at GM de Mexico over the firm's decision to grant union recognition in the new plant at Ramos Arizpe, Coahuila, to the CTM. This was contested by the GM union in Mexico City which claimed the right to the collective contract at the new plant. This was denied by the GM management and the union was eventually defeated.

The advantage to GM of having a weak, compliant union in its new plants in Northern Mexico is clear from a comparison of the collective contracts for the Mexico City and Ramos Arizpe plants. Wage rates in Ramos Arizpe are between 50 and 60 per cent of comparable rates in Mexico City, the working week is 7 or 8 hours longer there, and there are fewer paid holiday days. Moreover, whereas the union in Mexico City has imposed agreements on the company whereby workers automatically acquire permanent status after working 18 months in the plant, and requiring the company to inform the union in advance of any planned changes in the speed of the line, there are no such clauses at Ramos Arizpe (Davila Flores, 1982).

Thus the new pattern of accumulation in the Brazilian and Mexican motor industry poses a number of threats to the working class. It makes them more subject to competition from workers in other countries. Because of the nature of the new technology being introduced it reduces their control over the labour process, without any neo-Fordist concessions of the type which have been granted to workers in the European motor industry.[6] Finally by decentralizing production within the country, away from existing centres of auto production it enables the TNCs to incorporate less militant workers and divide their local labour forces internally as well as internationally.

Labour in the motor industry has been directly affected by the international crisis. In 1983 employment by the terminal firms in both Brazil and Mexico was virtually at the same level as it had been in 1974. Between 1980 and 1983 employment in Brazil had fallen by over 30 000, while in Mexico almost as many jobs had been lost in two years up to 1983 (*Motor Business*, 1984 p. 60; Micheli, 1984, p. 114). Thus closer integration with the world motor industry has done nothing to reduce the vulnerability of auto workers to the depredations of recession.

Terminal-suppliers relations

It was seen in Chapter 7 that the terminals in the motor industry complex enjoy a dominant position which enables them to appropriate surplus value from their suppliers. What changes are likely to be brought about in these relationships as a result of the changing patterns of capital accumulation which have characterized certain Latin American countries in the seventies and eighties?

Given the control which the terminals have over the market for vehicles and parts, particularly original equipment but also spare parts, (as was seen in Chapter 7), in the world's major vehicle markets, they are likely to be the crucial factor in the expansion of Latin American auto exports. This is in fact explicitly recognized in the regulations which require TNCs to export from Latin America, which have put pressure specifically on the terminal firms. However, this does not mean that they will necessarily be the firms which produce the exports in the first place. Two strategies are possible. One is for the terminals to produce parts for export to the parent company or other affiliate 'in plant' in Latin America as in the case of the engine exports from Brazil and Mexico. The other is for the terminal to provide access to its international network to a supplying firm, through the local subsidiary, as is the case with exports of transmissions by Tremec from Mexico. The choice of strategy will depend partly on the exact requirements imposed by the host government. In the Mexican case, for instance, 50 per cent of exports by the terminals must be of parts produced by local suppliers.

Their control over foreign markets can give the terminals an additional source of leverage over their suppliers. What is now at stake for a supplier when it negotiates with a terminal is not only access to the local original equipment market and that part of the domestic replacement market controlled by the terminals and their dealers, but also access to foreign markets. The decision to promote exports of parts and components may also further deepen the heterogeneity of the parts industry. It is the larger parts firms often linked to foreign capital themselves which are in the best position to supply the terminals. In the mid-seventies in Mexico ten companies were responsible for over 80 per cent of exports by the parts industry. Most of these companies were linked to foreign capital, although Mexican legislation requires majority local shareholdings in the parts industry (Bennett and Sharpe, 1979). A similar situation existed in Argentina where 6.8 per cent of parts firms accounted for 75 per cent of parts exports and these tended to operate in those sectors of the parts industry with the highest penetration by foreign capital (Nofal, 1983, p. 297).

The other factor that tends to affect the relationship between the terminals and suppliers is the policy of relaxing local content requirements which has accompanied both the export promotion strategy and the liberalization strategy. Increasing the margin permitted for imports and also removing the obligation of the terminals to incorporate locally produced parts where these are available, removes an important part of the protection received by the parts industry. With the changes in government regulations in the seventies, the threat by the terminals to import a particular part or component if a supplier does not offer it on acceptable terms becomes much more credible. This is another card in favour of the terminals in any negotiation, enabling it to pass on the costs of the new pattern of capital accumulation to the parts industry.

In fact there is some evidence that the terminals have reduced their reliance on the local parts industry in the late seventies. In Argentina the ratio of local purchases to the value of output fell from a peak of 65.2 per cent in 1974 to 47.6 per cent in 1978 even before the new liberalization measures were introduced (Nofal, 1983, table V.4). In Mexico there was a fall from 58.8 per cent to 44.9 per cent between 1974 and 1980 (AMIA). This seems to confirm the above analysis whereby the terminals are becoming less dependent on local suppliers which will improve their bargaining power with them.

3   LIBERALIZATION

As was seen in the last chapter, both Chile and Argentina embarked on the liberalization of their motor industries in the seventies. More recently, in 1980, Colombia and Peru have also taken steps to liberalize their domestic industries through permitting imports of CBU vehicles on less restrictive terms than in the 1970s. The most striking consequence of such liberalization measures have invariably been a sharp increase in the level of imports. As was seen in Chapter 10 the liberalization policies of the Chilean and Argentinian governments involved both a relaxation in local content requirements and reduced tariffs on CBU imports. As Table 11.9 indicates this led to an increase in imports of parts and vehicles between 1972 and the early 1980s. In the case of Argentina where the liberalization began in 1979, imports of parts per vehicle produced more than doubled by 1982 and imports of vehicles increased more than fivefold. In Chile the value of parts imports per vehicle produced locally had increased by almost 50 per cent between 1972 and 1980, reflecting the considerable decrease in local content requirements. There was an even larger increase in the value of vehicle imports which went up almost four times between 1972 and 1980.

TABLE 11.9   *Growth of motor industry imports, Argentina and Chile*

	Argentina			Chile		
	Imports of parts ($m)	*Imports of parts per vehicle produced ($)*	*Imports of vehicles ($m)*	*Imports of parts ($m)*	*Imports of parts per vehicle produced ($)*	*Imports of vehicles ($m)*
1972	80.9	301	4.3	26.2	997	61.8
1982						
(current prices)[1]	199.7	1512	54.3	88.5*	3025*	490.1*
(1972 prices)†	86.9	658	23.6	42.0*	1436*	232.7*

* 1980.
† Deflated by purchasing power of US dollar in producer prices.
Source   UN, *Yearbook of International trade Statistics*, various issues.

Increased vehicle imports are reflected in the declining share of the domestic market held by locally produced vehicles. In Chile their share fell to about a quarter in the late seventies. In Argentina imports, which had never exceeded 500 vehicles a year between 1972 and 1978 shot up to 11 279 vehicles in 1979, 68 351 in 1980 and 60 126 in 1981 (ADEFA). These represented 4 per cent, 20 per cent and 25 per cent of the total domestic market in these three years. A similar trend has been apparent in Colombia and Peru in the 1980s. The decision of the Colombian government to reduce import duties on cars to a level of 150 per cent led to a sharp rise in the share of the domestic market accounted for by imports from 6 per cent in 1979 to 25 per cent in 1980. The unexpectedly large increase in imports led to a partial reversal of policy in 1981 when imports of CBU cars valued at less than US $5000 were banned (Ronderos Tobon, 1981) but imports still accounted for almost a quarter of the market in 1982. In January 1980 the Peruvian vehicle market was also opened up to imports. By 1981 imports accounted for 55 per cent of the Peruvian market.

Growing import penetration in Latin America has reflected the changing structure of the international motor industry. Local production of vehicles, except in Peru, has been controlled almost exclusively by US and European capital, reflecting the dominant position which they enjoyed internationally in the late fifties and early sixties when production began. In contrast Japanese capital has taken the lead in penetrating these markets through exports in the late seventies and early eighties. In Chile, Japanese imports have taken 40 per cent of the local market and account for over half of all vehicle imports (Gwynne, 1983), while in Argentina in 1980 and 1981, 65 000 vehicles were imported from Japan, again accounting for over half of all imports (ADEFA). In Colombia Japan accounted for over 70 per cent of all vehicle imports in 1982, while in Peru in 1981 they made up over 40 per cent of imports as well as accounting for half the sales of locally assembled vehicles (MVMA, *Automobile International*).

Although one conventional rationale for a liberalization strategy is to make local industry more competitive internationally, there is little evidence of this having taken place in either Chile or Argentina. In Chile two of the remaining four companies, Citroen and Fiat, closed down in the face of competition from imports, and it is expected that the two which remain will terminate production by 1986 (Gwynne, 1983). Thus if existing policies are adhered to the prospect is the complete disappearance of the local assembly industry in Chile.

In Argentina the prolonged crisis of the industry together with the liberalization measures taken by the military regime, has led to major changes in the structure of the industry without making its total disappearance seem likely. The withdrawal of General Motors and Citroen, the merger between Fiat cars and SAFRAR (Peugeot) to form SEVEL and the acquisition of Chrysler and the state-owned IME by Volkswagen totally altered the structure of the Argentinian motor industry in the late seventies. The number of car producers was reduced from seven to four between 1978 and 1980 and the level of concentration in the industry increased considerably. Nevertheless these four firms continued to produce more than thirty models between them for a domestic market of less than 150 000 cars a year in the early eighties.

As a result there is little evidence that Argentinian car prices are approaching international levels. In the late 1970s and early 1980s Argentinian prices were between 4 and 5.5 times international levels and substantially higher than before the liberalization programme was implemented (Nofal, 1983, p. 144). Another indication of the fact that liberalization has not made the Argentinian motor industry more competitive on international markets is the decline in exports from the industry in the late seventies.

The balance of payments implications of a liberalization strategy are severe. Since imports tend to rise sharply while industry exports do not become internationally more competitive, the inevitable consequence is a growing trade deficit. In Chile in 1980 assembled vehicles accounted for 10 per cent of all imports and the sector's deficit was well in excess of US $500 million. In Argentina the industry accounted for almost 8 per cent of all imports and the trade deficit was running at around US $700 million in the early 1980s (Table 11.7).

In effect liberalization policies have led to a return to the situation which prompted many countries to promote the development of a local motor vehicle industry in the late fifties and early sixties. The high weight of the industry in terms of the composition of imports was one of the factors which made it a candidate for import substitution in the first place. In the 1980s with renewed balance of payments pressures, arising particularly from the need to service the growing foreign debt, the industry in those countries which pursue liberalization to its logical conclusion will have come full circle.

The most obvious consequences of liberalization for workers in both Chile and Argentina has been a sharp reduction in the number employed in the industry. Reduced local content and increased competition from imports both serve to displace labour from the industry. In Chile employment was cut from over 6000 in the early seventies to under 2000 in 1977 (ILO, *Yearbook of Labour Statistics*, 1982). In Argentina employment was reduced by over 25 000 in the terminal industry between 1977 and 1983 (ADEFA) while in the parts industry it fell by 80 000 between 1977 and 1981 (Nofal, 1983, table I.16, p. 151). In both these cases the ability of workers to resist dismissals on such a large scale was undermined by the repressive measures taken against workers' organizations by the military regimes which assumed power in 1973 and 1976, respectively. There is, therefore, a clear link between these liberalization measures taken in the motor industry and the authoritarian regimes in power.

The imposition of military rule also led to substantial falls in real wages in the industry even before the implementation of liberalization policies had a major impact on employment levels. In the Chilean motor industry real wages fell by 30 per cent in 1974 compared with the previous year, while in Argentina wages for unskilled workers were only a quarter of their 1975 levels by 1978 (calculated from ILO statistics). The implications of this in terms of the deteriorating living conditions of motor industry workers is obvious. From the point of view of capital it meant a considerable reduction in wage costs. In Argentina, for instance, the share of wages in the value added by the terminals (derived as production valued at prices to the dealers minus local purchases) fell sharply from over a half (53.9 per cent) in 1975 to less than one third (32.4 per cent) in 1978 (calculated from ADEFA statistics).

It is not only labour that is adversely affected by this type of policy. Liberalization hits the local parts industry particularly hard. They lose out both from the declining market share of locally produced vehicles and from the reduced purchases of the terminals which remain. In Argentina the share of local purchases in the value of output by the terminals fell to 34.8 per cent in 1981, the lowest level since 1961 when local production was just being initiated (Nofal, 1983, table V.4). The terminals on the other hand, are in a much stronger position since they are now able to incorporate more parts in the kits which they import, and can also choose between local production and CBU imports thus enabling them to widen the range of models on offer by supplementing local production with imports.

When liberalization has taken place, firms with local production facilities have often taken advantage of their established position in the domestic market in order to sell imported vehicles as well. In Argentina, for instance, Ford, Peugeot-Citroen and Chrysler-VW were among the major importers. In Peru following the liberalization measures over 40 per cent of imports in 1981 were accounted for by firms which had production facilities in Peru. Thus whereas the terminals are able to take advantage of the additional flexibility which liberalization offers them (although in some cases this flexibility leads to withdrawal from local production altogether) the parts industry, particularly that section controlled by local capital, sees its position weakened considerably. It is not surprising that in Argentina the Consejo Coordinador de la Industria de Autopartes vigorously opposed the liberalization of the late seventies and defended the 1971 Ley de la Reconversión de la Industria Automotriz (Sourrouille, 1980, p. 75).

4 THE ANDEAN PACT

Introduction

Before evaluating the consequence of the strategy of import substitution on a regional scale proposed by the Junta del Acuerdo de Cartagena, it is necessary to stress first of all the limited extent to which this strategy has been followed in the motor vehicle industries of the Andean Pact countries over the past decade. As was pointed out in the previous chapter, implementation of the terms of Proposal 45 and Decision 120 of the Andean Pact has been extremely slow, and the future prospects of the sectoral automotive programme are not bright.

One reflection of this is the limited extent to which trade in automotive products has developed among the member countries. Only a small fraction of all motor industry imports come from other Andean Pact countries. In 1980 such imports by Peru came to only US $0.2 million (0.1 per cent of total motor industry imports) and in Colombia to US $11.7 million (2.1 per cent of total imports). In 1978 Venezuela imported US $6.8 million from the Colombian motor industry, but this was only 0.5 per cent of the country's total imports of motor industry products in that year. The bulk of imports continue to be supplied from the advanced capitalist countries although the larger Latin American countries, particularly Brazil are also involved.

A further reflection is the limited extent to which local production of the more technologically complex parts and components (those classified as 'ECF *basicos*') has developed in the region. Apart from axles, for which there are a number of plants in Venezuela, there are very few plants producing these more complex components. In most cases there are no more than one between the three major Andean Pact countries. The most obvious deficiency is in engine production where the Andean Pact proposed that there should be eleven plants in Colombia, Peru and Venezuela, but so far only one exists. Similarly there have been shortfalls in the construction of plants to produce gearboxes and hydraulic steering equipment in the region. Thus an important aim of the sectoral programme, namely to raise the technological level of the local industry through the production of more sophisticated parts and components has fallen short of its goals.

Another indication of the limited extent to which import substitution has developed in the region is the slow growth of purchases by the terminal firms from local suppliers and the continued heavy reliance on imported parts and components. In Colombia, for instance, local purchases of parts and components by the terminals remained almost constant per vehicle produced in the seventies, only increasing from 19 000 pesos in 1970 to 20 600 pesos in 1979 (measured at 1970 prices) (Ronderos Tobon, 1981, table 3.1). In Venezuela in 1977 (the last year for which it has been possible to obtain information) 60 per cent of the inputs used by the terminals were imported (Fontanals and Porta, 1979, table 16). Between 1968 and 1977 local purchases of parts by the Venezuelan terminal industry appear only to have increased marginally in relation to the value of production from 27 per cent to 33 per cent (Fontanals and Porta, 1979, p. 7 and table 16). In all three larger Andean Pact countries imports of parts and components per vehicle produced remained high (see Table 11.10).

TABLE 11.10   *Imports of parts and components in Colombia, Peru and Venezuela, 1982*

	Imports (m $)	*Vehicles produced (no.)*	*Imports per vehicle ($)*
Colombia	213.5	35 567	6 003
Peru	101.1	21 977	4 600
Venezuela	860.2	155 108	5 546

SOURCES   UN, *Yearbook of International Trade Statistics*; MVMA, *World Motor Vehicle Data*.

Balance of payments

The policies pursued in the Andean Pact countries have not succeeded in improving the trade balance of the motor industry in the region. In fact, as can be seen from Table 11.11 the trade deficit in each of the three countries increased substantially in the 1970s and early 1980s. While exports have remained at extremely low levels throughout the period, imports have grown rapidly. As a result the industry's deficit has increased more than sixfold in Colombia between 1972 and 1982, sevenfold in Peru and fivefold in Venezuela. In the last country the deficit was running at well over US $1000 million a year in the early 1980s. In 1982 imports of automotive products accounted for 13.1 per cent of all Colombian imports, 14.0 per cent in Peru and 13.0 per cent in Venezuela. This represented an increase in the weight of imports of vehicles and parts in total imports of all three countries since the early seventies (cf. Table 8.5).

TABLE 11.11 Imports, exports and trade deficit of motor industry in Colombia, Peru and Venezuela, 1972, 1976, 1980, 1982 ($m)

	Colombia			Peru			Venezuela		
	Imports	Exports	Deficit	Imports	Exports†	Deficit	Imports	Exports	Deficit
1972	108.7	1.2	− 107.5	59.4		− 59.4	289.1	1.8	− 287.3
1976	252.3	7.1	− 245.2	149.4	0.7	− 148.7	953.3	n.a.	− 950.0*
1980	545.7	21.2	− 524.5	239.0	5.1	− 233.9	1165.0	22.1	− 1142.9
1982	714.1	16.8	− 697.3	412.5		− 412.5	1518.0	55.0‡	− 1463.*

NOTES   Figures refer to SITC 7115, 7294 and 732 unless otherwise indicated.

* Estimate.
† SITC 73 except 735.
‡ 1981.

SOURCE   Yearbook of International Trade Statistics, various issues.

Rationalization

An integral part of the automotive sectoral programme was a rationalization of the terminal industry in the region. It was proposed that eight models of passenger car would be produced, two in Colombia, one in Ecuador, two in Peru and three in Venezuela, and twelve different types of commercial vehicles covering the whole range of lorry sizes and a 4-wheel drive vehicle (see Table 10.1). In fact, however, the industry in the region continues to be highly fragmented in terms of both the number of terminal firms and the number of models produced (see Table 11.12). Although the situation has improved slightly compared with 1972, particularly in Venezuela which was the country with the greatest number of firms and variety of models, the industry is a very long way from achieving the kind of structure envisaged by the sectoral programme.

In the parts industry, far from rationalization there has been an increase in the number of plants producing many of the less complex parts and components. By the late seventies there were thirteen plants producing clutch systems and eleven each producing coils, alternators, starter motors and windscreen wipers in Colombia, Peru and Venezuela, while production in the region was less than a quarter of a million vehicles.

Arguably the rationalization which has taken place is the result of individual government policies and has little to do directly with the Andean Pact as such. In a sense this is inevitable since the programme envisages trade in vehicles between the member countries and that this would make it possible to plan production on a regional basis. Since such trade remains negligible. It has not been possible for individual countries to specialize in producing specific models in selected classes. As a result all the countries produce classes of passenger cars and of CVs which they have not been allocated. Indeed, in a number of cases exactly the same model of car or commercial vehicle is produced in more than one member country, a complete negation of planned rationalization.

Another way to look at the extent to which the motor vehicle industry has been rationalized within the Andean Pact is to compare the scale of output proposed for each model, with those actually achieved so far. For passenger cars the planned output per model in 1985 varied from 35 000 to 54 000 depending on the class. In the case of CVs it was 26 000 per model for those of less than 4.6 metric tons GVW, between 6000 and 9000 units for those between 4.6 and 17

TABLE 11.12 Number of firms and models produced in Andean Pact countries, 1981

	Cars			CVs		
	No. of firms	No. of models	Average output per model	No. of firms	No. of models	Average output per model
Colombia	3	16	1546	1	11	984
Peru	3	5	2619	3	15	618
Venezuela	5	37	2237	11	85	843

SOURCE MVMA.

metric tons GVW, and 2500 units for those over 17 metric tons GVW. A glance at Table 11.12 will show how far short of these production scales the Andean Pact countries were in the early 1980s. In cars for example only GM's Malibu Sedan, of which over 21 000 were produced in Venezuela, approached these levels while no other model was produced in more than 10 000 units.

Costs and prices

As was seen in Chapter 6 vehicle prices and costs were much higher in the early seventies in the Andean Pact countries, particularly Colombia and Peru, than in the countries of origin of the models produced locally. Unfortunately detailed cost comparisons of the kind available for the earlier period do not exist for the late seventies or early eighties.

However, there are reasons to believe that costs and prices have not become more internationally competitive in the region in the 1970s. In both Colombia and Peru vehicle prices have tended to rise faster than the consumer price index. In Colombia the index of vehicle prices deflated by the consumer price index was 118.5 in 1980 (1971 = 100).[7] In Peru the corresponding index increased by between a third and a half (depending on the class of vehicle) for cars between 1971 and 1978 (Fernandez-Baca et al., 1979, table 3b). In dollar terms vehicle prices increased almost threefold in Colombia between 1971 and 1980, and by about two-thirds in Peru between 1971 and 1978. This compares with an increase in US consumer prices for new cars of about 40 per cent between 1971 and 1978 and 65 per cent between 1971 and 1980.

In 1977 the price to the dealer of a car produced in Colombia varied from almost 150 per cent to 250 per cent of the price in the country of origin depending on the model (Sandoval et al., 1981, table 1.6). This represented an improvement over the situation found in 1970 when the average price of a Colombian vehicle was three times the price in the country of origin (ECLA, 1973, table 25). However, this reflects primarily the reduction in the tariff on CKD kits from an average of 115 per cent in 1970 (ECLA, 1973, table 24) to only 10 per cent by the late seventies (Sandoval et al., 1981, p. 32).[8] That there was no significant improvement in productivity and cost competitiveness in the industry is confirmed by evidence showing that the relative cost of Colombian made parts increased in the late seventies compared with the country of origin (Ronderos Tobon, 1981, table 3.5).

Venezuela has not fared any better in this regard than Colombia or

Peru. In 1970 prices to the dealer were on average 46 per cent higher than in the country of origin (ECLA, 1973, table 25). In 1973 the figure varied between 60 per cent and 80 per cent for a number of US models. By 1978 the prices of models subject to price control were between 40 per cent and 60 per cent more expensive than in the United States while for 'luxury' models exempt from price control the excess price ranged from 140 per cent to 155 per cent (Fontenals and Porta, 1979, table 4).

Employment and implications for labour

Proposal 45 of the Andean Pact envisaged an expansion of the labour force in the region's automotive industry to employ over 94 000 workers by 1980, of which over 73 000 would be engaged in the terminal industry. Although there has been some expansion in employment in the industry since the early seventies, this has fallen far short of the scale envisaged in the programme.

In fact as the earlier analysis of the balance of payments position of the Andean Pact countries illustrated, and as the limited employment created locally tends to confirm, the region remains primarily of interest to the auto TNCs as an area in which to realize surplus value through the export of CKD kits and components. The new plants which have been constructed in the region, in sharp contrast to those built in Brazil and Mexico in the seventies, have been almost entirely built with a view to the national or regional market, not the world market. They have therefore been small in relation to the minimum efficient scale of plant in the industry. For example, the engine plant built by Renault at Duitama, Colombia, in the early seventies had a capacity of only 40 000 engines a year working two shifts, only one-tenth of the output of the plants built in Mexico in the late seventies. The small scale of production led to the choice of universal machines for the plant, although it was modern for the scale of production envisaged (see Sandoval *et al.*, 1981, for more details on the Duitama plant).

As far as the labour force is concerned, the changes which took place in the Andean Pact countries in the seventies have certain parallels with the move towards integrated production in Brazil, Argentina and Mexico in the fifties and sixties. However, these moves are still not very far advanced as the continued high level of reliance on imported parts and components indicate. Differential tariffs between CKD and CBU imports, restrictions on imports of vehicles, licences for imports of parts, local content requirements and government controls on models produced and prices charged are the key determinants of profitability in the region's motor industry.[9] Thus the firms' relations with the state remain the top priority for management. Control of labour and labour productivity remain a secondary issue.

Implications for suppliers and transfers of surplus value

Had the proposals of the Junta del Acuerdo de Cartagena been fully implemented, they could have led to a significant improvement in the position of the parts industry in relation to the terminals. The decision to make the incorporation of certain locally produced parts and components by the assemblers obligatory for the terminals, rather than the more conventional approach of setting a local content requirement, reduced the flexibility of the terminals. They could not use the threat of importing a part as a negotiating ploy in order to obtain better terms from their suppliers. Thus, one source of competitive pressure on the parts industry would have been removed at least as far as those components whose incorporation was obligatory was concerned.

However, as was seen above, the development of production of the technologically more sophisticated components in the region has been extremely limited. Moreover, as far as simpler components such as windscreen wipers and starter motors are concerned there has been a tendency for the number of local producers to increase giving more scope for the terminals to play off one supplier against another. In practice, therefore, it is unlikely that the changes in the Andean Pact motor industry in the seventies have done anything to change the unequal relationship between suppliers and terminals described in Chapter 7.

5   CONCLUSIONS

From the discussion of this chapter it is clear that there has been a major restructuring of the Latin American motor industry in the seventies and early eighties. As in the late fifties and early sixties when changing international conditions, particularly intensified competition between US and European capital facilitated the development of manufacturing in certain Latin American countries and increasing levels of local content in others, so in the seventies new international conditions have again facilitated certain changes in the position of the Latin American motor industry in the international division of labour. This is not to imply that the restructuring which has taken place is a direct reflection of the interest of international capital in the form of the auto TNCs. It is, however, congruent with their emerging strategies. Thus the two countries which have most obviously changed the nature of their insertion in the international motor industry, Brazil and Mexico, have been able to do so for two fundamental reasons. First they have large, and until recently, growing domestic markets, which are a considerable attraction to the auto TNCs particularly in a period of world recession. Secondly their policies have taken into account the changing nature of the world motor industry in the 1970s.[10] As a result they have succeeded in attracting major new investments in the motor industry designed to produce for world markets.

This contrasts sharply with the lack of success on virtually all counts, of the Andean Pact's sectoral programme for the motor industry. First of all, the Andean Pact countries, even when taken together constituted a market about half the size of Mexico's or a quarter the size of Brazil's in the early 1980s. Secondly the policies of the Andean Pact countries have by and large not been adjusted to the changing patterns of accumulation in the international motor industry since the seventies (cf. Gwynne, 1980). As was indicated in Chapter 10 the TNCs themselves have suggested fundamental changes in the programme in order to bring it more in line with their own strategies. The result is that little success has been achieved in implementing Decision 120, and in the early eighties a number of member states have moved away from the spirit of the Andean Pact programme with the introduction of liberalization measures. There have been very few major new investments undertaken in the region as a result of the Andean automotive programme.

In conclusion, the contrasting experiences of Brazil and Mexico on the one hand and the Andean Pact countries on the other, highlight the importance of international conditions for developments in the Latin American motor industry. It is the international context which sets the bounds within which local accumulation and restructuring must take place in any particular period.

NOTES

1. The figures which we use here tend to exaggerate the degree of autarchy of the Brazilian motor industry since they do not include imports of capital

goods or of raw materials which as was seen in Chapter 8 were substantial in the early seventies. However, even taking our earlier estimates of total imports by the industry these only came to between 6 per cent and 9 per cent of the value of output.

2. Nor can this be accounted for by the growth of intra-regional trade within the Andean Pact. See Section 4.

3. Because of the lack of data on capital flows and their relatively small size compared with imports and exports of goods, this section will concentrate on the trade balance.

4. This is also reflected in the trade balances of the terminal TNCs all of which were in surplus by 1981 giving an aggregate surplus of US $1110 million in that year, US $812 million in 1982 and US $710 million in 1983 (data provided by E. Guimaraes).

5. Quiroz contrasts the professional worker of the older Mexican car plants with the mass worker characteristic of the newer plants (Quiroz, 1981).

6. It is interesting to note that GM in their new engine plant at Ramos Arizpe make extensive use of women workers in engine assembly (Davila Flores, 1982). This is one of the areas of production in which European firms such as Renault have introduced neo-Fordist methods (Coriat, 1980).

7. Own elaboration from Sandoval *et al.*, 1981, table 1.5.

8. If the import duty in 1970 had been 10 per cent and not 115 per cent then the Colombian price to the dealer would have been only slightly over twice the country of origin price instead of three times higher.

9. It is interesting to note in this context that in Colombia it is those vehicles which receive the highest tariff protection which also show the highest excess price in relation to the country of origin. These higher prices cannot be explained by higher costs either because of a higher level of local content (the local content tends to be lower) or because of duties on CKD imports which are low (Sandoval *et al.*, 1981, p. 27).

10. Guimaraes, 1981, p. 51 argues that the Brazilian government may have over-estimated the changes that were taking place in the international division of labour in the motor industry.

12 The Road Ahead

1 THE MOTOR INDUSTRY AND THE 'STYLE OF DEVELOPMENT'

It has been stressed in this study that the motor industry played a central part in the development strategies of most Latin American countries, whether these emphasized import substitution, the promotion of manufactured exports or regional integration. It is not surprising therefore that the impact of the motor industry complex extends well beyond the boundaries of the complex itself to the economy as a whole. As a leading sector it can in many ways be said to imprint itself on the whole 'style of development' of the Latin American countries.

In the advanced capitalist countries the growth of the motor industry has brought about a major transformation in patterns of work and living. By becoming a mass consumption good the car has totally altered much of everyday life. In Latin America the lower levels of per capita income and the higher price of cars has meant that cars are still a luxury good access to which is restricted to a minority of the population (see above Chapter 6). Nevertheless, despite this fact the allocation of resources to support private transport has led to very similar patterns emerging in Latin America to those found in the advanced capitalist countries.

In the advanced capitalist countries the development of the motor industry has been based primarily on the growth of private transport. In the United States the 'private affluence/public poverty' dichotomy (Galbraith, 1962, especially ch. 18) is nowhere more marked than in the field of transport with urban motorways jammed with cars and run down, inadequate public transport. While the United States is undoubtedly an extreme case the trend away from public transport towards increased reliance on private transport characterizes the advanced capitalist countries generally (Bhaskar, 1980, figure 3.2). Moreover, in the United States the Big Three car companies helped deliberately accelerate this trend by acquiring and running down public transport companies (NACLA, 1979, p. 9).

The TNC-led model of development being applied in the Latin American motor industry is tending in the same direction. With the establishment of manufacturing operations in the region in the fifties and sixties, the vested interests in favour of expanding the road network and developing the necessary ancillary facilities for car owner-ship were greatly strengthened. Large numbers of firms and workers became dependent on the industry and constituted a significant pres-sure group. In this situation a shift away from public transport is more than likely. In Mexico the proportion of total expenditure on transport and communications accounted for by public transport declined from around 85 per cent in the late fifties to less than 70 per cent in the early seventies (Bhaskar, 1980, figure 3.2). Another indicator of the same trend is the sharp increase in the ratio of cars to buses in the vehicle park of the major producing countries in the sixties and seventies. This rose from 28:1 to 65:1 in Argentina (1958–82), from 13:1 to 85:1 in Brazil (1957–82) and from 19:1 to 67:1 in Mexico (1960–82).

The extension of car ownership creates an important demand for greater expenditure on road improvements and new roads which in turn further fuels the demand for cars. In Argentina, for instance, public expenditure on road building in the five years after the beginning of manufacturing operations (1960–64) was double the level in the preceding five years, and there was a similar sharp increase in the length of road built (CIFARA, 1970, p. 163). Thus the development of a local motor industry implies not only the allocation of resources to produc-ing cars for a high income market, but also requires the commitment of substantial resources by the state to developing the necessary con-ditions for the use of these vehicles.[1] Moreover, as an increasing proportion of the rich and influential acquire cars, there is less and less pressure on the state to maintain an adequate system of public transport with the likely result that services deteriorate. This phenome-non acquires particular significance in Latin America where the bulk of the population does not own cars and are forced to rely on the inadequate public transport system.

The relationship between the growth of the motor industry and the 'style of development' was brought out very clearly in the debate over the plans for car production in Chile during the Popular Unity Government (1970–73). The socialist government was committed to a substantial measure of income redistribution and at the same time attempted to develop the Chilean motor industry through a rationalization of the number of producers and increased local content to include local production of the engine, gearbox and differential. According to the plan for the motor industry, car production was due to increase to 35 000 units in 1973 and 85 000 units by 1980. However, given that only a very small proportion of the Chilean population were in a position to buy cars, critics of the motor industry policy argued that with a substantial redistribution of income, the Chilean market would be incapable of absorbing the number of cars which the government planned to produce. Furthermore, such a policy would require the government to devote a large proportion of public funds to building new roads, remodelling urban centres and creating parking facilities. A socialist transport policy should on the contrary give much greater emphasis to the development of collective transport rather than continuing to increase private car ownership (Barkin, 1973).

The wider effects of the development of the motor industry is also illustrated by the Brazilian proalcohol programme discussed in Chapter 10. The attempt to substitute domestically produced ethanol for imported petroleum as a fuel for cars has led to substantial changes in agriculture in certain parts of the country. In order to meet government targets for ethanol production in 1985, 2.5 million hectares of sugar cane would be required (van der Plujim, 1983, table 5). Already by the early 1980s over 1.5 million hectares of new land, an area roughly the size of Wales had been put under sugar cane since 1975 (OU, 1983, p. 44). In some areas, for example, the state of Sao Paulo this expansion has partly been at the expense of food crops. It has also been accompanied by increasing land prices and growing concentration of land ownership (van der Plujim, 1983). Not only are major decisions on agricultural production being governed by the needs of the motor industry but substantial investment resources are also diverted to this end. Investment in distilleries alone was expected to be US $5 billion to meet the production target for 1985 and the government was financing 80 per cent of the cost at low interest rates (Colson, 1981, p. 63).[2]

In the major oil producing countries of Latin America, Mexico and Venezuela, the influence of the industry presents itself in a different fashion. The extremely low price of petrol at the pump in these countries subsidizes the private car user in a major way. In addition to its inequitable direct effects on the distribution of income, such a policy contributes to further rapid motorization in Latin America. Perhaps to an even greater extent than in the advanced capitalist countries, the costs of ownership to individual car users is substantially below the social costs when account is taken of the increasing pollution and congestion of many Latin American cities. Moreover, these costs and benefits are unevenly distributed between those few who benefit from car production and car ownership and the majority who bear a considerable part of the costs in the form of pollution, congestion and inadequate public transport services.

The central role of the motor industry in Latin America is unlikely to change while the private car continues to play such a major part. A style of development which seeks to emulate the consumption patterns of the advanced capitalist countries, guarantees a future for the industry in the region. The experience of Brazil is indicative of the extent to which governments wedded to such a development model will go in order to maintain the role of the private car, despite the most adverse circumstances, while that of Chile under the Popular Unity indicates that even an avowedly socialist strategy may still not break away from this pattern. What then are the trends which are likely to emerge in the industry in the foreseeable future?

2   THE FUTURE OF THE LATIN AMERICAN MOTOR INDUSTRY

The likely development of the Latin American motor industry over the next decade will obviously depend to an important degree on what happens in the international motor industry in this period. Prediction is a hazardous business at the best of times. It is particularly so at the moment for the motor industry which has been embroiled for the past decade in a world-wide crisis and an intense process of restructuring. As a result some commentators on the industry have constructed alternative future scenarios for the international motor industry (e.g. Jones, 1982).

A crucial issue is the likely developments in technology in the industry. As far as product technology is concerned, there is unlikely to be a radical change in the near future. The electric car, often canvassed as a replacement for the petrol driven car, still seems a long way from becoming a practical reality. A more probable course is the further incremental development of technology along lines which have already taken place such as the production of lighter, more fuel-efficient vehicles and the increased incorporation of electronic components. Production technology is likely to be characterized by an extension of automation and increasing use of robots, together with computer control of production. This will lead to further reductions in requirements for unskilled labour, which will only partly be offset by greater employment of specialists and maintenance workers. It may also increase flexibility in production permitting the production of a greater variety of models on one production line.

There is general agreement that the vehicle market of the advanced capitalist countries will show only very slow growth to the end of the twentieth century (see Tables 12.1 and 12.2). The most dynamic areas are expected to be in the Third World and to a lesser extent the socialist countries. The share of the Third World in total car demand is expected to rise from about 12 per cent in 1979 to over 20 per cent sometime in the 1990s, while the area's share of the world CV market is likely to be even higher. This implies that the less developed countries will account for over 40 per cent of the growth in world demand for cars and at least as much of the increased demand for CVs during the rest of the century.

The reason for this is that the advanced capitalist countries have already arrived at a stage of being mature markets when the level of vehicle ownership tends to level off, despite increases in income. As a result vehicle demand relies primarily on the replacement of vehicles as they are scrapped. In contrast the low level of vehicle density in most Third World countries means that ownership increases rapidly as incomes increase. Sales therefore have a substantial element of new demand which contributes to increasing the stock of vehicles on the road.

Concentration and centralization of capital has been a characteristic of the motor industry throughout its history. By 1983 a dozen manufacturers controlled almost 90 per cent of the capitalist world's vehicle production. Most analysts are agreed that this trend will continue in the future. Some go as far as to predict that six major groups will dominate the terminal industry before the end of the century (Bhaskar, 1980). The rising costs of designing and developing new models and investing in new facilities imply that only the largest firms can survive as major manufacturers, producing a full line of models. There is, however, an alternative, which has been resorted to particularly amongst European firms, namely the growth of joint ventures, joint research, joint production of components and joint design of models. It remains an open question whether these are a permanent solution to the firms' problems or whether they will turn out to have been merely a transitory phase of the process of concentration and centralization. However, further concentration and centralization

TABLE 12.1 Projections of future vehicle demand, 1990 and 2000

	Cars								
	OECD		Centrally planned economies		Third World*		Latin America		Total
	m	%	m	%	m	%	m	%	m
1979 actual	24.5	80.3	2.3	7.7	3.65	12.0	1.8	5.9	30.5
1990 projections									
Bhaskar	28.5	70.5	4.0	9.9	7.9	19.6	3.0	7.4	40.4
OECD	29.0	76.7	2.6	6.9	6.2	16.4	3.3	8.7	37.8
MIT	29.0	78.4	2.8	7.6	5.2	14.1	n.a.	n.a.	37.0
2000 projections									
OECD	32.2	70.2	3.9	8.5	9.8	21.4	5.4	11.8	45.9
MIT	33.1	67.8	4.2	8.6	11.5	23.6	n.a.	n.a.	48.8

Growth rates (% p.a.)	OECD	Centrally planned Economies	Third World	Latin America	Total
1979–90					
Bhaskar	1.4	5.0	7.3	4.8	2.6
OECD	1.5	0.9	4.9	5.7	2.0
MIT	1.5	1.6	3.3	n.a.	1.8
1990–2000					
OECD	1.1	4.1	4.7	5.1	2.0
MIT	1.3	4.1	8.3	n.a.	2.8

* Includes South Africa.

SOURCES Bhaskar (1981) exhibit 7(a); OECD (1983) table 3; Altshuler et al. (1984) tables 5.3 and 5.6.

TABLE 12.2   *Projections of future demand for commercial vehicles, 1990 and 2000* (m *units*)

	OECD	Centrally planned economies	Third World	Latin America	Total
1979 actual	7.5	1.6	1.7	0.6	10.8
1990 projections					
Bhaskar	5.9	2.1	4.8	1.2	12.8
MIT	9.2	2.0	3.0	n.a.	14.2
2000 projections					
MIT	10.8	2.5	4.7	n.a.	18.0
	Percentage of total				
1979 actual	69.4	14.9	15.7	5.6	100.0
1990 projections					
Bhaskar	46.1	16.4	37.5	9.4	100.0
MIT	64.8	14.1	21.1	n.a.	100.0
2000 projections					
MIT	60.0	13.9	26.1	n.a.	100.0
	Growth rates (% p.a.)				
1979–90					
Bhaskar	− 2.2	2.5	9.9	6.5	1.6
MIT	1.9	2.0	5.3	n.a.	2.5
1990–2000					
MIT	1.6	2.2	4.6	n.a.	2.4

SOURCE   As Table 12.1.

is unlikely to see the total disappearance of the smaller producers some of whom will be able to find specialized market niches as BMW have done in Europe.

Concentration and centralization is also likely to become increasingly marked in the parts industry, where large firms which have themselves become TNCs will enjoy considerable advantages in supplying the terminals in their world-wide operations. In the words of James Bere, president of Borg-Warner,

> this will be a challenging time, especially for those of us who are manufacturers of components. In the next decade, competition between component manufacturers will become, for the first time, truly international, will be more intense than ever, and the rules will be different. Many suppliers will fall into the abyss. But for those who survive the prospects will be good. (Quoted in Lifschitz, 1982a, p. 785.)

As the above quotation makes clear, concentration and centralization in the industry is related to further advances in the internationalization of capital. Although disputed by some, it seems likely that the process of standardization reflected in the increasingly similar nature of products manufactured in different parts of the world will continue. This does not exclude minor variations in design but implies that the design efforts of teams in subsidiaries in different countries will be pooled to produce common basic models using common components. GM and Ford are both developing a full line of seven or eight models of cars which will be produced world-wide, giving production runs of 2 million for the most widely used model and an average of around a million for others. GM is also standardizing i s engine production to produce four or five petrol engines and two diesel engines (Bhaskar, 1980, p. 73).

The proportions of output manufactured or assembled overseas by the major TNCs is likely to increase considerably. It is only by extending overseas operations that firms are likely to be able to obtain sufficient sales to remain competitive in terms of the introduction of new models and providing a wide model range. The TNCs are likely to maintain and consolidate their hold on markets outside the traditional producing countries because this is the area where market growth is likely to be concentrated. Moreover, the major Japanese firms, which continue to be exceptional among the leading auto TNCs in having minimal overseas production, are likely to have to follow their US and European counterparts in investing overseas, as government and trade union pressures against Japanese imports build up. This has already been recognized by the leading Japanese firms. Nissan's 'world strategy for the 1980s' according to its President Takashi Isihara is

> to limit our annual amount of domestic production to three million cars and to carry out overseas production in a positive way, with regard to production beyond that level (*Sunday Times*, 28/9/80).

Overseas expansion by the Japanese in the eighties will therefore either involve additions to the industry's capacity while other manufacturers continue with considerable excess capacity, or possibly tie-ups (eventually even leading to mergers) with other major producers, along the lines of the Honda–BL and Nissan–Alfa Romeo deals. In either case these moves are likely to result in an intense struggle for market shares.

At the same time the 1980s are likely to see a counter-offensive from Ford and GM. These two companies still controlled over a third of vehicle production outside the COMECON countries in 1983. The homogenization of markets described above will enable GM and Ford, by far the most diversified companies geographically, to standardize their international model ranges giving them greater potential for economies of scale and/or flexibility through dual sourcing than their competitors. As the General Director of Citroen has commented, GM will be in a particularly favourable position.

Consolidating on enormous industrial strength around a standardized range, GM will be in a position to wage a price war in the mid-1980s (X. Katchar, n.d.).

GM has also declared its intention to overtake Ford as the leading US manufacturer outside the United States (*Automotive Industries*, 1979; Forbes, 1979). The company plans to spend between $10 billion and $13 billion on investment abroad in the eighties, representing 20 to 25 per cent of its capital expenditure. This is not simply a response to the difficulties of the US domestic market. As international markets become more integrated it is logical for GM to try to make use of its US market dominance to expand overseas. GM's declared aim is to 'knock the hell out of the competition'. One of the key areas where GM is planning to do this is Europe where it has built a 300 000 car plant in Spain as well as an engine plant in Austria.

The major European car companies have also internationalized and have plans for further overseas expansion in the eighties. VW, Daimler-Benz and Renault are all expanding into the United States. Renault plans to increase its US sales from less than 20 000 in 1979 to 150 000 by 1985. European firms which saw their share of the US market decline in the seventies in the face of Japanese competition are likely to increase their market share in the eighties as a result of recent investments, intensifying the competitive struggle in the US market as well.

The parts industry is likely to follow the manufacturers in becoming increasingly internationalized in the eighties. As manufacturers move into international sourcing, an internationally organized operation will become a considerable advantage for suppliers. Moreover, as more countries in the Third World establish assembly plants and move from assembly to partial or full manufacturing, new markets will develop. Major groups such as Lucas and Bosch which in the past have tried to avoid competing in each other's markets are likely to do so more and more. Again the result will be an increased level of competition.

What are the implications of these changes for the international division of labour in the motor industry? Will the motor industry follow the pattern set by the textile industry and certain electrical and electronic industries, with a massive shift of production to low wage countries? There will undoubtedly be some changes in the geographic distribution of the industry internationally. The more rapid growth of demand for vehicles in the Third World is likely to be accompanied by an increase in these countries' share in world production and assembly, particularly as countries which were previously importers become assemblers and assemblers become manufacturers.

However, the real question is whether the Third World countries will emerge as major net exporters of motor industry products (vehicles or parts) as a result of their lower labour costs? There are several reasons for thinking that such a major relocation will not occur. First the industry has undergone considerable technological change in the past decade or so and it cannot be characterized as being at a point where the form of the product is stable and production technology static. Secondly the industry is subject to substantial economies of scale. In an unstable and uncertain world, the massive investments required in optimum scale plants would be very risky in countries where there was no significant domestic market and where the industry would have to rely almost exclusively on exports. Both the threat of protectionism and the generous incentives often offered by governments in the advanced capitalist countries, help to ensure that the bulk of production for these markets will be produced within the advanced countries. Thirdly the motor industry in the advanced capitalist countries has considerably increased labour productivity and reduced labour costs through automation in recent years. This is clearly an alternative to relocation as a means of reducing wage cost and as the industry becomes more capital intensive and the share of labour in total costs declines relocation becomes a less and less attractive strategy.

In this context it is important to stress that shifts in the international location of production will not be the outcome of the free play of market forces. As already mentioned state intervention or the threat of such intervention plays an important part in investment decisions in the motor industry. Moreover, the fact that a small group of companies controls vehicle production in most countries in the capitalist world implies that the strategies of the TNCs play an important mediating role between market forces and geographical relocation.

In a situation of intensified international competition, those countries which have large and growing markets are in a strong position to attract new investment in the industry, even beyond that required to supply the local market. This is facilitated by the development of 'world component strategies' by the major TNCs. With final assembly usually being undertaken near the market, it is more likely that the production of certain components for world markets will be decentralized to such countries, possibly with some exports of CKD kits for specific models. However, with production in these countries firmly under the control of the major TNCs, there is little likelihood of their becoming major net exporters of vehicles along the lines of Japan. Consequently the bulk of production is likely to remain within the advanced capitalist countries, and what production does take place in the Third World will be concentrated in a few highly favoured countries. This is borne out by the investment plans of the major TNCs. Somewhere between 5 and 10 per cent of their planned investment will be in the Third World, of which Brazil and Mexico receive the largest share, and together with Argentina account for up to three-quarters of the total (UNCTC, 1982, p. 294).

What then are the implications of these developments at the international level for the Latin American motor industry? Despite the drastic fall in vehicle production in the region from a peak of 2.2 million in 1980 to 1.5 million in 1983, the long term prospects are for a continued growth in demand in the region. Projections of the market for cars in Latin America in 1990, suggested that new registrations will reach 3 million cars or more (Table 12.1). This would represent between 7 per cent and 9 per cent of the world market for cars in 1990, compared with 5 per cent in the late seventies. By the year 2000 it has been predicted that Latin America will account for 11.6 per cent of world-wide car demand. In the case of commercial vehicles the forecast is for demand to reach over 1 million vehicles by 1990, again representing almost 10 per cent of the world market (Table 12.2). Such figures would make the Latin American demand for cars comparable with that of Japan and the CV market similar to that of Western Europe.

In view of what has been said earlier, it is reasonable to suppose that production in Latin America will not differ greatly from local demand. Bhaskar predicts that in 1990 a total vehicle market of 4.2 million will be matched by production of 4 million and a deficit of 0.2 million to be made up through imports (Bhaskar, 1981, exhibit 11). A major constraint on the growth of Latin American vehicle exports in the future, apart from factors such as high costs which have been a barrier in the past, is the control of regional production by the major TNCs. These companies already have substantial excess capacity in their plants in the advanced capitalist countries and will be reluctant to abandon these in favour of massive expansion of Latin American production. In 1980 the six major producers in Latin America (VW, GM, Ford, Fiat, Renault-AMC and Chrysler) had a world-wide production capacity for almost 30 million vehicles (Bhaskar, 1981, exhibit 12). Even if they maintain their current share of just over half the vehicles produced in the world (which seems unlikely in the light of past trends), they are unlikely to sell more than 27 million cars and CVs world-wide in 1990 (on the basis of a world market of 53.64 million vehicles in that year, see Table 12.1).

The trend to growing domination of the Latin American motor industry by a small group of TNCs is likely to continue. Between 1970 and 1983 the four largest firms in the region increased their share of total vehicle production from 70 per cent to 82 per cent, and in 1983 VW, GM and Ford alone accounted for 70 per cent of the region's output. With Fiat, the fourth firm in Latin America experiencing problems internationally, withdrawing from car production in Argentina and having serious financial problems in Brazil, and Chrysler restricting its Latin American operations to Mexico, the domination of the region by VW, GM and Ford is likely to increase in the future. Substantial new investment by Japanese capital in the region seems unlikely in the foreseeable future. Not only do the current difficulties of the motor industry act as a disincentive to investment at present, but the pressures on the Japanese TNCs to invest in Western Europe and the United States are likely to lead to their being fully occupied in expanding overseas elsewhere.[3]

A number of different patterns are likely to emerge in the Latin American motor industry in the next decade. Brazil and Mexico will continue to be the major markets and production centres in the region. Consequently the bulk of TNC investment will be concentrated in these two countries and they will enjoy a privileged role in the Latin American motor industry. Mexico seems set to achieve even closer integration with the US motor industry. The link-up between Renault and AMC and the decision by Nissan to invest in a light CV assembly plant in the USA, following the earlier VW investment, means that the six TNCs with operations in Mexico all now have plants in the United States as well.[4] All six firms have invested in Mexican engine plants which will supply their US operations, and other components are also being produced in Mexico for incorporation in vehicles built in the United States. As these plants come on stream exports will increase substantially and the industry's trade deficit is likely to be considerably reduced.[5]

Whereas Mexican exports are likely to be increasingly directed to the US market, the Brazilian motor industry can be expected to show a much more diversified pattern. However, as in Mexico, future export growth is likely to rely more on parts and components than on CBU vehicles and CKD kits. The TNCs are unlikely to permit their Brazilian subsidiaries to export on a major scale to their domestic markets, and as the Third World countries which have in the past provided Brazil with its major market for vehicles begin to build up their domestic industries, the scope for Brazilian exports is likely to narrow. The companies with export commitments to fulfil are likely to rely increasingly on exports of parts and components.[6] In the past these have been directed mainly to their parent companies and affiliates in North America and Western Europe. Brazilian subsidiaries may also be given a role in building up production in other Third World countries, as for example with the contract for VW do Brasil to provide a turnkey plant to Iran.

The growing integration of the Mexican and Brazilian motor industries with those of North America and Western Europe will make it increasingly necessary for workers in these countries to develop links in order to prevent capital from playing them off against each other. The new export oriented plants which have been set up in these countries make the conditions of workers in Mexico and Brazil much more like those of their counterparts in the advanced capitalist countries, and although this alone is by no means sufficient to ensure international solidarity, there may be a convergence in terms of problems, experiences and strategies for workers' struggles.

Elsewhere in Latin America the prospects of the motor industry seem rather limited. The ambitious plans of the Andean Pact countries have come to nothing and are unlikely to be revived in anything like their past form. Indeed, the continued existence of the Andean Pact itself is in question. As far as the motor industry is concerned the experience of the Andean Pact programme illustrates the difficulties of implementing a policy which is not at least compatible with the strategies of the major TNCs, particularly for countries whose markets even in aggregate remained relatively small. A fundamental problem of the Andean Pact proposals was that they were drawn up with the conditions of the sixties and early seventies in mind, a fairly stable product and technology and considerable competition to enter new markets. The shift in emphasis in the seventies as a result of the need to adjust to new international conditions, and increasing international integration of production rendered the proposals obsolete. It seems unlikely that the conditions for it to become viable again will emerge in the immediate future.

On the other hand, balance of payments pressures are likely to prevent these countries from relying heavily on imported vehicles in the long term. The most likely strategy therefore seems to be continued assembly for the local market, with a level of local content which falls well short of full manufacturing. Some TNCs with a particular interest in acquiring a foothold in the smaller markets of the region, may be willing to export a small number of parts in return for preferential treatment, along the lines of the deal between Renault and the Colombian government to export gearboxes from Colombia. However, their participation in the world market will remain marginal and they will continue to be net importers of motor industry products.

The only two Latin American countries whose markets might prove sufficiently attractive, if growth resumed, to achieve a more significant role are Argentina and Venezuela. In the case of Argentina only Renault and Ford amongst the TNCs appear to have a strong commitment to maintaining an important production base in the country. Of these, Renault is in a weak position in Latin America as a whole because it has no subsidiary in Brazil and only a small share of the Mexican market, while Ford's main bases in Latin America are Brazil and Mexico (see Nofal, 1983, pp. 321–6 for more details on the international integration of these companies' Argentinian operations). Venezuela where production has been stagnant since the mid-seventies does not at present appear to be well placed to attract major new investment in the industry, and its role is likely to be similarly reduced in international terms.

Between 1970 and 1983 the share of Brazil and Mexico in the total number of vehicles produced and assembled in Latin America increased from 64 per cent to 79 per cent. In the future the Latin American motor industry is likely to see further concentration of production, both in terms of ownership and geographically. While Brazil and Mexico become increasingly integrated into the evolving world motor industry as small but important cogs in the international wheel, the prospect for the remaining Latin American countries is to continue providing a market for the exports of kits, parts and components from the major centres of production.

NOTES

1. For example, between 1964 and 1970 an expressway linking downtown Lima to the richest residential areas absorbed half the total investment by the municipal government of Lima (Webb, 1975, p. 115).
2. In the early 1980s there was a reversal for the programme with production of alcohol-powered cars falling by a half in 1981 from a peak of over 250 000 vehicles in 1980. However, by 1983 a number of factors led to a revival in the market position of alcohol engines (UNIDO, 1984, p. 166).
3. It should be noted, however, that Nissan is expanding its activities in Mexico, partly in response to increased local demand, and partly in conjunction with its new investment in the United States.
4. Renault has now taken over AMC's shareholding in the seventh Mexican firm, VAM.
5. A new decree for the industry issued by the Mexican government in 1983 does not contain any radical changes which are likely to affect the industry in a major way. See Comercio Exterior, November 1983.
6. New BEFIEX agreements were signed with the major TNCs in 1983 which committed Ford to export $3000 million worth of vehicles and parts between 1983 and 1989, VW $2900 million, GM $1100 million and Fiat $1900 million (EIU, 1983, p. 47).

Bibliography

Abernathy, W. J. (1978) *The Productivity Dilemma* (Baltimore: The Johns Hopkins University Press).

Acuerdo de Cartagena (1983) *Evaluación del programa de reactivación y examen de la situación actual y perspectivas del proceso de integración subregional.* COM/XXXV/dt 2/Mod. 1.

ADEFA (1969) *La industria automotriz Argentina informe economico, 1969* (Buenos Aires: Asociacion de Fabricas de Automotores).

ADEFA (1970) *Industria automotriz Argentina, 1970* (Buenos Aires: Asociacion de Fabricas de Automotores).

ADEFA (1972) *Industria automotriz Argentina, 1972* (Buenos Aires: Asociacion de Fabricas de Automotores).

Aguilar, J. (1982) *La politica sindical en Mexico: industria del automovil* (Mexico DF: Ediciones Era).

Almeida, J. (1972) *A Implantacao da industria automobilistica no Brasil* (Rio de Janeiro: Fundacao Getulio Vargas).

Altshuler, A. *et al.* (1984) *The Future of the Automobile* (Cambridge: MIT Press).

AMDA, (1973) *La comercializacion automotriz* (Mexico DF: Asociacion Mexicana de Distribuidores de Automoviles).

AMIA (1976) *La industria automotriz de Mexico en Cifras* (Mexico City: Asociacion Mexicana de la Industria Automotriz).

AMIA (1982) *La industria automotriz de Mexico en Cifras* (Mexico City: Asociacion Mexicana de la Industria Automotriz).

Automotive Industries (1979) 'GM shooting for No. 1 Overseas', *Automotive Industries*, May 1979.

Baer, W. (1976) 'Technology, Employment and Development: Empirical Findings', *World Development*, vol. 4, no. 2.

Baer, W. and L. Samuelson, (eds). (1977) 'Latin America in the Post-import Substitution Era', *World Development*, Vol. 5, 1/2.

Baharona, E. *et al.* (1976) *Politica economica e inversion extranjera en el desarrollo de la industria automotriz Chilena (1962–1975)* (Universidad de Chile, Escuela de Economia. Thesis).

Baranson, J. (1969) *Automotive Industries in Developing Countries* (Washington, World Bank Staff Occasional Paper, No. 8).

Barkin, D. (1973) 'Automobiles and the Chilean Road to Socialism', in D. L. Johnson (ed.), *The Chilean Road to Socialism* (New York: Anchor Press/ Doubleday).

Baumgarten, A. L. (1972) 'Demanda de automoveis no Brasil', *Revista Brasileira de Economia*, vol. 26, Apr/Jul.

Behrman, J. (1972) *The Role of International Companies in Latin American Integration: Autos and Petrochemicals* (Lexington, Mass.: D. C. Heath).

Behrman, J. and H. Wallender (1976) *Transfers of manufacturing technology within multinational enterprises* (Cambridge, Mass.: Ballinger).

Bennett, D. and K. Sharpe (1979) 'Export Promotion and the Mexican Automobile Industry', *International Organization*, Spring 1979.

Bennett, D. and K. Sharpe (1979a) 'Agenda Setting and Bargaining Power: the Mexican State vs. Transnational Automobile Companies', *World Politics*, Vol. 32 (1).

Beynon, H. (1973) *Working for Ford* (Harmondsworth: Penguin).

Bhaskar, K. (1979) *The Future of the U.K. Motor Industry* (London: Kogan Page).

Bhaskar, K. (1980) *The Future of the World Motor Industry* (London: Kogan Page).

Bhaskar, K. (1981) *The Motor Industry – The Future*. Paper presented at the International Conference 'The Incidence of the External Environment on the Global Automotive industry', Breau-sans-Nappe.

Bhaskar, K. *et al.* (1984) *State Aid to the European Motor Industry* (Norwich, University of East Anglia).

British Overseas Trade Board (1974) *The Japanese Market for Vehicle Components and Accessories* (London).

Bueno, G. (1971) 'La industria siderurgica y la industria automotriz', in Instituto de Investigaciones Sociales. UNAM, *El Perfil de Mexico en 1980*, Vol. II (Mexico City: Siglo XXI).

Bueno, G. *et al.* (1971) *La transferencia internacional de tecnologia al Nivel de Empresa: el caso de Mexico*. (New York: United Nations, ESA/FF/AC2/10).

Central Policy Review Staff (CPRS) (1975) *The Future of the British Car Industry* (London: HMSO).

Chudnovsky, D. (1981) *Las subsidiarias en America Latina y el financiamiento de la inversion de las ET manufactureras de EUA* (Mexico, DF: ILET, DEE/D/59/e).

Chudnovsky, D. (1982) 'Las filiales estadounidienses en el sector manufacturero de America Latina. Sus cambiantes pautas de repatriacion de utilidades', *Comercio Exterior*, vol. 12, no. 7.

CIFARA (1970) *Estudio tecnico-economico de la industria nacional de transporte* (Buenos Aires: Camara Industrial de Fabricantes de Autopiezas de la Republica Argentina).

Cmillo, E. *et al.* (1973) *Acumulacion y centralizacion del capital en la industria Argentina* (Buenos Aires: Editorial Tiempo Contemporaneo).

Counter Information Services (n.d.). *Anti-report. The Ford Motor Company.*

Cohen, R. (1982a) *Internationalization of the auto industry and its employment impacts* (Detroit: SAE Technical Paper Series).

Cohen, R. (1982b) *International market positions, international investment strategies and domestic reorganization plans of the U.S. automakers.* Mimeo.

Colson, R. F. (1981) 'The Proalcool Programme – A Response to the energy Crisis', *Bank of London and South America Review*, vol. 15, no. 2.

Commission des Communautes Europeenes (1977) *Etude sur l'evolution de la concentration dans l'industrie des pneumatiques en France* (Brussels: EEC).

Commission des Communautes Europeenes (1979) *Etude sur l'evolution de la concentration dans le secteur des equipements automobiles en France* (Brussels: EEC).

Commission of the European Communities (1977) *A study of the evolution of concentration in the manufacture and supply of tyres, sparking plugs and motor vehicle accumulators for the United Kingdom* (Brussels: EEC).

CONADE (1966) *La Industria automotriz (Analisis Preliminar)* (Buenos Aires: Consejo Nacional de Desarrollo).

Connor J. M. and W. F. Mueller (1977) *Market Power and Profitability of Multinational Corporations in Brazil and Mexico*. Report to the Subcommittee on Foreign Economic Policy of the Committee on Foreign Relations, United States Senate, US Government Printing Office, Washington.

Coriat, B. (1980) 'The Restructuring of the Assembly Line: a New "Economy of Time and Control"'. *Capital and Class*, 11.

Coronil, F. and J. Skurski (1982) 'Reproducing Dependency: Auto Industry Policy and Petrodollar Circulation in Venezuela', *International Organization*, vol. 36, no. 1.

Crandall, R. (1968) 'Vertical Integration and the Market for Repair Parts in the United States Automobile Industry', *Journal of Industrial Economics*, July.

Cruz, H. da and M. da Silva (1982) *Evolucao tecnologica em uma firma de processo productivo continuo no setor metal – mecanico Brasileiro* (Buenos Aires: Programma de Investigaciones sobre Desarrollo Cientifico y Tecnologico en America Latina, Monografia de Trabajo, No. 58).

CSE Microelectronics Group (1980) *Microelectronics: Capitalist Technology and the Working Class* (London, CSE Books).

Cuadernos del Dialogo (1971) *La civilizacion del Automovil* (Madrid: Editorial Cuadernos para el Dialogo).

Davila Flores, M. (1982) *El Complejo Automotriz de Ramos Arizpe, Coahuila*, mimeo, Universidad Autonoma de Coahuila.

Direccion Nacional de Estudios Industriales (DNEI) (1969) *Situacion Actual y perspectivas de mercado de automoviles en la Republica Argentina* (Buenos Aires: Ministerio de Economia y Trabajo).

Dos Santos, T. (1973) 'The Crisis of Development Theory and the Problem of Dependence in Latin America', in H. Bernstein (ed.), *Underdevelopment and Development* (Harmondsworth: Penguin).

Duncan, W. C. (1973) *US – Japan Automobile Diplomacy* (Cambridge, Mass.: Ballinger Publishing Co).

ECLA (1970) *The Demand for Motor Vehicles in Latin America*. Working Group on Economies of Scale in the Latin American automotive industry, Santiago, Chile, Information Paper No. 1.

ECLA (1973) *Perspectivas y modalidades de integracion regional de la industria automotriz en America Latina* (ECLA/DI/DRAFT/92. Division de Desarrollo Industrial).

Economist (1979) 'A Survey of Commercial Vehicles', *The Economist*, 27 October.

Edelberg, G. S. (1976) *The Procurement Practices of the Mexican Affiliates of Selected U.S. automobile firms* (New York: Arno Press).

EIU (1977) *The U.S. Market for Motor Vehicles, Parts and Accessories* (London: Economist Intelligence Unit, Special Report No. 40).

EIU (1978) *The automotive components industry of the U.K.* (London: Economist Intelligence Unit, Special Report No. 58).

EIU (1983) *Motorizing the Third World* (London, Economist Intelligence Unit, Special Report No. 131).

EIU (1983a) *Foreign Outsourcing by US Auto Manufacturers* (London: Economist Intelligence Unit, Special Report No. 151).

Ensor, J. (1971) *The Motor Industry* (London: Longman).

Evans, J., D. James and P. Hoffel (1979) *Labor in the Argentine Motor Industry* (paper presented at a Workshop on the Auto Industry in Latin America, Boston).

Evans, J., D. James and P. Hoffel (1984). 'Reflections on the Argentine Autoworkers and their Unions', in R. Kronish and K. Mericle, *The Political Economy of the Latin American Motor Vehicle Industry* (MIT Press).

Fernandez-Baca Llamosas, *et al.* (1979) *El complejo automotor en Peru* (Mexico DF: ILET).

Foncerrada Moreno, J. and H. Vazquez Tercero (1969) *Informe Economico* (Mexico DF: Asociacion Nacional de Distribuidores de Automoviles).

Fontanals, J. and F. Porta (1979) *El complejo automotriz en Venezuela.* Paper presented to the ILET-CLACSO-SSRC Seminar, Mexico City, January, 1980.

Forbes (1979) 'GM Gets Ready for World Car', *Forbes*, 2nd April 1979.

Fox, J. (n.d.) Unpublished manuscript on the Latin American motor industry.

Frank, A. G. (1972) *Lumpen-bourgeoisie, Lumpendevelopment* (New York: Monthly Review Press).

Friedman, A. (1977) *Industry and Labour: Class Struggle at Work and Monopoly Capitalism* (London: Macmillan).

FTC (1966) *Economic Report on the Manufacture and Distribution of Automotive Tires* (Washington DC: Federal Trade Commission).

Galbraith, J. K. (1975) *Economics and the Public Purpose* (Harmondsworth: Penguin).

Galbraith, J. K. (1962) *The Affluent Society* (Harmondsworth: Penguin).

Gartman, D. (1979) 'Origins of the Assembly Line and Capitalist Control of Work at Ford', in A Zimbalist (ed.), *Case Studies on the Labour Process* (New York: Monthly Review Press).

Gudger, W. M. (1975) *The Regulation of Multinational Corporations in the Mexican Automotive Industry.* (Unpublished PhD. dissertation, University of Wisconsin).

Guimaraes, E. (1980) *Industry, Market Structure and the Growth of the Firm in the Brazilian Economy* (PhD thesis, University of London).

Guimaraes, E. (1981) *The Brazilian passenger car industry.* Paper presented to the International Conference on the Incidence of the External Environment on the Global Automotive Industry, Breau-sans Nappe.

Gwynne, R. N. (1980) 'The Andean Group Automobile Programme: an Interim Assessment', *Bank of London and South America Review*, August.

Gwynne, R. N. (1983) *Multinationals and 'Apertura' in Latin America* (paper presented to a meeting on 'Multinational Companies and the Third World' organized by the Developing Areas Research Group and the Industrial

Activity and Area Development Study Group of the Institute of British Geographers).

Hermele, K. (1982) *The Knack or How to Get the Work Done: Discipline and Control in the Auto Industry.* Working Group for the Study of Development Strategies (AKUT), Department of Development Studies, University of Uppsala.

Hermele, K. (1982a). *Swedish Auto Firms in Latin America: Case Study of Saab-Scania and Volvo in Peru and Brazil.* Mimeo. Research Policy Unit, Lund.

Humphrey, J. (1982) *Capitalist Control and Workers' Struggle in the Brazilian auto industry* (Princeton University Press).

Humphrey, J. (1984) *Car Production in Britain and Brazil. A Comparison.* Mimeo.

IBRD (1978) *The World Rubber Economy: Structure, Changes, Prospects* (Washington, World Bank/FAO).

IKA (1963) *La Industria automotriz Argentina* (Buenos Aires: Industrias Kaiser Argentina).

IMF (1964) *World Automotive Industry* (International Metalworkers Federation Automotive Conference, Frankfurt on Main, 16–19 November).

IMF (1976) *2nd IMF Latin American and Caribbean automobile and agricultural implement Conference Report.* Valencia, Venezuela. 27–29 September.

International Automotive Review, 1982/83. 'The developing Role of Third World Countries in the Vehicle Industry', *International Automotive Review*, 4th Quarter 1982/1st Quarter 1983.

International Automotive Review, 1984. 'Export Activities of Japanese Vehicle Manufacturers' *International Automotive Review*, 3rd Quarter, 1984.

Isla, L. de la (1968) *Mercado nacional de vehiculos automotores* (Thesis, Univesidad Nacional Autonoma de Mexico, Escuela Nacional de Economia).

Islas, H. (1983) 'Una Industria en Busca de Soluciones: la Automovilistica', *Comercio Exterior*, Nov.

IWC Motors Group (1978) *A Workers' Enquiry into the Motor Industry* (London: CSE Books).

Jenkins, R. (1977) *Dependent Industrialization in Latin America* (New York: Praeger).

Jenkins, R. (1979) *Foreign firms, Exports of Manufactures and the Mexican Economy* (Norwich, University of East Anglia, Development Studies Monograph, No. 8).

Jenkins, R. (1984) *Transnational Corporations and Industrial transformation in Latin America* (London: Macmillan).

Jenkins, R. (1984a) 'The Rise and Fall of the Argentinian Motor Vehicle Industry', in R. Kronish and K. Mericle (eds), *The Political Economy of the Latin American Motor Vehicle Industry* (MIT Press).

Johnson, L. J. (1967) 'Problems of Import Substitution: the Chilean Automobile Industry', *Economic Development and Cultural Change*, vol. 15, no. 2.

Jones, D. (1981) *Maturity and Crisis in the European Car Industry: Structural Change and Public Policy* (University of Sussex, Sussex European Papers No. 8).

Jones, D. (1982) *Adjustment Strategies and Policy Issues in the Automobile Industry*, quoted in TIE, 1983.

Jones, D. and S. Prais (1978) 'Plant-size and Productivity in the Motor Industry: some International Comparisons', *Bulletin of the Oxford University Institute of Economics and Statistics*.

Juarez, A. (1979) *Las Corporaciones Transnacionales y los Trabajadores Mexicanos* (Mexico City: Siglo XXI).

Karssen, W. J. (1968) 'Concentration in the Automobile Industry of the USA', in US Congress, Sub-committee on Antitrust and Monopoly, *Economic Concentration*, vol. 70.

Katchar, X. (n.d.) *The Automobile in 1985, the New American Challenge*. Mimeo.

Kommission der Europaischen Gemeinschaften (1979) *Untersuchung der Kozentrationsetwicklung in der Reifenindustrie sowie ein branchbild der Kraftfahrzeug-elektrikindustrie in Deutschland* (Brussels, EEC).

Krutzky, J. (1977) *The Impact of International Influences on the Domestic Distribution of Power: the Situation in the French Auto Industry* (PhD thesis, Columbia University).

Larriva, J. J. and A. Vega (1982) 'El Comercio Exterior de la Industria Automovilistica en Mexico. Evolucion y Perspectivas', *Comercio Exterior*, December.

Lenicov, J. (1973) 'Algunos Resultados de la Politica Desarrollista (1958–64). El Caso de la Industria Automotriz', *Economica*, vol. 19, no. 3.

Leyton-Brown, D. (1980) 'The Mug's Game: Automotive Investment Incentives in Canada and the United States', *International Journal*, vol. 35.

Lifschitz, E. (1978) *Bases Para el Estudio de la Penetracion Transnacional en el Complejo Sectorial Automotor* (Mexico DF: ILET).

Lifschitz, E. (1979) *El Complejo Automotor en Mexico* (Mexico DF: ILET).

Lifschitz, E. (1982) *Los Complejos Automotores en America Latina (version preliminar)* (Mexico DF: ILET, DEE/R/123).

Lifschitz, E. (1982a) 'Comportamiento y Proyeccion de la Industria de Automotores en America Latina: los Casos de Argentina, Brasil y Mexico', *Comercio Exterior*, July.

Lustig, N. (1979) 'Distribucion del Ingreso, Estructura del Consumo y Caracteristicas del Crecimiento Industrial', *Comercio Exterior*, May.

Macdonnell, S. and M. Lascano (1974) *La industria automotriz: aspectos economicos y fiscales* (Direccion General Impositiva, Departamento de Estudios, Division Planes, Buenos Aires).

Maxcy, G. (1981) *The Multinational Motor Industry* (London: Croom Helm).

Maxcy, G. and A. Silberston (1959) *The Motor Industry* (London: Allen and Unwin).

Menge, J. A. (1962) 'Style Change Costs as a Market Weapon', *Quarterly Journal of Economics* vol. LXXVI.

Mericle, K. (1978) *The Political Economy of the Brazilian Motor Vehicle Industry* (paper presented to the SSRC Working Group Seminar on the Transnational Automobile Industry in Latin America).

Mericle, K. (1984) 'The Political Economy of the Brazilian Motor Vehicle Industry', in R. Kronish and K. Mericle (eds), *The Political Economy of the Latin American Motor Vehicle Industry* (MIT Press).

Micheli, J. (1984) 'La Produccion Automovilistica en Mexico y su Contexto Internacional', in CIDE, Estudios de Caso, Serie Economia Internacional, num 1, *Mexico en la division internacional del trabajo*.

Middlebrook, K. (1978) *Union structure and labor participation in the Mexican automobile industry* (paper presented to the SSRC Working Group Seminar on the Transnational Automobile Industry in Latin America).

Monopolies Commission (1963) *Report on the Supply of Electrical Equipment for Mechanically Propelled Land Vehicles* (London: HMSO).

Monopolies Commission (1968) *Clutch Mechanism for Road Vehicles* (London, HMSO).

Moore, R. M. (1967) *The Role of Extrazonally Controlled Multinational Corporations in the Process of Establishing a Regional Latin American Automotive Industry: a Case Study of Brazil* (PhD thesis, Fletcher School of Law and Diplomacy).

Morley, S. and G. Smith (1973) 'The Effect of Changes in the Distribution of Income on Labour, Foreign Investment and Growth in Brazil', in A. Stepan (ed.), *Authoritarian Brazil* (New Haven: Yale University Press).

Morley, S. and G. Smith (1977) 'The Choice of Technology: Multinational Firms in Brazil', *Economic Development and Cultural Change*, vol. 25, no. 2.

Motor Business (1960) 'The U.K. Vehicle Components Industry', *Motor Business*, no. 22, April.

Motor Business (1964) 'The Structure of the French Vehicle Components Industry', *Motor Business*, no. 39.

Motor Business (1965) 'The International Operations of the U.S. Motor Manufacturers', *Motor Business*, July.

Motor Business (1965a) 'The Structure of the West German Vehicle Components Industry', *Motor Business*, no. 42.

Motor Business (1984) 'The Brazilian Motor Vehicle Sector, Part I', *Motor Business*, no. 2, 1984.

Müller, R. and D. Moore (1978) *Case One: Brazilian Bargaining Power Success in BEFIEX Export Promotion Program with the Transnational Automotive Industry*. Paper prepared for UN Centre on Transnational Corporations, New York.

Munk, B. (1969) 'The Welfare Costs of Content Protection: The Automotive Industry in Latin America', *Journal of Political Economy*, vol. 77.

NACLA (1979) 'Car Wars'. *NACLA Report*, July/August.

NAF INSA (1960) *Elementos para una Politica de Desarrollo de la Fabricacion de Vehiculos Automotrices en Mexico* (Mexico City: Nacional Financiera).

NEDO (1971) *Japan: Its Motor Industry and Market* (London, HMSO).

Nofal, M. B. (1983) *Dynamics of the Motor Industry in Argentina* (PhD thesis, The Johns Hopkins University).

Nowicki, A. G. (1968) *Automobile Demand in Developing Countries* (UNIDO, ID/WG, 13/23).

Nun, J. (1979) 'Dismissals in the Argentine Automobile Industry: a Case Study of the Floating Surplus Population', *Labour, Capital and Society*, vol. 12, no. 2.

OECD (1978) *Long Term Perspectives of the World Car Industries* (Paris, OECD Interfutures).

OECD (1983) *Long Term Outlook for the World Automobile Industry* (Paris, Organization for Economic Cooperation and Development).

Oliveira, F. de, *et al.* (1979) *El Complejo Automotor en Brasil* (Mexico DF: ILET/ Nueva Imagen).

OU (1983) *Industrialisation and Energy in Brazil*, Third World Studies, Case Study 6, Milton Keynes, Open University Press.

Partridge, H. (1980) 'Italy's FIAT in Turin in the 1950s', T. Nichols (ed.), *Capital and Labour* (London: Fontana).

PEP, (1950) *Motor Vehicles: a Report on the Organization and Structure of the Industry, its Products and its Market Prospects at Home and Abroad* (London: Political and Economic Planning).

Phelps. D. M. (1936) *The Migration of Industry to South America* (New York: McGraw-Hill).

Pratten, C. (1971) *Economies of Scale in Manufacturing Industry* (Cambridge University Press).

Pratten, C. and A. Silberston (1967) 'International Comparisons of Labour Productivity in the Automobile Industry, 1950–1965', *Bulletin of the Oxford University Institute of Economics and Statistics*.

Price Commission (1979) *Prices, Costs and Margins in the Manufacture and Distribution of Car Parts* (London, HMSO).

Quijano, A. (1974) 'The Marginal Pole of the Economy and the Marginalized Labour Force', *Economy and Society*, vol. 3(4).

Quijano, J. M. (1979) 'Mexico: Credito y Desnacionalizacion', *Economia de America Latina*, no. 3, Sept.

Quiroz, O. (1980) 'Proceso de Trabajo en la Industria Automotriz', *Cuadernos Politicos*, Oct–Dec.

Quiroz, O. (1981) *Tecnologia, Reestructuracion Capitalista y Composicion de Clase en la Industria Automotriz Mexicana*. Mimeo.

Raddavero, E. (1972) 'Analisis de la Transferencia de la Tecnologia Externa a la Industria Argentina: el caso de la Industria Automotriz', *Economica*, vol. 18.

Rae, J. S. (1959) *American Automobile Manufacturers* (New York: Chilton).

Rhys, D. G. (1972) *The Motor Industry: an Economic Survey* (London: Butterworth).

Rodrigues, L. M. (1970) *Industrializacao e atitudes Operarias* (Sao Paulo: Brasilense).

Ronderos Tobon, A. (1981) *The Automotive Industry in Colombia* (MA dissertation, School of Development Studies, University of East Anglia).

Rothschild, E. (1974) *Paradise Lost: the Decline of the Auto-industrial Age* (New York: Vintage Books).

Roxborough, I. (1984) 'Labour in the Mexican Motor Vehicle Industry', in R. Kronish and K. Mericle (eds), *The Political Economy of the Latin American Motor Vehicle Industry* (MIT Press).

Roxborough, I. (1984a) *Unions and Politics in Mexico. The Case of the Automobile Industry*, Cambridge University Press.

Sanchez Marco, C. (1968) *Industry study: cost benefit analysis of car Manufacturing in Mexico (1)* (Paris: OECD Development Centre).

Sanchez Marco, C. (1968a) *Industry Study: Cost Benefit Analysis of Car Manufacturing in Mexico (2)* (Paris: OECD Development Centre).

Sandoval, P. *et al.* (1981) *Analisis de la trayectoria de una planta automotriz en Colombia: el caso de SOFASA* (Buenos Aires: Programa de investigaciones sobre Desarrollo Cientifico y Tecnologico en America Latina).

Sarli, W. (1979) *El Complejo Automotor en Uruguay* (Mexico DF: ILET, DEE/ D131).

Semmler, W. (1982) 'Theories of Competition and Monopoly', *Capital and Class*, 18.

Sepulveda, B. and A. Chumacero (1973) *La Inversion Extranjera en Mexico* (Mexico City: Fondo de Cultura Economica).

Sicard, C. (1970) *Les Relations Cout-volume dans l'industrie Automobile.* (UNIDO, ID/WG 76/17).

Silberston, A. (1965) 'The Motor Industry, 1955–64', *Bulletin of the Oxford University Institute of Statistics*, vol. 27, no. 4.

Sinclair, R. and D. F. Walker (1982) 'Industrial Development via the Multinational Corporation: General Motors in Vienna", *Regional Studies*, vol. 16.6.

Sinclair, S. (1983) *The World Car: the Future of the Automobile Industry* (London: Euromonitor Publications Ltd).

SMMT (1961) *The Motor Industry of Great Britain, 1961* (London: Society of Motor Manufacturers and Traders).

Sotelo, A. and A. Artega (1981) *La Crisis Mundial del Automovil y sus repercusiones en la Industria automotriz Mexicana.* Paper presented to II Congreso de los Economistas del Tercer Mundo, Havana, Cuba.

Sourrouille, J. (1980) *El Complejo Automotor en Argentina* (Mexico City: ILET/Editorial Nueva Imagen).

Stubbs, P. (1972) *The Australian Motor Industry: a Study in Protection and Growth* (Melbourne).

Sylos-Labini, P. (1962) *Oligopoly and Technical Progress* (Cambridge, Mass.: Harvard University Press).

TIE (1983) *Left-hand drive. Shopfloor internationalism and the auto industry.* Transnational Information Exchange, No. 16.

Toder, E. J. *et al.* (1978) *Trade Policy and the U.S. Automobile Industry.* (New York: Praeger).

Trajtenberg, R. (1977) *Un enfoque sectorial para el estudio de la penetracion de empresas transnacionales en America Latina* (Mexico City, ILET).

Trajtenberg, R. and R. Vigorito (1981) *Economia y Politica en la Fase Transnacional: Algunas Interrogantes* (Mexico: D.F.: ILET, DEE/D/58/e).

UAW (1970) *Survey of Latin American auto contracts* (United Auto Workers: International Affairs and Information Systems Departments).

UNCTC (1978) *Transnational Corporation in World Development. A Reexamination* (New York: United Nations).

UNCTC (1981) *Transnational Corporation Linkages in Developing Countries: the Cases of Backward Linkages via Subcontracting* (New York: United Nations).

UNCTC (1982) *Transnational Corporations in the International Auto Industry* (New York: United Nations).

UNCTC (1983) *Transnational Corporation in World Development: Third Survey.* (New York: United Nations).

UNIDO (1984) *International Industrial Restructuring and the International Division of Labour in the Automotive Industry* (Vienna: United Nations, UNIDO/IS4D).

US Senate (1973) *Hearings of the Sub-Committee on International Trade of the Committee on Finance* (Washington).

Vaitsos, C. (1973) *The Changing Policies of Latin American Governments Towards Economic Development and Direct Foreign Investment.* Paper presented to the Conference on Latin American-US Economic Interactions, The University of Texas, Austin.

Vaitsos, C. (1974) *Inter-country Income Distribution and Transnational Enterprise* (Oxford: Clarendon Press).

Van der Pluijm, T. (1983) 'Energia versus alimentos? El programa de etanol en Brazil', *Comercio Exterior* (May).

Vaupel, J. W. and J. P. Curhan (1969) *The Making of Multinational Enterprise* (Boston: Harvard Business School).

Van Ginneken, W. (1980) *Socio-economic Groups and Income Distribution in Mexico* (London: Croom Helm).

Vázquez Tercero (1975) *Una Decada da Politica Sobre Industria Automotriz* (Mexico DF: Editorial Tecnos).

Vila, A. J. (1962) *La Industria Automotriz Argentina* (Buenos Aires).

Webb, R. (1975) 'Government Policy and the Distribution of Income in Peru, 1963–1973', in A. F. Lowenthal (ed.), *The Peruvian Experiment* (Princeton University Press).

Wells, J. (1977) 'The Diffusion of Durables in Brazil and its Implications for Recent Controversies concerning Brazilian Development', *Cambridge Journal of Economics*, vol. 1.

West, P. (1977) *The Tyre Multinationals: a Study of Foreign Investment and Technology Transfer in Latin America* (PhD thesis, University of Sussex).

West, P. (forthcoming) 'International Expansion and Concentration of the Tyre Industry and Implications for Latin America', in R. Newfarmer (ed.), *Profits, Progress and Poverty: Studies of International Industries in Latin America* (Notre Dame University Press).

White, L. J. (1971) *The Automobile Industry since 1945* (Harvard University Press).

White, L. J. (1977) 'The Automobile Industry', in W. Adams (ed.), *The structure of American Industry*, 5th ed. (New York: Collier-Macmillan).

Widdick, B. (1976) 'Work in Auto Plants, Then and Now', in B. Widdick (ed.), *Auto Work and its Discontents* (Baltimore: Johns Hopkins University Press).

Wierzynski, G. H. (1968) 'The Battle for the European Auto Market', *Fortune*, 77.

Wilkins, M. (1974) *The Maturing of Multinational Enterprises* (Cambridge, Mass.: Harvard University Press).

Wilkins, M. and F. Hill (1964) *American Business Abroad* (Wayne State University Press).

Wong Gonzalez, P. (1984) *The New International Division of Labour and Spatial Organization in Mexico. Some Implications of the Motor Industry Restructuring* (M.Sc dissertation, London School of Economics).

Wurtele, W. (1977) *International Trade Union Solidarity and the Internationalization of Capital: the Role of the International Metalworkers' Federation in Latin America* (paper presented at the seminar on Third World Strikes, Institute of Social Studies, The Hague).

Wurtele, W. (1979) 'Volkswagen no Brasil: Adjuda ao Desenvolvimiento', *Revista de Cultura en Politica* (August).

Young, S. and N. Hood (1977) *Chrysler, U.K. A Corporation in Transition* (New York: Praeger).

Young, S. and N. Hood (1980) 'Recent Pattern of Foreign Direct Investment by British Multinational Enterprises in the United States', *National Westminster Bank Quarterly Review* (May).

Index

assembly 68; casting 67;
forging 65; machining 70;
stamping 65, 67, 68
productivity 94, 165, 167
profits 126, 165, 182
research and development 169
restructuring and internationalization of
capital 170–81
restructuring and state support for
capital 181–4
state intervention 165, 248
tariffs 42, 144
technology 166
terminal supplier relations in advanced
capitalist countries 119–26
unions 80, 81, 167
vertical integration 70, 94, 125
workforce (composition of) 65, 68
working conditions 167
wages 125, 126, 168, 220
Italy 3, 27, 93
import restrictions 171
imports 32
labour control strategies 80
parts industry 123
state intervention 182
tyre industry 121
ITT 173

Japan
exports 39–40, 46, 164, 171, 184, 226
foreign capital 39–40
imports 40
investment 250
joint ventures 39
MITI 39
motor industry 3, 12, 27, 28, 38–40
overseas production 184
parts industry 120, 121, 123
production: costs 164, 215;
growth 38; under licence 38
productivity 39, 93, 95, 164, 165
profits 125
quality control circles 81
replacement market 124
takeovers 39
tyre industry 121, 178–9
unionization 81
Junta del Acuerdo de Cartagena 198,
202, 229, 236

Kleber-Colombes 165
Koni 173

LAFTA 107, 113
Latin American Motor Industry
accumulation of capital 149–53
balance of payments 99, 198, 216–17,
227, 230, 252: capital flows 153–5;
trade balance 155–8
centralization 206
competition 101, 106, 111, 190, 226
concentration 2, 127–8, 142, 206, 250
consumer credit 111
cost of production 189, 249
debt equity levels 137
deletion allowances 141
demand conditions and problems of
realization 98–102
economies of scale 113–14, 116
employment 57, 83, 136
exports 155, 207, 208–16, 230, 249
foreign capital 17–22, 56, 63, 127, 226,
250
foreign debt 227
future of industry 242–52
import restrictions 21–2, 58, 99, 193
import substitution 3, 55–7, 189, 190,
198–204, 227, 229–30
imports 16, 21, 153, 155, 207, 208, 216,
226, 230, 249
income distribution and demand for
cars 102–6
income elasticity of demand 102
integration into world motor
industry 206–8
internationalization of capital 2, 4, 7,
18, 19, 20, 22
intervention of the state 58–9, 190–8
labour control strategies 78–98
labour force militancy 3, 82
labour force structure 76–8
linkages 57
local content 3, 56–8, 62–4, 71, 82, 114,
127, 146, 202
mechanisms of domination 130–4:
technology 130–2; ownership 132;
markets 133–4
motor industry and style of
development 239–42
new labour processes 217–23
output 249–50
parts industry 20, 22, 56, 63–4, 126–30
price elasticity of demand 101, 102
production processes 71–6
productivity 83, 89–96, 106, 113, 142,
213, 214
profit remittances 150, 154